Broken Gospel?

Broken Gospel?

Christianity and the Holocaust

Peter M. Waddell

James Clarke & Co.

James Clarke & Co.

P.O. Box 60
Cambridge
CB1 2NT
United Kingdom

www.jamesclarke.co
publishing@jamesclarke.co

Hardback ISBN: 978 0 227 17847 8
Paperback ISBN: 978 0 227 17845 4
PDF ISBN: 978 0 227 17846 1
ePUB ISBN: 978 0 227 17844 7

British Library Cataloguing in Publication Data
A record is available from the British Library

First Published by James Clarke and Co., 2022

Shall your loving kindness be declared in the grave,
your faithfulness in the land of destruction?

Psalm 88:11

Contents

Acknowledgements

There are many people who have contributed to the publication of this book, and to whom thanks are owed. Family, friends and parishioners have read chapters and had long discussions on everything from grammar to the most involved questions of history and theology. I am almost bound to have omitted some, but special mention must go to all those who ploughed through draft material: Max Beber; Michael Briant; Bernice Compton; Jamie Franklin; David Ford; Julie Gittoes; Neil Gardner; Brian Hibberd; Alex Hughes; Richard Lamey; Roland Maxted; Neil Messer; Jeremy Morris; Thomas Norgaard; Nick Sagovsky; Adrian Smith; Christine Smith; Liz Stuart; Simon Reynolds; Poppy Roper; Fabian Richter; Tony Rindl; David Shervington; Helen Shepherd; Martin, Tom and David Waddell; Justin White; Andrew Williams; Trevor and Joyce Williams; and Rowan Williams. Of course, while each of them has helped to make the book better, none of them agree with everything in it or are responsible for any of its flaws.

Although it is invidious to single anyone out, special mention must go to Dr Neil Titman, who gave of his time and talent with really exceptional generosity to a friend of a friend. He always had confidence that there was a book here waiting to be published, when not everyone did. I am also deeply grateful to Adrian Brink and Sam Fitzgerald of James Clarke Press who were also finally convinced and brought *Broken Gospel?* to publication. Dorothy Luckhurst must also be thanked for her copyediting – a task that would try the patience of a saint.

Writing books in full-time parish ministry has become rare, for obvious reasons. I could not have done it without a hugely supportive parish, above all, my clergy colleagues and churchwardens: Vanessa Kerswill, Maxine Howarth, Bill Sanderson, Jane McHugh, Andrew Taylor, Tom Betteridge and Carol Higgs. Thanks are also due to the Diocese of St Albans – not least for the period of extended study leave in early 2022 which allowed me, at last, to finish!

One of the challenges in writing a book of this nature away from a university setting is finding ready access to sources. I am immensely grateful to the University of Winchester for appointing me a Visiting Research Fellow, giving me full access to all of their online resources. It is also a great pleasure to pay tribute to Hertfordshire County Council Libraries and Archives Service, and to the staff at the Abbots Langley Library – who never raised an eyebrow at some of the strange titles the vicar was requesting.

I was delighted when Ally Barrett, priest and artist, agreed to create this book's cover illustration. The bloodied hands holding shards of a shattered clay jar recall St Paul's words in 2 Corinthians 4:7 contrasting the glory of the Gospel with the fragile fallibility of believers and the Church. The Hebrew word אי־כבוד ('Ichabod') means 'the glory is departed', and in 1 Samuel 4:21 expresses just the sort of lament over catastrophe that much of *Broken Gospel?* is about. And yet, all failure is held against the constant backdrop of Jesus' promise: 'blessed are those who mourn, for they will be comforted.' (Matthew 5:4). In the end, there is always grace.

Finally, once again, thanks and love must go to Lisa, Sam and Ben. They have borne the brunt of this book being written. My hope is that as the boys and their generation grow they will find here some resource for believing that, despite everything, the Gospel still endures.

Introduction

The Holocaust is, in my judgement, the greatest tragedy for Christians since the crucifixion. In the first instance, Jesus died; in the latter, Christianity may be said to have died. Will there be, can there be, a resurrection for Christianity? That is the question that haunts me. Am I part of a religion that is in fact a fossil rather than a living entity? Can one be a Christian today, given the death camps that, in major part, were conceived, built and operated by a people who called themselves Christians?

Henry James Cargas[1]

I have been meaning to write this book since I sat in church as a teenager, listening to a sermon about prayer and how God answers it. The preacher was well-educated, well-meaning and clear. God cared about His people so much, we were assured, that He would look out for us in the smallest details of life. Indeed, on several occasions, when the minister had been driving around the city in urgent need of a place to park, he had said a prayer and – lo and behold – God had provided one.

I had not yet encountered Rabbi Irving Greenberg's rule that, after the Holocaust, 'no statement, theological or otherwise, should be made that would not be credible in the presence of burning children'.[2] Yet, I knew instinctively even then that a religion which thought God found parking spaces for His believers whilst letting the Holocaust happen

---

1. Henry James Cargas, *Shadows of Auschwitz: A Christian Response to the Holocaust* (New York: Crossroad, 1990), p. 1.
2. Irving Greenberg, "Cloud of Smoke, Pillar of Fire: Judaism, Christianity, and Modernity After the Holocaust", in Eva Fleischer (ed.), *Auschwitz: Beginning of a New Era?* (New York: Ktav Publishing House, 1977), p. 23.

lacked moral credibility. If that was Christianity, it deserved nothing but decline and death.

The question about prayer and Providence was, however, only the question that had struck me first. Others were at least as important, and as testing. In the wake of the Holocaust, for instance, what sense could be made of the Christian language of hope, salvation, heaven and reconciliation? Is there hope for the killers, or must we imagine them tormented forever in some kind of post-mortem concentration camp – or (perhaps even more difficult) believe they are somehow reconciled to their victims? To what extent could Christian theology itself be blamed for what had happened to the Jews – a question which might seem out-rageous at first, but is increasingly reasonable the more one absorbs (to take but one instance) Jesus' reported rebuke to the Jews: 'You are from your father the devil, and you choose to do your father's desires. He was a murderer from the beginning, and there is no truth in him' (John 8:44).[3] Can there be a Christianity which does not rely on the denigration of Judaism and encourage hatred of Jews? Moreover, even if there can, given that actual Christianity has in fact done both, has the Church's wickedness been so thorough that the truth of the Gospel itself is called into question? All these questions are addressed in the second section of this book.

It is of course possible, for a while, to live in denial of at least some of them. It might be argued that Christianity had nothing to do with the Holocaust: that the genocide was committed by neo-pagans driven by half-digested and perverse readings of Darwin and Nietzsche, who hated Christianity as much as they did Judaism and who would eventually have turned their killing machine in the Church's direction. Attention might be focussed on the stories of those heroic Christians who resisted the killers, hiding Jews even to the point of sacrificing their own lives. The Holocaust, it might be suggested, poses no sharper questions to Christianity than does any other instance of terrible suffering through radical evil.

As the first section of this book will show, this rosy view stems from ignorance about the Holocaust itself and the centuries preceding it. It is true, of course, that Nazism and Christianity are not the same thing, and that leading Nazis became increasingly hostile to Christianity over time – murderously so. It is also true that there were many instances of Christian resistance to the killing. However, the resisters represent

---

3. Unless otherwise stated, biblical quotations are taken from the New Revised Standard Version (NRSV).

but a tiny minority of European Christians. Most, whether through intimidation or inertia, did nothing. It is not plausible, as we shall see, to say that they did not know what was happening: they may not have known precise details and locations but, by the end of 1942 at the very latest, it was common knowledge that mass slaughter was under way (and, long before that, that it was likely). Many Christians, of course, did more than turn a blind eye. They drew up lists, manned cordons, made arrests, drove trains. They killed.

We cannot console ourselves that those Christians involved in the killing were merely 'nominal' believers, born and raised in historically Christian societies but lacking personal faith. Even if that were so, things would be bad enough: had European Christianity been *so* ineffectual that those raised within it saw no problem with genocide? In fact, though, things are worse. At the level of political leadership, one of the Nazis' most enthusiastic collaborators in the genocide was the President of Slovakia, Jozef Tiso, a Catholic priest (never disciplined by the Vatican for his actions). The most notorious concentration camp in Croatia, Jasenovac, was at one stage under the command of a Franciscan friar, Miroslav Filopovic-Majstorovic – known to the prisoners as 'Brother Satan' for his unusual cruelty. He presided over the murder of more than 40,000 Jews and Serbs, killing many personally. Executed for war crimes in 1946, he went to the scaffold in his Franciscan robes. Protestants were no better: one Wehrmacht chaplain, on trial in 1958, justified his involvement in the mass executions of Jews thus: 'These acts were the fulfilment of the self-condemnation which the Jews had brought upon themselves before the tribunal of Pontius Pilate.'[4] These were not nominal Christians, but serious believers – indeed, public representatives of the faith.

Such men inherited a long history of Christian justification for the hatred and persecution of Jews. It is ignorance of that history which allows Christians today to imagine that the Holocaust poses no special challenge to their faith. Most people nowadays, for instance, are well aware of how the Nazis proceeded by stages: how the deportations and extermination camps were preceded by the forcing of Jews into ghettoes and by marking them out with yellow stars. It comes as a shock to most Christians, however, to learn that such measures were simply a revival of old Church laws. As far back as 1215, the Fourth Lateran Council enforced ghettoisation and required all Jews in Christian Europe to wear a yellow badge – measures which, unsurprisingly, served as the

---

4. Cited in Robert Michael, *Holy Hatred: Christianity, Antisemitism, and the Holocaust* (London: Palgrave Macmillan, 2006), p. 174.

prelude to extensive anti-Jewish violence. Contemporary Christianity's forgetfulness of this (and, as the first chapter of this book shows, much else) allows it to pretend that Nazi anti-Semitism came out of nowhere. The truth, however, is that Christianity in both Roman Catholic and Protestant forms had for centuries set the Jews up as ready victims. The Church primed Europe not to care about the murder of the Jews and even, to some extent, to welcome it. The Holocaust was not a Christian crime in the same direct sense as, for instance, was the burning of witches or heretics. Others took the lead out of a variety of motives, sometimes explicitly anti-Christian. Yet, the bitter truth remains: without Christianity, the Holocaust would never have happened.

What does all that mean for Christianity today? There is an ironic echo of the traditional Christian view of Judaism as a spiritually bankrupt religion. It should, the Church said, have come to an end with the coming of Jesus: perversely, inexplicably the Jews chose to reject him and so they staggered on throughout history, spiritually paralysed, bereft and barren. This was, of course, a grotesque misrepresentation of Judaism. It may, however, seem hauntingly accurate as a description of post-Holocaust European Christianity. We have staggered on, largely in denial of our history, without facing the fundamental questions raised by our historic blood-guilt, refusing radical revision of our faith. Christianity is still here, yet, we inchoately sense it is terribly and perhaps even mortally wounded. It is haunted by unconfessed guilt, vitiated of spiritual power, trapped in half-conscious self-loathing and a sense of overwhelming futility. This is true to some extent of European culture as a whole, and even more so of the religion that gave that culture its moral and spiritual foundation. Rabbi Eliezer Berkovits delivers the verdict: the Holocaust means 'bankruptcy – the moral bankruptcy of Christian civilisation and the spiritual bankruptcy of Christian religion ... a moral and spiritual collapse the like of which the world has never witnessed before for con-temptibility and inhumanity'.[5]

There has, of course, been some reckoning with this. The blood-guilt is not entirely unacknowledged. Indeed, in one respect (traced in chapter five) the Holocaust has prompted a theological revolution in Christianity, with an astonishing *volte-face* on historic teaching about Judaism. Equally, the Church has to some extent engaged with the complicity of Christians in genocide. As we shall see in chapter three, however, that engagement has in many respects been somewhat half-hearted and not

5. Rabbi Eliezer Berkovits, *Faith after the Holocaust* (Jerusalem: Maggid Books, 1973), p. 39.

searching enough. It is also questionable how far repentance has really gone. Many grassroots Christians remain far too keen to accept the most comforting narratives of the Church's involvement with the Holocaust; far too ready, even now, to perpetuate caricatures of Jews, whether of Jesus' day or our own; far too complacent that Christian teaching and practice can continue essentially unchanged by the Holocaust. A suspicion of bankruptcy may lurk somewhere deep in our souls, but it has not yet attained radical clarity in most Christian minds. This book is written in the conviction that, if there is hope for the resurrection of Christianity, it will only be through such clarity: through the most honest accounting of quite how far adrift from God we have come and a willingness to radically rethink our theology. Dry bones can indeed live again, but not through any pretence that they *deserve* to. If there is a future for Christianity, it will be through grace alone.

Grace, of course, is also the key to the most important question of all. 'No statement should be made, theological or otherwise, that is not credible in the presence of burning children', said Rabbi Greenberg. One hesitates to write another sentence. Silence might indeed be the only course. Greenberg's rule remains the single most serious challenge to any kind of religious faith today – and not only of the parking space variety.

Yet … if ultimately there is nothing but silence, then there is nothing but burning children. We would be confessing that at the heart of things, there is finally only torment and death. For all that Christianity needs to repent and change, in this respect at least this book remains stubbornly Christian. It is written in the conviction that futility is not the end, that there is something – Someone – who meets even extinction, who goes into its depths and lights them up with hope. Who on a Roman cross made it so that no one must end in the execution pits or crematoria, and the world will not end in defeat. Christianity may indeed be terribly broken. Jesus Christ remains. In Him nothing is doomed, and hope lights up the destiny of all.

The Feast of the Annunciation, 2022

Chapter 1

Barabbas and His Afterlife

In the Gospel, when Pilate refuses to crucify Jesus, the Jews call out to him: 'His blood be upon us, and upon our children's children.' Perhaps I shall have to put this curse into effect.

Adolf Hitler (1938)[1]

The Story of Barabbas

Now at the festival the governor was accustomed to release a prisoner for the crowd, anyone whom they wanted. At that time they had a notorious prisoner, called Jesus Barabbas. So after they had gathered, Pilate said to them, 'Whom do you want me to release for you, Jesus Barabbas or Jesus who is called the Messiah?' For he realized that it was out of jealousy that they had handed him over. While he was sitting on the judgement seat, his wife sent word to him, 'Have nothing to do with that innocent man, for today I have suffered a great deal because of a dream about him.' Now the chief priests and the elders persuaded the crowds to ask for Barabbas and to have Jesus killed. The governor again said to them, 'Which of the two do you want me to release for you?' And they said, 'Barabbas.' Pilate said to them, 'Then what should I do with Jesus who is called the Messiah?' All of them said, 'Let him be crucified!' Then he asked, 'Why, what evil has he done?' But they shouted all the more, 'Let him be crucified!'

1. Cited in Michael, *Holy Hatred*, p. 172.

> So when Pilate saw that he could do nothing, but rather that a riot was beginning, he took some water and washed his hands before the crowd, saying, 'I am innocent of this man's blood; see to it yourselves.' Then the people as a whole answered, 'His blood be on us, and on our children!' So he released Barabbas for them; and after flogging Jesus, he handed him over to be crucified.
>
> Matthew 27:15-26 (NRSV)

'His blood be on us, and on our children!' Those words have justly been deemed as 'responsible for oceans of human blood and a ceaseless stream of misery and desolation'.[2] There could not be a pithier summary of what would become the predominant Christian view of the Jews: they had killed Christ, and *they* meant not only the Jewish leaders in Jesus' day or the fickle Jerusalem mob, but *all* Jews. For many Christian centuries, as we shall see, this meant that, at best, the Jew was destined to wander like Cain, allowed to live but bearing eternal guilt and shame, their blighted existence a strange witness to the truth of the Gospel. At worst, Christ's followers decided his blood called for vengeance and were only too pleased to take it.

The Barabbas story is not, of course, the only text in the New Testament which has led in the same direction. Its books are unsurprisingly marked by the increasingly bitter 'parting of the ways' between early Christianity and rabbinical Judaism. The picture is complicated, of course, by the fact that the authors were all themselves Jews – but, to put it mildly, their writings contain much ammunition for later anti-Jewish hatred. St Paul wrote that: 'the Jews ... killed both the Lord Jesus and the prophets, and drove us out; they displease God and oppose everyone by hindering us from speaking to the Gentiles so that they may be saved. Thus they have been constantly filling up the measure of their sins'(1 Thessalonians 2:15-16). According to John's gospel, the Jews – at least those who do not welcome Jesus as the Messiah – 'are from your father the devil, and you choose to do your father's desires. He was a murderer from the beginning' (John 8:44). Most hauntingly, there is John's depiction of Judas (his very name suggesting 'Judah' and so a wider reference to his people), the betrayer of Christ, staggering into the night (John 13:30). George Steiner comments:

---

2. Claude Montefiore, cited in Raymond E. Brown, *The Death of the Messiah: From Gethsemane to the Grave: A Commentary on the Passion Narratives in the Four Gospels, Volume 1* (London: Doubleday, 1994), p. 831.

Judas goes into a never-ending night of collective guilt. It is the sober truth to say that his exit is the door to the Shoah. The 'final solution' proposed, enacted, by National Socialism in the twentieth century is the perfectly logical, axiomatic, conclusion to the Judas-identification of the Jew. ... That utter darkness, that night within night, into which Judas is dispatched and commanded to perform 'quickly', is already that of the death ovens.[3]

The Barabbas story, then, is far from unique in its anti-Jewish venom. That said, there are good reasons for choosing it as our starting point. The blood-curse of Matthew 27:25 captures how the Jews were to be seen for most of Christian history: as collectively bearing the responsibility for, and the consequences of, Jesus' death. It was only at the Second Vatican Council of the 1960s (examined fully in chapter five) that this theory of collective guilt was repudiated by the Roman Catholic Church. What is more, examining the Barabbas story also forces Christians to address difficult questions of what really happened in the last days of Jesus – and whether the darkest of poisons flowed not only in later Christian interpretation of the gospel story, but in its very first telling.

What Really Happened?

Christians often seem oblivious to the remarkably odd character of the Barabbas tradition. Pontius Pilate, from what little we know, was a tough and even rashly provocative Roman governor.[4] It seems unlikely that he would have submitted to a custom whereby he was obliged to release to the Jerusalem mob a prisoner of their choice – and not just any prisoner, but one who 'had been put in prison for an insurrection that had taken place in the city, and for murder'. (Luke 23:19). That he would do so at Passover time, when Jerusalem would have been a tinderbox of militant anti-Roman sentiment, is odder still. Raymond Brown's conclusion after an extensive study of Roman and Jewish amnesty/pardon traditions is telling: 'There is no good analogy supporting the historical likelihood

---

3. George Steiner, *No Passion Spent: Essays 1978-1996* (London: Faber & Faber, 1997), p. 417.

4. Philo of Alexandria complains of 'the briberies, the insults, the robberies, the outrages and wanton injuries, the execution without trial constantly repeated, the ceaseless and supremely grievous cruelty' committed by Pilate (*On the Embassy to Gaius*, 302).

of the custom in Judea of regularly releasing a prisoner at a/the feast [of Passover] as described in the three gospels.'[5] Rome just did not do this kind of thing. There is a good *prima facie* case for saying that the Barabbas story is deeply implausible as history. However, if it is not history, what is it?

Well, perhaps, deliberate fabrication. The Gospels were created by a Church desperate to commend itself to the people and authorities of the Roman Empire. The Cross of Jesus was a great stumbling block to this project because crucifixion was, everyone knew, a Roman punishment for political rebels. If Jesus was a rebel, how could his followers be harmless? If he was not, how did he end up on a cross? The early Church devised an answer: it was all the fault of the wicked Jews. They had forced the hand of a well-intentioned but weak Roman governor. He had kept the peace by granting their wish. They had even admitted their guilt, calling down the blood of Jesus upon them and their children.

The fabrication also served a theological purpose. What were Christians to make of Judaism? One New Testament answer (dominant throughout Church history) is to say it is simply over: spiritually bankrupt, dead. A mid-second-century Christian might find support for this view in the fate that had befallen the Jews after Jesus' crucifixion. They rose in rebellion against Rome in the 60s and the catastrophic end of that was the destruction of their Temple in 70 CE, the subsequent razing of Jerusalem and their mass expulsion from the Promised Land. They had rejected the real Messiah, preferring the false promises of violent nationalism, and look – the Christian apologist might say – where it has got them. One could not imagine a story more pregnant with all that than Barabbas and the blood-curse. E.P. Sanders suggests that imagining it is precisely what the early Church did: the tale is not history but 'Christian propaganda'.[6]

For many Christians such a conclusion would be deeply shocking. It poses a stark challenge to those theories of biblical inspiration which maintain that, if the Bible says something happened, then it really happened. Some would claim that holds for every single detail of every single incident; many more would restrict the claim to meaning that, in broad outline, the biblical authors are trustworthy witnesses to history. Nearly all Christians, however, would find it difficult to accept that the

---

5. Brown, *Death of the Messiah*, p. 818.
6. E.P. Sanders, *The Historical Figure of Jesus* (London: Penguin Books, 1993), p. 274.

gospel writers had simply made the whole story up – especially if they did so for spiritually poisonous reasons.

But might Christians simply need to face reality? Jeremy Cohen is scathing about Raymond Brown's categorisation of the Barabbas story as 'not impossible' – the most sceptical judgement the cautiously orthodox Brown allows himself.[7] Brown admits there is no independent evidence for the amnesty tradition and sees the oddity in imagining that Pilate would have behaved this way, but still wants to maintain the basic historical trustworthiness of the narratives. Someone without a similar existential investment in the Gospels being fundamentally trustworthy might well be driven by the same facts to see fabrication here. Of course, the story is not strictly impossible but Cohen suggests the more natural next step is to admit it is highly implausible, and probably false.

The Gospels, after all, contain other apparently straightforward claims about history which on closer inspection seem much more likely to be theology/ideology dressed up in narrative form. Matthew 27:52-53 says that when Jesus died there was a great earthquake, during which 'the tombs also were opened, and many bodies of the saints who had fallen asleep were raised. After his resurrection, they came out of the tombs, and entered the holy city and appeared to many.' There is no report of this in any other New Testament book or other contemporary document. Would not something so astounding, so memorable and so public have been mentioned elsewhere? Yet the historically suspect story expresses a profound theological conviction: the death of Christ meant the undoing of death and the opening of a glorious future for all God's people – even those whom the world had crushed. One commentator notes, 'Matthew is not interested in satisfying our natural curiosity or answering empirical scepticism. He tells the story for its symbolic significance.'[8] Quite so: and perhaps also in the case of Barabbas. There, however, the symbolism was not life for all but death to the Jews.

The difficult question, of course, is how much of what looks like gospel history is actually theological symbolism: doctrine in the form of story with little or no actual historical reference behind it. Some read the story of the visit of the Magi to adore the infant Jesus like this; others might include even stories at the very heart of faith, like the virginal conception and the bodily resurrection of Jesus. Believers will draw the

---

7. Jeremy Cohen, *Christ Killers: The Jews and the Passion from the Bible to the Big Screen* (Oxford: Oxford University Press, 2007), p. 22.

8. France, R.T., *The Gospel of Matthew: The New International Commentary on the New Testament* (Grand Rapids, MI: Eerdmans, 2007), p. 1081.

line at different places, but most will allow some degree of theologically imaginative reconstruction of history in the New Testament. Indeed, many would now allow that the whole gospel tradition is to be read as a fusion of genuine historical memory with theological interpretation: what might be called 'meditated history'. At some points, the history is minimal. At others, it is maximal. Working out the balance in each particular element of the tradition is one of the principal challenges for biblical scholars, theologians and ordinary believers.

However, there are good reasons – beyond the believer's reluctance to challenge orthodoxy – to hesitate before consigning the Barabbas story to the firmly unhistorical category.

Firstly, if the Evangelists shaped the story of Jesus' death to maximise Jewish guilt whilst minimising Roman responsibility, they did so very ineffectively. Not only does the brute fact of the Cross loom too large to exculpate Rome (it was Romans who crucified people, not Jews), but the Evangelists emphasise the vicious treatment that Jesus received at Roman hands. It was Roman soldiers who beat him, flogged him, mocked him and crowned him with thorns. It was Pilate who put up the sign mockingly proclaiming Jesus King of the Jews, and peremptorily dismissed the high priests when they protested. The Romans do not come out of this story well. Maybe exonerating them was not, after all, the point of the exercise – but, if that is so, then the supposed motivation for the alleged fabrication of the Barabbas story is called into question.

It is also worth noting the things the Evangelists do not fabricate. One of the great issues facing the early Church was whether Gentile converts to Christianity needed to be circumcised (so committing themselves to keeping the whole Mosaic Law) or not. Nothing would have been more convenient than a directive from Jesus which would settle the matter. Yet, the Evangelists report nothing. They refuse to provide something which would be highly convenient but has no historical basis. Indeed, for an early Church seeking to win converts among the Gentiles, they complicate matters by recording highly awkward sayings of Jesus like, 'I was sent only to the lost sheep of the house of Israel' (Matthew 15:24). Once again, it seems, the Evangelists may be more faithful to history than is often supposed.

Moreover, there is, of course, nothing intrinsically implausible about some Jewish involvement in and responsibility for the death of Jesus. Rome governed its provinces, when it could, with the consent and collaboration of a native leadership: in first-century Judea, the high-priestly caste connected with the Temple. Jesus came into sharp conflict with this local elite. It is quite possible that they co-operated with or even initiated his death at the hands of the Romans. That is what ruling classes and collaborators with empires do: it is not anti-Semitic to suggest that a Jewish elite might behave as many others have done.

The historicity of the Barabbas story may also be supported by the fact that – unlike the stories of the visit of the Magi, or the dead saints wandering around Jerusalem – it occurs in all four Gospels. Such multiple attestation is usually taken by scholars to indicate (not prove) that *something* akin to what is recorded probably happened. Of course, if one accepts that Matthew and Luke were dependent upon Mark, then there are only actually two independent witnesses – Mark and John. However, even two sources represent impressive evidence for a minor detail of ancient history, especially when one (John) shows no sign of wanting to exploit the story for symbolic significance. He passes hurriedly over the Barabbas incident (18:39-40) as if he has heard of it and wants to record it as part of the historical tradition, but he has no special interest in it. All of which suggests that we may, after all, be confronted with real history here.

Furthermore, note the different way each Evangelist handles the material. Matthew alone records the blood-curse and speaks of the 'people as a whole' calling it down, using the Greek *laos* which often signifies Israel or the Church understood as a theological whole.[9] Mark's account, by contrast, simply speaks of 'the crowd' (*oxlos*). Matthew has polished the scene to draw out the dreadful import he sees: this is Israel solemnly repudiating its God. Yet, paradoxically, he drops all reference to Barabbas being connected with murder and insurrection – he is simply a 'notorious prisoner' (27:16). Mark said that Barabbas had been in prison with those who had committed murder during the insurrection; Luke went further by twice identifying Barabbas himself as charged with murder (23:19, 25). It is easy to understand why Mark and Luke make this connection: to choose the rebel murderer over the true Messiah demonstrates perfectly the fateful choice the Evangelists think Israel made that morning. Why, however, did Matthew *not* do the same? It would have suited his purposes magnificently. One obvious possibility is that he did not know the connection between Barabbas and murder – that the version of the story he had heard first had not included it. Perhaps Matthew restricted himself to the version he had first received, precisely so as *not* to fabricate history. This would give us a possible three independent witnesses, and another suggestion of Matthean conservatism in handling tradition. All this is speculative,

9. As noted by France, *Gospel of Matthew*, p. 1057, n. 44.

of course, but it does provide some caution against the 'pure propaganda' theory.

That the Barabbas story is pure propaganda with no historical reference whatsoever seems unlikely. That things transpired exactly as Matthew says seems even more so. What, then, really happened? We are reduced to a reasonable conjecture: there was indeed a Barabbas, who was swept up in a wave of arrests following anti-Roman violence in Jerusalem. He is unlikely to have been seriously suspected by the authorities of killing Romans. He was probably on the edge of the troubles, perhaps just unlucky enough to be in the wrong place at the wrong time. His imprisonment and possible execution became something of a *cause célèbre* in Jerusalem that year. In the end he was released – possibly through a very local, and otherwise invisible to history, amnesty tradition that the Gospels describe; possibly just because Pilate was clearing out the cells. Barabbas was small fry. If you could ease feeling in the city by releasing him, so much to the good. Perhaps it was even a way of giving Pilate's local collaborators some much-needed street credibility – all their cosying up to Rome could produce results.

At the same time, Jesus of Nazareth was condemned – and far from helping him, the priests and their people egged the Romans on. Perhaps there was an actual moment when you had to shout for either Barabbas or Jesus; perhaps not. Either way, a choice was made and Christians like Matthew would have brooded on that choice and thought that, after all, were not the high priests the symbolic representatives of the whole people? Did the subsequent decades not make it ever clearer that collectively Israel's choice had indeed been for the way of Barabbas, not Jesus? Had not the catastrophic consequences of that choice been a clear manifestation of divine judgement upon Israel? Matthew would meditate on that little, half-remembered moment of chaotic history – Barabbas' release and Jesus' condemnation – and his meditation would crystallise into his gospel story. Not pure history, but not pure propaganda either: meditated history, which for the Jews would turn out to be the most lethal kind.

Bearing the Blood: The Consequences of a Story

According to all three Synoptic Gospels, at the moment of Jesus' death the curtain shielding the Holy of Holies in the Temple was torn in two. We may justly doubt whether this actually happened (how did the Evangelists know? why did the Temple priests not become Christians on the spot?) and suspect that this is yet more doctrine presented as history. Like the blood-curse, however, the torn curtain captures in an especially vivid way something of the New Testament's essential teaching concerning Judaism. The Temple has been divinely desecrated and its cult replaced by what had happened on the Cross. As Hebrews 10:9 puts it, contrasting the Temple sacrifices with the new covenant inaugurated by Christ's death: '[God] abolishes the first in order to establish the second.' At least insofar as it is a religion of Temple sacrifices, from this Christian point of view Judaism is finished.

Paul (studied in more depth in chapter five) shares a similar perspective. According to him, all the promises made to and about Israel have come to fruition in Jesus, and the new people of God are now the family of Jews and Gentiles who accept him as the Messiah. Those Jews who do not are subject to a mysterious spiritual 'hardening' (Romans 11:25). Paul confidently hopes that in the end they too will acknowledge Jesus and be reunited with the people of God but, insofar as they remain Jews rather than Christians, 'to this very day, whenever Moses is read, a veil lies over their minds' (2 Corinthians 3:15). The Jews, he thinks, are beloved of God because the gifts and calling of God once made to them are irrevocable (Romans 11:29) but the Judaism he knew had run into a dead end, becoming a spiritually bereft and desolate way of life. The blood-curse called down on Good Friday morning had devastated it.

A Christian who thought this way would find it almost impossible not to see the history of the Jewish people in subsequent decades as enacting the divine judgement upon that nation. The Temple had been razed by Vespasian's troops in 70 CE and Jerusalem's Jewish population expelled. The traditional financial offerings to the Temple were forcibly redirected towards pagan worship, and in 119 CE Emperor Hadrian even banned circumcision, effectively dooming Jewish existence.[10] Following the merciless suppression of the Bar Kokhba Jewish revolt of 132-35, things grew grimmer still. The Jews were expelled from Judea itself, which was then merged with Galilee to form the new province of Syria Palaestina. The change of name indicated the underlying purpose: to dissolve any connection between Jewish people and Jewish land (and, ultimately, to abolish both concepts). The *coup de grâce* was the erection of a new temple in Jerusalem, dedicated to Jupiter, Juno and Minerva. These were the patron divinities of the new Roman city Aelia Capitolina,

---

10. Simon Schama, *The Story of the Jews: Finding the Words 1000 BCE-1492 CE* (London: Vintage, 2014), p. 182 – though Schama notes that Hadrian's laws lasted a mere three years.

populated now largely by demobbed Roman soldiers and many Gentile Christians. To most Christians, it was obvious: the Jews were bearing their blood-guilt.

Most of this suffering, though, had not been inflicted by Christians or in the name of Christianity. Christians, shaped by the bitterness in their founding stories, may indeed have been strongly prejudiced against Jews. Thus far, however, they lacked the power to do much with their anti-Judaism. Jewish blood was shed by Roman swords, which were not yet Christian ones. The Romans killed the Jews not because of the latter's alleged role in the death of Jesus, but for their stubborn refusal to assimilate to the Empire and its gods and for their armed resistance when the point was pressed. Not all anti-Judaism – in the first or the twentieth century – was Christian.

Nonetheless, Christians were growing rapidly more anti-Semitic and more powerful. Melito of Sardis, writing in the second half of the second century, marks a crucial step as he brings together two Christian convictions – that Jesus was God incarnate and that the Jews were responsible for his death – to make a lethally logical third. The Jews were guilty of killing God (deicide):

> The one who hung the earth in space, is himself hanged; the one who fixed the heavens in place, is himself impaled; the one who firmly fixed all things, is himself firmly fixed to the tree. The Lord is insulted, God has been murdered, the King of Israel has been destroyed by the right hand of Israel.[11]

This charge would stalk the Jewish people for at least the next eighteen hundred years. Nearly all Christian tradition up to the Second Vatican Council in the 1960s asserted it emphatically. John Chrysostom (c.350-407 CE) set the tone for many. The Jews were Christ-killers, not just then but now, and so their continued existence as Jews was an insult to God: 'Where Christ-killers gather, the cross is ridiculed, God blasphemed, the Father unacknowledged, the Son insulted, the grace of the Spirit rejected.'[12] The Jews had made themselves 'fit for slaughter.'[13] It was but a small step further to Christians violently anticipating the final vengeance of God upon the Jews.

---

11. Melito of Sardis, *On the Pascha*, 96.
12. St John Chrysostom, *Sermons against the Jews*, 1.6.3.
13. Ibid., 1.2.6.

That next, murderous step was not taken often in the first Christian millennium. The chief reason for this was the doctrine of St Augustine. Augustine agreed with all the early Fathers of the Church that Judaism was now spiritually worthless and the Jews themselves at best frozen, 'stationary in useless antiquity'.[14] At worst, they 'linger in the same danger of destruction' as afflicted their ancestors.[15] However, Christians must not unleash this destruction. God may, in God's time, but the Church should take its cue from Psalm 59:11: 'do not kill them, or my people may forget'. The Jews in their current bereft state were useful for the Church. They were witness to the history from which Jesus sprang and the people, culture and religion with which he engaged. Their miserable existence also served as a terrible warning: Christians should contemplate them, pity them and resolve not to merit similar condemnation themselves.

The Augustinian line held for several centuries, but in the second millennium the already sombre picture darkened sharply. As with any large-scale cultural phenomenon, there are a myriad of causes and consequences at play here, and a full analysis of the evolution of Christian anti-Semitism requires an analysis beyond the scope of this book. However, the trajectory is clear. Until very roughly 1000 CE, the Jews occupied a reasonably safe – if subordinate and precarious – position in Christian society. By the mid-1500s, that security had been eroded to vanishing point. There were few Jews left in Western Europe and those who remained were in acute danger.

One key reason for this transformation was the grand vision of the medieval Church pursued by Pope Innocent III (r. 1198-1216) and the Fourth Lateran Council (1215). Their project was to reinvigorate Christendom as a truly cohesive Christian society, where every element in society took its place within the ordered whole, all under the authority of God, Jesus and the papacy. This was a totalitarian conception of society, in the sense that the Christian vision was to be all-embracing and embraced by all: you could not really belong to this society without accepting its fundamental premises and sharing its basic allegiance. It was thus marked by persecution of any who did not fit readily underneath the papal monarchy. As Cohen notes, 'No room existed for infidels. Such trends in the political and religious thought of the thirteenth century

---

14. Augustine of Hippo, *Treatise against the Jews* (*Tractatus adversus Iudaeos*), in *Fathers of the Church*, Volume 27 (Washington, DC: Catholic University Press of America, 1955), ch. 6, pp. 387-414.
15. Ibid., ch. 8.

certainly made the climate ripe for the exclusion of the Jews, the infidels most deeply imbedded in the society, from Christendom.'[16]

The most brutal sign of this changed climate was the pogrom: mass killings of Jews, often incited by the ecclesiastical authorities. There had been pogroms before, but in the early medieval period their number, scope and intensity accelerated dramatically. In 1096, the First Crusade was proclaimed by Pope Urban II. Principally directed against the Muslim occupation of Jerusalem, this and subsequent crusades also unleashed waves of violence against the enemies of Christ in Christianity's European heartlands – both Christian heretics, such as the Cathars, and, supremely, the Jews. The latter were close to hand, militarily weak and their very existence mocked Jesus and God: 'We have set out on a long march across vast distances against the enemies of God in the East, even though we have right here, before our eyes, the Jews, the worst enemies of God. To ignore them is preposterous and foolish.'[17] Many thousands of Jews were killed. Robert Michael notes, 'If the Crusaders possessed the same organisation and technology of death as the Nazis, they would have achieved a final solution of the European Jewish problem a thousand years earlier than the Nazis.'[18]

Such anti-Jewish violence, like the wider crusading effort, had many causes. However, these included theological developments which under-mined the old Augustinian 'defence' of the Jews. In Augustine's view, the Jews remained a useful visual aid: setting forth the old covenant, against which the new shone out all the more brightly. Yet, in the medieval era, Christian scholars were increasingly noticing that Judaism was no longer the religion of the Old Testament alone. The Talmud – the collection of rabbinic writings drawn together during the fifth and sixth centuries of the Christian era – had assumed central importance. Judaism was not, after all, frozen in aspic: it was a living, breathing religion. This recognition was not, however, a positive development in Christian appreciation of Judaism. Rather, to Christians, for Judaism to change was simply further evidence of Jewish wickedness. Having abandoned God, they were now abandoning the religion of their fathers – and the only precarious basis for their existence in Christendom. Christian scholars, suddenly alive to Judaism as more than a cipher, concentrated their fire on the Talmud – a campaign which culminated in its prohibition by the

---

16. Jeremy Cohen, *The Friars and the Jews: The Evolution of Medieval Anti-Judaism* (Ithaca, NY: Cornell University Press, 1984), p. 255.

17. Cited in Michael, *Holy Hatred*, p. 61.

18. Ibid., p. 183.

Inquisition in 1240, and in mass public burnings of it and other Jewish writings. Pope Innocent IV explained why:

> [The Talmud] is a big book among them, exceeding in size the text of the Bible. In it are found blasphemies against God and His Christ, and obviously entangled fables about the Blessed Virgin, and abusive errors, and unheard-of follies. But of the laws and doctrines of the prophets they make their sons altogether ignorant. They fear that if the forbidden truth, which is found in the Law and the Prophets, be understood, and the testimony concerning the only-begotten Son of God, that he appeared in the flesh, be furnished, these [children] would be converted to the Faith and humbly return to their Redeemer.[19]

Thus, in his view, so immured were the Jews in wickedness and blindness, they would rather substitute a new holy book for the Bible than be confronted with the obvious truth of Christianity. Christians might – perhaps – still refrain from killing Jews, but against this latest Jewish perversion no quarter could be given.

The conviction of Jewish malignancy gathered strength in other ways too. Augustine had agreed that Jews bore responsibility for the death of Jesus, yet declined to charge them with intentional deicide. They had never thought Jesus was divine; their sin, though terrible, was therefore to some extent one of ignorance.[20] Most theologians concurred until the medieval era, when Thomas Aquinas (1225-74) effectively reversed the position. The ignorance of those who killed Christ actually magnified their sin, because 'it was, in a sense, voluntary ignorance. For they beheld the blatant signs of his divinity, but they corrupted them out of hatred and jealousy of Christ; and they wished not to believe his words, by which he proclaimed himself to be son of God.'[21] Far from excusing the Jews, such wilful ignorance condemned them still further.

So taught, most medieval Christians could not look at contemporary Talmudic Jews with anything like compassion or pity. These were people who had wilfully murdered the incarnate God, and who continued to mock Him. Anything could be believed of them: even that they would

---

19. Cited in Cohen, *The Friars and the Jews*, p. 68.
20. Cited in Cohen, *Christ Killers*, p. 76.
21. St Thomas Aquinas, *Summa Theologiae*, 3.47.5.

abduct Christian children and bleed them to death (often in a parody of crucifixion), using their blood to make bread for the Passover meal. The grisly, imaginary, fate of William of Norwich in 1144 was an early example of this extremely potent 'blood-libel'.[22] Potent and enduring: Cohen notes that in the late nineteenth and early twentieth centuries 'dozens of ritual murder allegations were levelled against Jews in France, Germany, Moravia, Bulgaria, Austria-Hungary, Russia and elsewhere. According to one recent calculation, the years 1870-1940 gave rise to more accusations of ritual murder, crucifixion and cannibalism than all previous centuries combined!'[23] Indeed, even in the twenty first century, the 'blood libel' continues to resurface occasionally in the Arab press.[24]

In the medieval era, such allegations were often accompanied by another charge which seemed almost as horrible: the deliberate desecration by Jews of bread consecrated at the Eucharist. In 1215, the Fourth Lateran Council had promulgated the dogma of transubstantiation: that after consecration the bread is no longer mere bread, but in its innermost reality nothing other than the real body of Jesus. To spit on, to stab or pour boiling water over a consecrated host was to torture Jesus anew. As far as many medieval Christians were concerned, this, like ritual child murder, was just the sort of thing Jews did: 'Jews allegedly committed such acts as an expression of their Christ-killing identity.'[25]

Jews, then, were a horrible, murderous presence in the bosom of Christendom: quite literally, agents of Satan. They had to be rigorously controlled. In most European towns the were concentrated in walled ghettos. The Fourth Lateran Council banned Jews from holding all public office and required them to wear distinctive dress or a badge so that they (and, admittedly, the very few Muslims in Europe) could be clearly identified. All this made the next step – systematic killing and expulsion – easier. When the Black Death ravaged Europe in the fourteenth century, the Jews were the prime suspects. In retaliatory violence many of their communities in Germany were completely exterminated. This, combined with the expulsions from England (1290),

---

22. Thomas of Monmouth, *The Life and Passion of William of Norwich*, trans. with an introduction by Miri Rubin (London: Penguin, 2014).

23. Cohen, *Christ Killers*, p. 115.

24. See, for instance, the Saudi government daily paper Al-Riyadh for 30 October 2002, cited at https://www.jewishvirtuallibrary.org/the-blood -libel-in-saudi-arabia (accessed 17 July 2020).

25. Cohen, *Christ Killers*, p. 105.

France (1306), Spain (1492) and elsewhere, meant that by the mid-1500s most of Western Europe had no Jews at all. In Nazi terminology, much of the region was *Judenrein* – 'clean of Jews'.

That did not stop Jews from occupying a central place in the European psyche – and, especially, that of Martin Luther. Hitler himself would later praise the reformer's recommendations for how Germany should deal with its remaining Jews.[26] Luther set out his programme in his 1543 work *On the Jews and Their Lies*:

> First, to set fire to their synagogues or schools and to bury and cover with dirt whatever will not burn, so that no man will ever again see a stone or cinder of them. ...
>
> Second, I advise that their houses also be razed and destroyed. ... Instead they might be lodged under a roof or in a barn, like the gypsies. This will bring home to them the fact that they are not masters in our country, as they boast, but that they are living in exile and in captivity, as they incessantly wail and lament about us before God.
>
> Third, I advise that all their prayer books and Talmudic writings, in which such idolatry, lies, cursing, and blasphemy are taught, be taken from them.
>
> Fourth, I advise that their rabbis be forbidden to teach henceforth on pain of loss of life and limb. ...
>
> Fifth, I advise that safe-conduct on the highways be abolished completely for the Jews. ...
>
> Sixth, I advise that usury be prohibited to them, and that all cash and treasure of silver and gold be taken from them and put aside for safekeeping. ...
>
> Seventh, I recommend putting a flail, an ax, a hoe, a spade, a distaff, or a spindle into the hands of young, strong Jews and Jewesses and letting them earn their bread in the sweat of their brow, as was imposed on the children of Adam (Gen. 3 [:19]). For it is not fitting that they should let us accursed Goyim toil in the sweat of our faces while they, the holy people, idle away their time behind the stove, feasting and farting, and on top of all, boasting blasphemously of their lordship over the Christians by means of our sweat. ...
>
> But if we are afraid that they might harm us or our wives, children, servants, cattle, etc., if they had to serve and work

---

26. Michael, *Holy Hatred*, p. 169.

for us ... then let us emulate the common sense of other nations such as France, Spain, Bohemia, etc., compute with them how much their usury has extorted from us, divide this amicably, but then eject them forever from the country. For, as we have heard, God's anger with them is so intense that gentle mercy will only tend to make them worse and worse, while sharp mercy will reform them but little. Therefore, in any case, away with them![27]

This anti-Semitic diatribe had an interesting afterlife: by the early twentieth century it had sunk into obscurity. It was not included in the standard version of Luther's works used by German clergy in the early twentieth century and most, Eberhard Bethge claims, would have been quite unaware of its existence.[28] It was the Nazi propagandist Julius Streicher who brought it back to public attention, as part of his efforts to claim Luther as a spiritual patron of Nazism. Indeed, at his trial in 1946, Streicher pleaded in his defence that the Allies would have had even Luther in the dock.

However, we need to resist too close an identification of Luther's intense Christian anti-Semitism and Nazism. Whilst only too pleased to exploit Luther's anti-Semitism, the leading Nazis were not themselves primarily motivated by traditional Christian hatred of Jews. As we shall see in the next chapter, their relationship to Christianity generally ranged from ambivalence to deep hostility. In many respects, Nazism can be regarded as a *post-Christian* phenomenon, rather than as a resurgence of Lutheran or Catholic hatred of Jews. Of course, religiously motivated anti-Semitism continued to exist. One might even allow that its continued potency was an indispensable condition for the Holocaust. However, its hold over the European imagination had undoubtedly been weakened in the centuries following Luther. The Enlightenment had seen not only an assault upon the teaching authority of the Church in general, but also a new regard for individual human rights and the need for tolerance of different religions. Most *philosophes* ridiculed such notions as collective or inherited guilt which lay at the root of much

27. Martin Luther, *On the Jews and their Lies* (1543), Parts 11-13, available at: https://www.ccjr.us/dialogika-resources/primary-texts-from-the-history-of-the-relationship/luther-1543 (accessed 12 January 2021).
28. Eberhard Bethge, 'Dietrich Bonhoeffer: One of the Silent Bystanders?', *European Judaism: A Journal for the New Europe* 25, no. 1 (Spring 1992), pp. 33-40, see esp. p. 36.

traditional Christian anti-Semitism. The puzzle is to explain why it was modern, post-Enlightenment Germany which, four centuries later, fulfilled Luther's bloodiest fantasies.

The sense of paradox deepens when one notes that the immediate impact of the Enlightenment was, initially, hugely positive for the Jews. Across Western Europe the story of the seventeenth to the nineteenth century was of the physical return of the Jewish people and of their gradual emancipation from Christian prejudice and discrimination.[29] By the end of the nineteenth century, this had been accomplished in full – at least in legal terms – in most European countries. Europeans were becoming more and more receptive to the idea that the degradation of Jews was based in superstition and ran contrary to the new ideals of human dignity and religious toleration.

However, another central Enlightenment value was freighted with difficulty for the Jews. Enlightened thought held that societies and states functioned best when governed by concepts of reason and universally applicable law. This tended to involve the dissolution of particular identities other than that of 'citizen': classically, the French Republic (always in the vanguard of the project) saw its people as simply *French* – not Protestants, not Catholics, not Jews. So, emancipation was a double-edged sword: whilst granting Jews the same rights as all other individuals, it simultaneously sought to erode the institutions and practices which made Jews different. 'Jews', argued the champion of their emancipation in France, Clermont-Tonnerre, 'should be denied everything as a nation; granted everything as individuals … the existence of a nation within a nation is unacceptable to our *patrie*.'[30]

This was worrying enough for the Jewish future: what made it more so was that the programme only partially succeeded. Conditions for Jews in Central Europe improved dramatically, in terms of their prosperity and civic rights. Yet, in many ways Jews remained stubbornly *other*. They maintained their own social structures (often now societies for self-improvement, to take best advantage of the new opportunities), their own religious identity (now often featuring grand, impressive synagogues), distinctive political preferences (voting solidly Left, because the Left favoured emancipation) and, because education was taken very seriously in the Jewish community, prominent representation in the top professions.

---

29. The story is well told in Simon Schama, *The Story of the Jews: Belonging 1492-1900* (London: Vintage, 2017), esp. chs 9 and 10.
30. Cited in ibid., pp. 393-94.

The overall result was a community still readily identifiable as different and dangerously exposed as a target for resentment.

Of which, there was much. To many, the Enlightenment meant the vaunting of reason and technology, the disenchantment of the world, the abandonment of tradition, the replacement of agricultural society and its norms and hierarchies by urbanism, democracy and egalitarianism. The strong reaction was typified in England by the likes of Wordsworth and Blake in their polemics against soulless modernity. In Germany, the reaction was especially pronounced and took on a sharp anti-French and nationalist edge, because the Enlightenment project was fatally associated with the national humiliation of the Napoleonic invasion. As the French armies had brought Jewish emancipation, German reaction also tended to be sharply anti-Semitic. Jews became the alien against which resurgent, conservative German nationalism came to define itself. They were no longer cast out so much on grounds of deicide, as because they were essentially un-German: culturally, spiritually and, ultimately, in a spuriously scientific twist, in terms of racial biology. No amount of assimilation could ever make a Jew German.

This new kind of exclusion was the lethal ingredient in the Nazi Holocaust. When Germany had been defined in such a way as to exclude a whole group, when that group was an obvious target for resentment and when the nation had suffered humiliating and traumatic defeat, genocide beckoned. Traditional Christian anti-Semitism indeed remains a *sine qua non* for the Holocaust: the Jews could not have been such convenient victims had not the Christians long made them so and, though weakened, Christian tradition still retained much sway over European and German minds. However, Beller places the immediate, primary responsibility elsewhere: 'Monolithic, conformist nationalism, apparently the most advanced form of modernity in mid-20th-century Europe, was the root cause of this political and moral disaster.'[31]

The root cause? Zygmunt Bauman concurs that the rise of nationalism was indeed a crucial factor in the modern mix that created the Holocaust. However, he identifies a range of other, also characteristically modern, tendencies which were in play. Quite apart from the reliance of the killers on modern technology (railways and poison gas), the Holocaust dwarfs previous genocides because it was run via the machinery of modern, rational bureaucratic planning. The mass slaughter was not due to an

---

31. Steven Beller, *Antisemitism: A Very Short Introduction*, 2nd edn (Oxford: Oxford University Press, 2015), p. 121.

explosion of primitive mob prejudice, but was a carefully organised, largely dispassionate, systematic operation: precisely because of this the Nazi scheme 'towers high above past genocidal episodes in the same way as the modern industrial plant towers above the craftsman's cottage workshop'.[32] Even more profoundly, the decision to exterminate was itself an expression of the quintessentially modern conviction that, at last, through wise government and scientific power the world can be perfected – through the elimination of the unwanted:

> It is difficult, perhaps impossible, to arrive at the idea of extermination of a whole people without race imagery; that is, without a vision of endemic and fatal defect which is in principle incurable and, in addition, is capable of self-propagation unless checked. It is also difficult, and probably impossible, to arrive at such an idea without the entrenched practice of medicine (both of medicine proper, aimed at the individual human body, and of its numerous allegorical applications), with its model of health and normality, strategy of separation and technique of surgery. It is particularly difficult, and well-nigh impossible, to conceive of such an idea separately from the engineering approach to society, the belief in the artificiality of social order, institution of expertise and the practice of scientific management of human setting and interaction. For these reasons, *the exterminatory version of anti-Semitism ought to be seen as a thoroughly modern phenomenon*; that is, something which could only occur in an advanced state of modernity.[33]

Bauman's overall verdict on the culpability of modern civilisation for the Holocaust is almost identical to what has often been said about Christianity's own culpability: 'Modern civilisation was not the Holocaust's *sufficient* condition: it was, however, most certainly its *necessary* condition. Without it, the Holocaust would be unthinkable. It was the rational world of modern civilisation that made the Holocaust thinkable.'[34] Whatever the grave responsibility of Christianity for the

---

32. Zygmunt Bauman, *Modernity and the Holocaust* (Cambridge: Polity Press, 1989), p. 89.
33. Ibid., p. 73.
34. Ibid., p. 13.

killing, then – and we have certainly seen that it is grave – the Church is not in the dock alone.

Indeed, what hold Christian doctrine retained upon modern European culture sometimes acted as a (not very effective) brake upon the slaughter. The Nazis were repeatedly frustrated by the lack of enthusiasm that several otherwise soundly anti-Semitic countries displayed for the genocidal project. French or Italian anti-Semitism was too often constrained, it seems, by the traditional Christian character of their societies. Twentieth-century German anti-Semitism, Goldhagen observes, was stronger stuff:

> No other country's anti-Semitism was at once so widespread as to have been a cultural axiom, was so firmly wedded to racism, had as its foundation such a pernicious image of Jews that deemed them to be a mortal threat to the *Volk*, and was so deadly in content, producing, even in the nineteenth century, such frequent and explicit calls for the extermination of the Jews, calls which expressed the logic of the racist eliminationist anti-Semitism that prevailed in Germany. ... German anti-Semitism was *sui generis*.[35]

Equally, no other country than Germany had been quite so influenced by Nietzsche's 'transvaluation of values' and the overthrow of traditional Christian morality:

> Such quaint concepts as individual human rights, and the sanctity of human life, [seemed] outmoded relics of an age when a 'slave religion' – Christianity, heir of Judaism – had perverted modern ethics. The murder of Jews in an industrial process thus could be seen as part of a breaking of false, traditional taboos in the pursuit of a higher form of Germanic modernity that dispensed with the superficial restrictions of mere Western civilisation.[36]

Christianity, then, is not the only, nor, perhaps, even the pre-eminent, reason that the Holocaust happened. Other factors featured in the

---

35. Daniel J. Goldhagen, *Hitler's Willing Executioners: Ordinary Germans and the Holocaust* (London: Abacus, 1996), p. 419.

36. Beller, *Antisemitism*, p. 96.

genocidal mix. Still, the basic truth remains: there could have been no Holocaust without Christianity. A direct, if twisting, line between the Barabbas story and the Final Solution remains. The Holocaust was not the Church's fault alone, but it was indeed the Church's fault. That fault goes right back to the shaping of the gospel record itself. It continued during the days of the killing, in the 1930s and 1940s – to which we shall turn in the next chapter.

Coda: Reading the Barabbas Story Today

Knowing all this, how should we now read the Barabbas story?

Perhaps we simply should not. Perhaps the spiritual catastrophe tradition has made of this story – a catastrophe invited by the texts themselves – makes any ethically responsible reading today impossible. This option, however, is not a live one for Christians who hold that in some sense Scripture has authority over them – even if that authority means simply that these are the texts with which Christians must continually wrestle, and which cannot simply be edited according to our tastes. Certainly, we must be alert to the great spiritual danger they pose: a sermon about the Barabbas story which did not condemn its later deployment would be scandalous indeed. However, merely to excise it from the record is to abandon any notion that God might speak through Scriptures which seem strange or appalling and, thus, effectively to make ourselves rather than Scripture the locus of authority. For most Christians, this is unacceptable.

Another possibility would be to read the story ironically, as communicating a truth quite unknown to the human author. Pope Benedict XVI (r. 2005-13) coyly does not offer a view on what Matthew thought he meant, but is clear on what his text really means: 'The Christian will remember that Jesus' blood speaks a different language from the blood of Abel (Heb. 12:24): it does not cry out for vengeance and punishment; it brings reconciliation. It is not poured out *against* anyone; it is poured out *for* many … these words are not a curse, but rather redemption, salvation.'[37] Rowan Williams, by contrast, suggests that Matthew did mean to impute collective guilt, but proposes that he thus unintentionally furnishes a further example of what his whole trial scene is about: 'a question to religious power and religious fluency, a question to all who are

---

37. Joseph Ratzinger, Pope Benedict XVI, *Jesus of Nazareth: Holy Week: From the Entrance into Jerusalem to the Resurrection* (London: Catholic Truth Society, 2011), p. 187.

insiders, all who are familiar with speaking about God'.[38] By blaming the Jews, Matthew simply reproduces the fault his story lays bare in Caiaphas: the tendency of those with religious power to become more interested in power than in God, in excluding others than recognising their own need before God and, hence, laying waste to their own spiritual lives. In Williams' hands, the story becomes less a source for what Christians should think about Jews, and more an example of how the Cross subverts *all* claims to religious authority based on excluding others – even those made by an Evangelist.

The idea of biblical inspiration does indeed allow that the apparently obvious meaning of a text need not be the only, or even the controlling, meaning. As T.S. Eliot suggests, 'If the word "inspiration" is to have any meaning, it must mean just this: that the speaker or writer is uttering something which he does not wholly understand – or which he may even misinterpret when the inspiration has departed from him.'[39] There can be many layers of meaning and theological depth in a text, and some are deeply buried. It is a perfectly proper approach to the Barabbas story to call attention to such possibilities.

However, it is another matter to claim that a writer not only wrote more than he knew, but wrote that which in its unfathomed depths contradicted his intended meaning. It would be odd to say that Matthew 27:25 is 'really' about how religious power goes wrong, or about the Jews being redeemed by the blood of Christ, if we think St Matthew would be mystified or even offended at such a reading. We have instead at least to ask what might be true (not just historically, but theologically) in Matthew's 'meditated memory' that the people as whole called down Jesus' blood upon them.

At which point it is helpful to remember both how little Matthew actually says, and how much the wider New Testament constrains our theological interpretation of that little. Matthew reports the cry of the crowd, without telling us how to interpret it and without telling us whether God grants the wish of the crowd and curses their children. Arguably, the rest of the New Testament suggests He cannot have done, even given its pervasive hostility to 'the Jews'. Luke's Jesus prays, 'Father, forgive them, for they know not what they do' (23:34). Paul insists that even Jews who do not accept Jesus as Messiah 'are beloved for the sake

---

38. Rowan Williams, *Christ on Trial: How the Gospel Unsettles Our Judgement* (London: Fount, 2000), p. 33.

39. T.S. Eliot, *On Poetry and Poets* (New York: Octagon Books, 1975 [1957]), p. 137.

of their ancestors; for the gifts and the calling of God are irrevocable' (Romans 11:28-29). Set in the context of the whole New Testament, Matthew 27:25 cannot teach that the Jews of all time and places are cursed by God. It does not say so, and the rest of the New Testament suggests otherwise.

Perhaps then we can hear anew what Matthew 27:25 actually says – which may remain deeply uncomfortable but is not obviously wicked and anti-Semitic. The leadership of the Jewish people at the time of Jesus made a choice. For whatever reason, and with whatever level of understanding, they chose to reject Jesus and to collaborate in his execution. Israel as a whole continued to drift towards the politics of militant religious nationalism which would explode in violence three decades later. It was, however dimly recognised, a choice – one with fateful consequences. Rejecting the call of God in Jesus, and embracing the way of Barabbas, spelled disaster for the nation.

That is all we need understand Matthew as trying to say: we do not need notions of collective guilt or of God taking vengeance for his Son's blood. We simply need the thoroughly biblical and Jewish understanding that, when nations stray from the way of God and adopt the politics of power and violence, disaster follows.

Chapter 2

Reaping the Whirlwind: The Christian Churches and the Killing

On Christmas night 1943, the Einsatzkommando IIb received an order to kill 3000 Jews and Gypsies in Russia. The order was executed doubly quick in order to enable the soldiers to go to Midnight Mass.[1]

In the summer of 1944, a German army chaplain named Walter Höchstädter, deeply distressed by reports of mass killings of Jews, circulated a powerful protest among his fellow troops. He wrote:

> The anti-Jewish madness which in the Middle Ages raged in all its fury has now entered its acute stage. The Church, the congregation of Jesus Christ, has to make confession. If she does not do so, then she has failed in her trust, just as she failed when she encouraged the persecution of witches. The blood of millions of slaughtered Jews, men, women and

---

1. The incident is reported in Didier Pollefeyt, 'Auschwitz, or How Good People Can Do Evil: An Ethical Interpretation of the Perpetrators and Victims of the Holocaust in Light of the French Thinker Tzvetan Todorov', in G. Jan Colijn and Marcia Sachs Littell (eds), *Confronting the Holocaust: A Mandate for the 21st Century* (Lanham, MD: University Press of America, 1997), p. 98.

children cries aloud to heaven. The Church must not remain
silent.[2]

It would be good to write that Höchstädter was typical and that,
despite its dismally anti-Semitic history, the Church offered brave
resistance when the supreme moral test came. He was not and the
Church did not. There were indeed brave individuals who either spoke
out against the genocide or quietly took action to save Jews from it.
Often, they acted from deep Christian motives. As Martin Gilbert
observes, the rescuers:

> are central to the story of a Nazi-dominated Europe within
> which righteous acts testified to the survival of humane
> values, and to the courage of those who saved human life
> rather than allow it to be destroyed. In every country under
> Nazi rule or occupation, the desire to help remained strong,
> despite widespread hostility or resistance. Six million Jews
> were murdered, but tens of thousands were saved.[3]

However, as those numbers suggest, the rescuers were the splendid
exception rather than the rule. The murder of six million people was
not possible without the direct involvement of tens if not hundreds of
thousands of Germans and their allies, and the acquiescence or support
lent them by the surrounding culture – that of Christian Europe. Henry
Huttenbach writes:

> it must be remembered that those who did escape camps
> ran away into societies poisoned by anti-Semitic sentiments.
> The vast majority perished at the hands of collaborators with
> Germany's scheme to exterminate the Jews, whether Swiss
> border guards refusing entrance to anyone over sixteen, or
> the French police arresting foreign Jews, or Poles refusing to
> hide escapees from ghettoes, or Russian partisans who killed
> Jews seeking to join them in their fight against the Germans.[4]

---

2. Cited in Richard Gutteridge, *Open Thy Mouth for the Dumb: The German Evangelical Church and the Jews 1879-1950* (Oxford: Basil Blackwell, 1976), p. 248.
3. Martin Gilbert, *The Righteous: The Unsung Heroes of the Holocaust* (London: Black Swan, 2003), p. 15.
4. Cited in Gilbert, *The Righteous*, p. 14.

Nor should the refusal of many other nations, the United Kingdom included, to grant asylum to the vast majority of German Jews be forgotten.[5] The likes of Höchstädter are pinpricks of light in a sea of darkness.

It is simply impossible to give a fully adequate account of the Church's role during the killing years in a book of this nature. One inadequate way is that chosen here: to focus on the statements and action of the official representatives of Christianity – the clergy, both Protestant and Catholic. That is not wholly unreasonable, insofar as these are representative figures charged with the moral and spiritual leadership of their communities. However, it does carry the risk that the 'big picture' is lost and the big picture is terribly simple: people raised in a broadly Christian culture either killed or failed to stop six million people being killed for no reason other than being Jewish. Nearly all the killers were baptised; many of them were believers. As historians such as Christopher Browning and Daniel Goldhagen have shown, they were not forced to become murderers, indeed many took grim pride in their work.[6] Beyond the killers themselves, millions more stood by approving – or, at least, not disapproving enough to do anything to stop it. These too were Christians.

The central conclusion of this chapter is therefore inescapable even from the start. At the very least, the Holocaust marks a catastrophic failure of Christianity. The failure is so catastrophic that a later chapter must face the question: is the Gospel itself disproved? Can the Church be so poisoned and poisonous that the Gospel itself becomes incredible? We postpone that question for the moment and turn to the evidence. How did the leadership of Christianity, Protestant and Catholic, respond to the supreme moral crisis of the Holocaust?

Pius XII: Hitler's Pope?

If it is inadequate to assess Christian behaviour during the Holocaust with reference to the clergy only, it may seem even more illegitimate to focus on one man – even if he was Pope. Many Protestants would

---

5. Louise London, *Whitehall and the Jews 1933-1948: British Immigration Policy and the Holocaust* (Cambridge: Cambridge University Press, 2000).

6. See Christopher R. Browning, *Ordinary Men: Reserve Police Battalion 101 and the Final Solution in Poland* (London: Penguin, 2001), and Goldhagen, *Hitler's Willing Executioners*. The two disagree sharply on whether a uniquely German anti-Semitism caused the Holocaust but agree that the killers required little coercion.

strenuously deny that the Pope in any sense represents them. Furthermore, the Roman Catholic Church itself is vastly complex and, papal fantasies notwithstanding, has never been utterly defined by the policies and personalities of Peter's successors.

Nevertheless, the exercise is not futile. The Roman Catholic Church is the largest Christian Church in the world, and the Pope holds an utterly central place in its self-understanding. Moreover, this particular Pope, Pius XII, was deeply immersed in the European conflict of which the Holocaust formed part – and the Holocaust came right to his doorstep, as the Nazis rounded up the Jews of Rome. Given the claims Catholics make for the papacy, how he acquitted himself is of critical importance for them at least. Moreover, other Christians should be realistic: globally, the Pope is Christianity's foremost representative. They, too, have a stake in the verdict on Pius XII. Did he deserve the eulogy of Golda Meir, Israel's then foreign minister, who said on his death in 1958 that 'when fearful martyrdom came to our people in the decade of Nazi terror, the voice of the Pope was raised for the victims. The life of our times was enriched by a voice speaking out on the great moral truths'? Or was he, as the title of one damning indictment puts it, 'Hitler's Pope'?[7]

The Case for the Defence

The central charge against Pius XII is that, *pace* Meir, he was silent in the face of genocide unfolding all around him. Popes have been famously good, throughout history, at denouncing things – especially the wicked ways of secular governments. Yet, during the Holocaust: silence. This was, admittedly, not absolute. Pius' defenders point to his Christmas broadcast in 1942, in which he lamented 'those hundreds of thousands who, without any fault of their own, sometimes only by reason of their nationality or their race, are marked down for death or gradual extinction'. When he spoke those words, the Pope knew in broad terms what was happening at Auschwitz and the other camps.[8] Consequently, the broadcast seems oblique: could there not have been a much clearer denunciation of the Nazis? Interestingly, at least one official in the main

---

7. John Cornwell, *Hitler's Pope: The Secret History of Pius XII* (London: Penguin, 1999).

8. See Kevin Madigan, 'Appendix A: The Vatican and the Final Solution: What Was Known, and When', in Judith H. Banki and John T. Pawlikowski OSM (eds), *Ethics in the Shadow of the Holocaust: Christian and Jewish Perspectives* (Chicago: Sheed and Ward, 2001), pp. 175-210, pp. 199-200.

security office of the German Reich thought otherwise, noting furiously that 'in a manner never known before, the Pope has repudiated the National Socialist New European Order ... here he is virtually accusing the German people of injustice towards the Jews, and makes himself the mouthpiece of Jewish war criminals'.[9]

It is not clear how representative this note is of wider Nazi reaction to the Pope's remarks. Certainly, no forceful retaliation followed. On other occasions, such as the deportation of Rome's Jews in September 1943, the Pope earned plaudits from the German ambassador to Rome for doing 'everything he can in this delicate matter not to strain relations with the German Government'.[10] Pius was ever the diplomat (having served as papal ambassador to Germany and as Vatican Secretary of State before becoming Pope). As Michael Marrus observes, his Vatican did not even condemn Nazi Germany directly 'for the imprisonment of hundreds of priests in Dachau, Mauthausen, Sachsenhausen, and elsewhere; and it refrained from criticising the Germans by name for their genocidal policies in Poland, with the attendant murder of some twenty percent of the Catholic clergy there'.[11] Fiery denunciation was simply not Pius' style.

This restrained, delicate approach might also be attributed to fear: of how the Nazis might retaliate against a more interventionist Pope personally, against the Church more widely and, indeed, against the Jews. Frank Coppa notes the contrast that is frequently drawn between Pius XII's post-war ferocity against Communism (imposing instant excommunication on any who supported or joined the Party), and the delicacy of his approach to the Nazis. Simple geography, Coppa judges, played its part 'in permitting Pius to take a more fervent stance against the Soviet Union, which was hundreds of miles away, while Hitler's Germany was next door and its Italian ally virtually surrounded Vatican City. ... [W]as Pacelli's boyhood fear of martyrdom a factor in the papal decision?'[12] Michael Phayer suggests that Pius' principal fear was for the

---

9. Gilbert, *The Righteous*, p. 434.

10. Guenter Lewy, 'Pius XII, the Jews and the German Catholic Church', in Robert P. Ericksen and Susannah Heschel, *Betrayal: German Churches and the Holocaust* (Minneapolis: Fortress Press, 1999), pp. 129-48, p. 146.

11. Michael R. Marrus, 'We Remember: The Vatican and the Holocaust in Historical Perspective', in Banki and Pawlikowski (eds), *Ethics in the Shadow of the Holocaust*, pp. 117-32, p. 128.

12. Frank J. Coppa, *The Life and Pontificate of Pope Pius XII: Between History and Controversy* (Washington, DC: Catholic University of America Press, 2013), p. 256.

physical integrity of Rome. He could not invite the destruction of the Eternal City, of which he viewed himself the guardian.[13]

These speculations seem unconvincing. After all, at one point, Pius actually involved himself in seeking Allied support for a putative German generals' plot against Hitler, which would have seen the latter deposed and peace terms struck.[14] More publicly, he also strongly urged American Catholics not to oppose Roosevelt's extension to the USSR of the Lend-Lease programme of military aid.[15] This contravened the clear teaching of his predecessor, Pius XI, who in *Divini Redemptoris* (1937) had said bluntly: 'Communism is intrinsically wrong, and no one who would save Christian civilisation may collaborate with it in any undertaking whatsoever.' The fact that Pius XII nonetheless did so (appealing to the distinction between aiding the Russian people and aiding the Communist state) disproves any charge that he was 'Hitler's Pope' and shows that he was not averse to running huge risks.

What of fear for the Jews? Would papal denunciation have sparked even fiercer Nazi violence against them? After the event it is easy to respond that nothing could have made the persecution worse. However, as Michael Burleigh notes:

> As long as [Pius XII] did not know that the intention was to kill every Jewish man, woman and child in Europe – and that intention was not clear at the start – then the desire not to make matters worse may have been a crucial consideration. It is easy, with hindsight, to object that matters could not have been much worse, but this is an utterly unhistorical approach to events that for Pius were either in the present or the future rather than sixty years in the past.[16]

Indeed, perhaps even with hindsight things are not entirely clear: because – awful as they were – things *could* have been worse. The

---

13. Michael Phayer, 'Ethical Questions about Papal Policy' ', in Carol Rittner and John K. Roth (eds), *Pope Pius XII and the Holocaust* (London: Continuum, 2002), pp. 221-32, pp. 224-26.

14. Michael Burleigh, *Sacred Causes: Religion and Politics from the European Dictators to Al Qaeda* (London: Harper Collins, 2006), pp. 225-26.

15. See Harold H. Tittman Jr, *Inside the Vatican of Pius XII: The Memoir of an American Diplomat during World War II* (New York: Doubleday, 2004), pp. 56-68, for a full account of this.

16. Burleigh, *Sacred Causes*, p. 252.

deportations from Rome have already been mentioned: the most striking thing about these, however, is that four out of five Roman Jews escaped, either into the Vatican or religious houses across the city.[17] That is why, after the war, the Jews of Rome raised a statue to Pius XII and (controversially) the chief rabbi of the city converted to Catholicism and took the Pope's name in baptism. What if the Pope had chosen instead to confront Hitler with all rhetorical guns blazing? Quite possibly, the SS would have launched an assault on the Vatican, those Roman houses, and all the other refuges across Western Europe where Jews were hiding. There were some – very fragile – political and diplomatic constraints on how the Holocaust unfolded: unequivocal papal condemnation might have finally thrown these off.

Defenders of the Pope point to an example which weighed heavily on Pius. In the summer of 1942, the Catholic Archbishop of Utrecht led the denunciation of the deportation of Dutch Jews. The Nazi response was to expand the programme: Jewish converts to Catholicism, hitherto exempted, were now deported. Hindsight tells us that, ultimately, they would have been killed anyway, but all Pius could see was that dramatic ecclesiastical intervention had made things worse.[18] It is also worth noting that two years later, when the full scale of Nazi intent was even more clearly visible (and, arguably, the Nazi ability to retaliate was diminishing) Pius' envoy in Hungary, Archbishop Angelo Rotta, was dramatically more active in seeking to prevent deportations than had been the case previously in other countries. As John Pawlikowski notes, 'there is no doubt that if one is to point to a bright spot in the official Catholic response to the plight of the Jews under the Nazis, Hungary would be it'.[19] If we are charitable and say that Rotta's actions should be considered as the Pope's, then there may be grounds for thinking that, when Pius thought he really could make a difference, he was eager to do so.

Before Hungary in 1944, however, what would dramatic intervention against the Nazis really have accomplished? The risk was only worth running if, by speaking, the Pope could actually change things. The Nazis did not pretend to be Catholics: there was no prospect that Hitler would simply bend the knee to papal authority. Nor could the broad

---

17. Gilbert, *The Righteous*, p. 442.
18. Burleigh, *Sacred Causes*, pp. 249-52.
19. John T. Pawlikowski, 'Reflections on Pope Pius XII: The Known and the Unknown', in Rittner and Roth (eds), *Pope Pius XII and the Holocaust*, pp. 56-69, p. 60.

mass of German Catholics be relied upon. To come out unequivocally against Nazism, when this would have been understood as condemning a Germany fighting for her life against Stalin, and to do so on behalf of the Jews, whom the Church had denigrated for centuries, this might provoke a great withdrawal of German Catholics from the Church.[20] Far better, some would say, to do all one practically could behind the scenes to actually save Jews, and not say anything to jeopardise this work. If the cost is being branded 'Hitler's Pope' by those with little historical understanding – so be it.

The Case for the Prosecution

There is however a darker possibility. Whilst the Nazis may not have owed Catholicism any kind of allegiance, many of their collaborators did. The leaders of Vichy France, for instance, approached the Vatican for endorsement of their anti-Semitic legislation and were relieved when it was given (though it is worth noting that the Vatican drew the line at approving deportations from France – which, nevertheless, continued apace).[21] The collaborationist government of Slovakia, notable for its vigorous participation in the annihilation of the Jews, was actually headed by a priest, Monsignor Jozef Tiso, upon whom no kind of papal discipline was ever imposed.[22] There *were* politicians, policemen, soldiers, civil servants and ordinary citizens who might have paid heed to a clarion call to resistance from Rome – or even to a discreet papal instruction. Why did it never come?

Daniel Goldhagen voices the suspicion in devastating terms:

> I am not saying that the Pope and the clergy in general actively wanted the Jews to die. But aside from the small percentage of clergy who aided the Jews, we cannot be sure that the Catholic clergy in general opposed the mass annihilation. We cannot be sure that if they did, then they opposed it unequivocally and with all their hearts. We cannot be sure that they beheld the killing of the Jews, whom many of them deemed guilty of the greatest offences, unambiguously as a crime and a sin. And we have such doubts because of the widespread antisemitism

---

20. Harold Tittman recalls Pius XII effectively admitting this to a group of Allied diplomats, *Inside the Vatican of Pius XII*, pp. 124-25.
21. Sergio I. Minerbi, 'Pope Pius XII: A Reappraisal', in Rittner and Roth (eds), *Pius XII and the Holocaust*, pp. 85-104, p. 96.
22. Ibid.

among them, and because of the things that many of them did. We can be sure that a significant number of bishops and priests willingly contributed to the annihilation of the Jews. We can also be sure that the Pope and the clergy's stunning lack of public sympathy for the Jews, their aid for critical acts of criminality, their support for so many more, and their extensive political blame and guilt definitively implicate the Catholic Church broadly and deeply.[23]

The case for the prosecution of Pius XII might begin by taking seriously the context within which he was formed. He was marinated in the long tradition of Christian anti-Semitism traced in our last chapter, which had reached a particular intensity in the late nineteenth and early twentieth centuries. This period is characterised by the Church's fierce struggle against the ideas and energies of revolutions, first French and later Russian. The tone is best caught by Pius IX's *Syllabus of Errors* (1864) which, amongst many other things, condemned the proposition that the Pope should reconcile himself to ideas of 'progress, liberalism and modern civilisation'. Goldhagen notes that anti-Semitism was a key weapon in the Church's armoury for this struggle: 'appealing to all people beholden to embattled institutions, practices and traditions, the Church sought to mobilise the vast reservoir of European anti-semitism in its political battle against modernity … if modernity could be identified with Jews, then half the battle against it was won'.[24]

It was not, of course, difficult to identify Jews with progressive and revolutionary forces in the early twentieth century: unsurprisingly, they were prominent in movements that promised liberation from the oppression of *ancien régime* Christian anti-Semitism. Pius XII came up against this personally in 1919, when he was based in Munich as papal nuncio to Germany. Power in Bavaria had been briefly seized by Communists. In his report to Rome, Pius described the scene when his deputy went to negotiate with the revolutionaries for the protection of diplomatic residences:

The confusion totally chaotic, the filth totally nauseating; soldiers and armed workers coming and going, the building, once the home of a king, resounding with screams, vile

---

23. Daniel J. Goldhagen, *A Moral Reckoning: The Role of the Catholic Church in the Holocaust and Its Unfulfilled Duty of Repair* (New York: Vintage, 2003), p. 221.

24. Ibid., p. 119.

language, profanities. Absolute hell. An army of employees were dashing to and fro, giving out orders, waving bits of paper, and in the midst of all this, a gang of young women, of dubious appearance, Jews like all the rest of them, hanging around in all the offices with lecherous demeanour and suggestive smiles. The boss of this female rabble was Levien's mistress [Levien was the communist leader], a young Russian woman, a Jew and a divorcee. ... Levien is a young man, of about thirty or thirty-five, also Russian and a Jew. Pale, dirty with drugged eyes, hoarse voice, vulgar, repulsive, with a face that is both intelligent and sly.[25]

Perhaps the Nuncio was simply passing on the impressions of his deputy, but there is nothing in the letter – which is, after all, Pius' own report – to distance himself in any way from the clear linking of Jews and revolution or, as Cornwell observes, from 'the repeated references to the Jewishness of these individuals, amid the catalogue of epithets describing their physical and moral repulsiveness, [which] gives an impression of stereotypical anti-Semitic contempt'.[26] Richard Rubenstein notes that the experience of the Bavarian Soviet Republic was seared into Pius XII's soul:

[for him] the Communist revolution was not something that happened in distant Russia. He experienced it directly. He also saw the right-wing nationalist forces that suppressed the revolution as defenders of Christian civilisation against the assault of rootless, godless Communists, many of whom were Jews. That lesson was never to leave him. If he had any doubts concerning the destabilising consequences of Jewish emancipation and the Jews' entrance into European intellectual and political life before Munich 1919, he had none thereafter.[27]

The Church's fear of revolutionary modernity, which in Russia and Spain had brought with it intense anti-clerical violence, 'all but guaranteed that, in Germany, Italy and elsewhere, the Nazis, Fascists

---

25. Cited in Cornwell, *Hitler's Pope*, p. 75.
26. Ibid.
27. Richard L. Rubenstein, 'Pope Pius XII and the Shoah', in Rittner and Roth (eds), *Pope Pius XII and the Holocaust*, pp. 175-202, p. 184.

and rightist tyrannies would be greeted by churchmen with relief if not acclaim'.[28] The authoritarian right, of course, presented its own problems. Much of Pius' energies as Nuncio to Germany following the ascent of the Nazis would be devoted, for instance, to defending the independence of Catholic education and youth work against totalitarian pressure. However, it is not surprising that the Church shared in the general willingness of conservative Europe in the early 1930s to see the Nazis and those like them as not quite as bad as Communists and as a bulwark in that larger struggle. As Frank Coppa puts it, 'While the Holy See had few illusions about National Socialism, it had absolutely none about Bolshevism. The first persecuted the Church; the second prohibited its existence within its borders.'[29]

It is in this context that the Concordat signed between the Roman Catholic Church and Nazi Germany in 1933 should be understood. From the Vatican's point of view, this treaty was of vital importance in establishing a limited measure of freedom and security for the Church, especially in the field of education and youth work. However, a high price had been exacted. Essentially, the Church acquiesced in the 'political castration of Catholicism in Hitler's Germany'.[30] The Catholic Centre Party (still a formidable electoral force) was dissolved and Hitler left unchallenged as Führer. In the view of Cardinal Faulhaber of Munich:

> At a time when the major nations in the world faced the new Germany with cool reserve and considerable suspicion, the Catholic Church, the greatest moral power on earth, through the concordat expressed its confidence in the new German government. This was a deed of immeasurable significance for the reputation of the new government abroad.[31]

Hitler himself said: 'one should only consider it a great achievement. The concordat gave Germany an opportunity and created an area of trust that was particularly significant in the developing struggle against international Jewry.'[32]

---

28. Goldhagen, *A Moral Reckoning*, pp. 174-75.
29. Coppa, *The Life and Pontificate of Pope Pius XII*, p. 167.
30. Eamon Duffy, *Saints and Sinners: A History of the Popes* (New Haven, CT: Yale University Press, 2001), p. 341.
31. Cardinal Faulhaber of Munich, speaking in 1937. Cited in Goldhagen, *A Moral Reckoning*, pp. 179-80.
32. Cited Cornwell, *Hitler's Pope*, p. 7.

The reference to the Jews is especially striking since at no point did Nazi treatment of the Jews arise in the negotiations preceding the Concordat, nor in subsequent diplomatic exchanges. Robert Ventresca writes that, even as Nazi anti-Semitism grew more radical and aggressive, the Vatican:

> continued to cling to the same principle that had dictated [its] response to Nazi anti-Semitism since 1933 – that, while the persecution of Jews or any other group on religious or racial grounds was decidedly un-Christian, ultimately it was a political matter, the purview of the civil authorities, and therefore not something the church had any standing to address.[33]

We shall see an identical distinction being drawn between the political and the religious spheres by many German Protestants, with identical results: either silence about the Jews, or active collaboration in their destruction.

The Vatican often had cause to complain that the German Government did not honour its side of the Concordat. On occasion, the strain burst into open hostility – most famously in 1937, when Pope Pius XI issued the encyclical *Mit brennender Sorge* ('With Burning Anxiety'). It was a response to the steady encroachment of Nazism upon the Church's liberties and has been described by Michael Burleigh as 'an immensely astute critique of everything that Nazism stood for'.[34] Although the encyclical pre-dates Pius XII's papacy, the then Cardinal Pacelli was one of those closely involved in the preparation of the document. Its dismissal of key tenets of Nazi ideology is contemptuous: 'The peak of the revelation as reached in the Gospel of Christ is final and permanent. It knows no retouches by human hand; it admits no substitutes or arbitrary alternatives such as certain leaders pretend to draw from the so-called myth of race and blood.'[35] This does not sound like 'Hitler's Pope'.

However, there is no explicit denunciation of anti-Semitism in *Mit brennender Sorge*. Robert Ventresca notes that the encyclical's:

> real target was not so much Nazi racial theory as it was the persistent violation of the letter and the spirit of the 1933

---

33. Robert A. Ventresca, *Soldier of Christ: The Life of Pope Pius XII* (Cambridge, MA, and London: Belknap Press of Harvard University, 2013), p. 147.
34. Burleigh, *Sacred Causes*, p. 190.
35. *Mit brennender Sorge*, Encyclical of Pius XI, 14 March 1937, para. 17.

> Concordat, of the Hitler government's incessant attempts to interfere with, curtail, or repress altogether the full and free expression of German Catholic life in its varied dimensions.[36]

The Jews are striking by their absence, apart from (in passing) the standard charge of Christ-killing.[37] There is no critique, for instance, of the recently passed Nuremburg Laws. This silence endures through all of Pius XII's encyclicals, even *Communium Interpretes Dolorum*, issued in April 1945. This brief reflection on the war years makes no explicit mention of the Jews or the Holocaust. Such reticence could perhaps be defended in 1942 on the grounds that it saved lives: that argument is difficult to make either in 1937, when the Holocaust was not yet underway, or in 1945, when Nazi power was collapsing. Yet, still, reticence reigned.

It might be argued that the implications of denouncing the mythology of race and blood, or of *Mit Brennender Sorge's* insistence that 'human laws in flagrant contradiction with the natural law are vitiated with a taint which no force, no power can mend', are so clear that they need hardly be called implications. Who, reading this, could not understand that Nazi anti-Semitism stood condemned? The answer, tragically, is perhaps those long steeped in Christian anti-Semitism, which effectively (if not consistently in theory) had removed the Jews from the category of ordinary human beings entitled to basic dignities and protection. Besides, Pius XII was capable of being crystal clear when the human dignity of those he really cared about was attacked. In *Mystici Corporis Christi* (1943), he unequivocally condemned the Nazi programme of euthanasia:

> Conscious of the obligations of Our high office We deem it necessary to reiterate this grave statement today, when to Our profound grief We see at times the deformed, the insane, and those suffering from hereditary disease deprived of their lives, as though they were a useless burden to Society. ... [W]ho that is possessed of sound judgment does not recognize that this not only violates the natural and the divine law written in the heart of every man, but that it outrages the noblest instincts of humanity?[38]

---

36. Ventresca, *Soldier of Christ*, p. 117.
37. *Mit brennender Sorge*, para. 16.
38. *Mystici Corporis Christi*, Encyclical of Pius XII, 29 June 1943, para. 94.

Here we see not only that Pius was prepared to speak out firmly against Nazi crimes, but that this speaking had some effect. It formed part of a widespread Catholic campaign against the 'T4' euthanasia programme, spearheaded by Bishop Galen of Münster who in August 1941 unequivocally denounced it as murder. Joseph Goebbels, the Nazi Propaganda Minister, told his post-war interrogators that the regime had judged it politically impossible to punish Galen: 'the population of Münster could have been regarded as lost during the war, if anything were done against the Bishop, and in that fear one safely could include the whole of [the state of] Westphalia'.[39] Instead, T4 was temporarily shelved and later restarted only under more secretive conditions.

Could concerted Catholic resistance to the Nazi assault on the Jews have had a similar effect? The answer is uncertain. Hatred for the Jews was more fundamental to Nazism than the euthanasia programme, and the regime may have been less willing to grant even the appearance of compromise. By the early 1940s, the stakes for both Jewish and Catholic lives were so high that the Church was perhaps right to decline the gamble. However, the critically important truth is that, in the earlier stages of the assault, such concerted resistance on behalf of the Jews was impossible – because neither the leadership of the Church nor the faithful at large saw the fate of the Jews as supremely important. In fact, there was significant Catholic (and, of course, broader Christian) support for the preliminary stages of Nazi anti-Semitic persecution. As Richard Rubenstein observes:

> there was nothing in the anti-Semitic policies of the Nazis concerning the Jews *before* World War II to which the Church would or could object as long as baptised Jews were excluded from the Nazi mandated disabilities. In effect, the Nazis were implementing a long-cherished Vatican goal, the disenfranchisement of non-believing Jews in Christian Europe and their ultimate return to the ghetto.[40]

So it was that, even when there was a clear possibility of overturning Nuremburg-style anti-Jewish measures, the Church sometimes failed to support it. Goldhagen records how in August 1943 the papal Nuncio to Italy met with the new anti-Fascist government in Rome to press for the exemption of Jewish converts to Catholicism from the anti-Jewish laws.

---

39. Cited in Goldhagen, *A Moral Reckoning*, p. 80.
40. Rubenstein, 'Pope Pius XII and the Holocaust', p. 198.

Asked by Jewish bodies to lobby for the repeal of all such laws, he refused, reporting to the Vatican that some had merit and should be confirmed.[41] There is no reason to think Pius would have dissented from that view. Like his nuncio, he was shaped by a religious and political formation in which discrimination against Jews seemed perfectly reasonable.

It is that mindset, Pius' accusers say, which means that the fate of the Jews simply failed to strike with sufficient force upon the Pope's conscience. There was, for Pius, a bigger issue at stake: the defence of the Church and Christian civilisation against revolutionary modernity, especially in its Russian Communist form. He had no love for Nazism; he was fully aware of the menace it posed to the things he cherished. However, it is hard to shake the perception that, for him, it was not quite as frightening and evil as the Communist threat. Nazis were never to be opposed with quite such vehemence and radicalism, because (at least outside Poland) they were not so murderously destructive of the Church. As for the Jews, you must work behind the scenes to alleviate, as much as you could, the worst of their plight. You must hope for what eventually happened: the defeat of Nazism in the West by more civilised powers. After that, indeed, one could even work with some elements of the old Fascist and Nazi regimes to continue the anti-Communist struggle. The fate of the Jews was for Pius but one factor – and far from the most important – in a morally and politically complex world-situation. It was not the supreme test, by which the Church would stand or fall. Eighty years on, it is that basic misjudgement which seems most culpable. We turn now from the successor of Peter to the Protestants. Was their response to Nazi genocide any more creditable?

The Protestants and the Killing

In early 1933, the leading German Protestant theologian Emmanuel Hirsch enthusiastically welcomed Hitler's appointment as Chancellor. 'All of us who stand in the present moment of our *Volk*', he wrote, 'experience it as a sunrise of divine goodness after endless years of dark misery.'[42] Hirsch would remain an enthusiastic backer of the Nazi Party until the bitter end. He was a Patron Member of the SS, committed to giving regular financial support to the organisation. He was an

---

41. Goldhagen, *A Moral Reckoning*, pp. 197-98.
42. Cited in Robert P. Ericksen, 'Assessing the Heritage: German Protestant Theologians, Nazis, and the "Jewish Question"', in Ericksen and Heschel (eds), *Betrayal*, pp. 22-39, p. 26.

influential adviser to Ludwig Müller, the even more committed Nazi *Reichsbischof* – a new post which, in line with Nazi ideology, radically centralised the leadership of the largely autonomous German regional churches. Strikingly, Hirsch's welcome of Hitler's rise to power was by no means untypical of German Protestant reaction. This was in 1933, well before the police state and its repressive methods were firmly entrenched. The adulation was unforced. Why?

German Protestants did not exist in a separate political universe from Catholics, and the biggest single factor in explaining both communities' response to Hitler and the Holocaust is a shared one. Like Catholics, Protestants were preoccupied by the Communist threat, and they found it equally difficult to disentangle this from more general liberal and democratic trends. There was a deep sense that an old and established order faced radical threat on multiple fronts and, crucially, this old order was not that of the democratic Weimar Republic. That polity was new and suspect, especially to those who had been formed and trained to defend the pre-war Bismarckian order. Richard Gutteridge observes that 'the vast majority of the Protestant clergy viewed the post-war democratic set-up with suspicion and dislike, as quite unacceptably international and liberal'.[43]

In the 1920s, that opposition crystallised into support for the *Deutschnationale Volkspartei* (DNVP), which up to 80 per cent of Protestant clergy supported. The party sought a national renaissance, a German people reunited and reborn in strength and self-confidence. The nation needed to overcome the enemy within – all that tended to factionalism, all that dissolved traditional social roles and identities, all that was insufficiently German. As Gutteridge observes, such politics fed on suspicion of the 'modern, liberating, sophisticated and cosmopolitan': all that tended towards national disintegration.[44] The Jew provided a convenient symbol for all this: the citizen of nowhere, the rootless, disloyal outsider. Anti-Semitism thus formed a fundamental part of the DNVP's rhetoric and strategy. Neither Hitler, nor the Protestant welcome for him, came out of the blue.

In several key ways, German Protestants were even more susceptible to the attractions of Hitler than their Catholic counterparts. Michael Burleigh attributes this to the different organisational structures of the two traditions, and their relations to wider culture. German Catholicism had rigid lines of internal authority and was institutionally embedded

---

43. Gutteridge, *Open Thy Mouth for the Dumb*, p. 35.
44. Ibid., p. 38.

in the global Church. Structurally, it was not prone to blow readily with the prevailing wind in any particular national culture, and there were fewer maverick individuals who might compromise its overall witness. German Protestantism, by contrast, was on principle decentralised and committed to the primacy of individual conscience. It was also sharply conscious of a vocation to be the Church of the German *Volk*: not just the Church *in* Germany, but truly *of* Germany. Thus, there was both a reluctance to be too radically out of step with the wider culture and greater freedom to move away from unfashionable traditional positions. In the case of euthanasia, for example:

> a highly decentralised Protestant Church seems to have lost interest in controlling its own charitable apparatus, to the extent that pro-eugenic professional enthusiasts within its ruling councils went increasingly unchallenged as the Depression made their arguments for sterilisation seem economically compelling. Protestantism was generally more prone to worrying about seeming out of step with scientific modernism – and other secular trends – than a Catholicism steeped in natural law doctrines, and in which the autonomy and integrity of the family was so central.[45]

All this suggests why, as James Hawes notes, Protestants were much more likely than Catholics to vote for the Nazis, and why a senior SS officer could observe in 1939 that 'one can declare with certainty that the Lutheran part of the population has a better understanding of the struggle and mission of the SS than the Catholic part'.[46] It also explains why one aspect of the Protestant response to Hitler has no real Catholic parallel – the self-styled 'German Christians'. This movement sought to synthesize Nazism and Christianity through a fundamental recasting of traditional religion.[47] So, for instance, German Christians often held that Jesus was not actually Jewish at all, but Aryan. St Paul had reinvented him as a Jew, meaning that large swathes of the New Testament had to be ignored as fundamentally misleading – whilst the Old Testament was of

---

45. Burleigh, *Sacred Causes*, p. 180.
46. James Hawes, *The Shortest History of Germany* (London: Old Street Publishing, 2017), pp. 164-65, pp. 178-79.
47. See Doris L. Bergen, *Twisted Cross: The German Christian Movement in the Third Reich* (Chapel Hill: University of North Carolina Press, 1996), for an overview of this movement.

no use whatsoever to Christians. It is worth noting that the latter point only restated in a highly provocative way a thesis advanced some years previously by the highly respected father of German liberal Protestant theology, Adolf von Harnack.[48] Nevertheless, taken as a whole, the German Christian agenda proved too much even for mainstream Protestantism's cultural flexibility.

It was easy, however, to embrace Nazi anti-Semitism. In the immediate aftermath of *Kristallnacht*, the regional church council of Thuringia reminded its clergy that, '[given] the German people's position towards Jewry, it is out of the question for a pastor, through ministry to Jews, to offer even the slightest impression that the church ... might hinder the state's measures for the final elimination of Jewry from German cultural life'.[49] The Bishop, Martin Sasse, went further still, noting the happy coincidence of *Kristallnacht* with the anniversary of Luther's birthday. To mark it, he issued a booklet of Luther's most extreme anti-Jewish utterances, with a preface hailing the recent burning of the synagogues as 'the crowning moment of the Führer's divinely blessed fight for the complete emancipation of the German people'.[50] Increasingly violent Nazi anti-Semitism was not a reason to oppose Hitler but the reverse.

Sasse, whilst not an isolated figure, does stand at one extreme – and it is very instructive in this connection to look at another figure at the other end of the spectrum.

Dietrich Bonhoeffer and 'the Jewish Question'

Dietrich Bonhoeffer is widely and justly considered a martyr of the Protestant anti-Nazi resistance. His opposition to Nazism extended to assisting in the escape of several Jews to Switzerland and to participation in a plot to overthrow Hitler and end the war.[51] He grasped from the earliest days of the regime that the clash between Christianity and Nazism was stark, fundamental and irreconcilable. This was in large

---

48. Harnack's dismissal of the Old Testament evolved over his career, reaching its climax in his *Marcion* (1921) (reissued, Eugene, OR: Wipf & Stock, 2007).
49. Cited in Wolfgang Gerlach, *And the Witnesses Were Silent: The Confessing Church and the Persecution of the Jews* (Lincoln: University of Nebraska Press, 2000), p. 176.
50. Gutteridge, *Open Thy Mouth for the Dumb*, pp. 190-91.
51. The standard biography is Eberhard Bethge, *Dietrich Bonhoeffer: Theologian, Christian, Contemporary* (London: Collins, 1970).

measure, though not exclusively, because of the latter's murderous hatred of Jews. Two of Bonhoeffer's closest friends were from Jewish families. His reaction to *Kristallnacht* was one of horror and anger: it may have been at this time that he first coined a saying which impressed itself upon his theological students – 'only he who cries out for the Jews may sing Gregorian chants'.[52] Another commentator notes his reflection: 'when today the synagogues are set on fire, tomorrow the churches will burn'.[53] It was also around this time that Bonhoeffer began to distance himself from what Bethge calls the 'defeated remnants' of church opposition to Hitler in large measure because he was ashamed by the timidity of its response to the persecution of the Jews. As James Rudin notes, 'At a time when there were so few models of Christian courage, at a moment in history when the Church seemed to be an accomplice, at worst, or a silent witness, at best, of the Nazi movement, Dietrich Bonhoeffer is a powerful corrective.'[54]

Sadly, however, even such an iconic figure has a complicated record on anti-Semitism. This is apparent from Bonhoeffer's one extended piece of writing on the question: 'The Church and the Jewish Question'.[55] In September 1933, the general synod of the Evangelical Church of the old-Prussian Union – the decision-making body for one of the largest of Germany's regional churches – passed the 'Church Law Relating to the Legal Position of Clergy and Church Officers'. This barred those of Jewish descent from holding office in the Church. It was not forced upon the Church by the State but proposed from within the Church itself. The Church's vocation to be truly the German Church, the argument went, meant its ministers needed to be truly German. How could racial aliens, such as Jews, effectively minister to the *Volk*? The new law provoked widespread opposition, prompting the formation of a Pastors' Emergency League, which would in due course grow into

52. Bethge, *Dietrich Bonhoeffer*, p. 512.
53. Kenneth C. Barnes, 'Dietrich Bonhoeffer and Hitler's Persecution of the Jews', in Ericksen and Heschel (eds), *Betrayal*, pp. 110-28, p. 123.
54. James A. Rudin, 'Dietrich Bonhoeffer: A Jewish Perspective', paper presented at the Evangelische Akademie Nordelbien, Hamburg, Germany, 17 June 1987. Unpublished, available online at https://www.jamesrudin .com/publications--reviews/dietrich-bonhoeffer-a-jewish-perspective (accessed 5 Dietrich February 2021), p. 10.
55. Bonhoeffer, 'The Church and the Jewish Question', in Dietrich Bonhoeffer, *Berlin: 1932-1933: Dietrich Bonhoeffer Works, Volume 12*, ed. by Larry L. Rasmussen, trans. by Isabel Best, David Higgins and Douglas W. Stott (Minneapolis: Fortress Press, 2009), pp. 361-71.

the 'Confessing Church'. Taking its stand on the Barmen Declaration of 1933, drafted in part by Bonhoeffer and Karl Barth, this movement asserted the spiritual independence of the Church and its right to order its own life – especially on the controversial question of who could or could not be admitted to the pastorate. Bonhoeffer wrote his essay to provide theological weight to those refusing to countenance a *Judenrein* church.

He begins by enquiring about the fundamental vocations of State and Church. The State exists in order to secure law and order; the Church to proclaim the Gospel. Both must respect each other's distinct vocations and activities. This is simply a restatement of the traditional Lutheran doctrine of the 'two kingdoms'. Therefore, the State has no right to force the Church to exclude baptised Jews from Christian congregations, or to prohibit mission to the Jews, or to say that Jews cannot be ordained ministers of the Church. Furthermore, to make a particular racial identity a prerequisite of full membership of the Church is wholly to undermine the Gospel. This is exactly the battle the apostle Paul fought against those in his day who wanted make circumcision and Jewish identity a precondition of being Christian. Those who make Aryan purity a similar precondition are, says Bonhoeffer, ironically, the truly 'Jewish' ones.[56]

So far, Bonhoeffer's emphasis is on the limits of the State's mandate. The Church, he argues, has a duty to remind the State of these limits and constantly to ask the State whether its actions are truly within its mandate. This means not only checking the State when it overreaches, but also rebuking the State when it under-reaches: when it fails to secure law and order, so that individuals and groups are then deprived of fundamental rights. It matters not who these people are: 'The church has an unconditional obligation to the victims of any societal order, even if they do not belong to the Christian community.'[57] So, when the State fails to protect Jews, or even assaults Jews, the Church has a duty to support them. Such support may even extend beyond charity: 'not just to bind up the wounds of the victims beneath the wheel, but to seize the wheel itself'.[58] When the State flagrantly and unrestrainedly betrays its own vocation to bring law and order, then the Church might need to actively resist the State. Bonhoeffer is on unconventional ground for a Lutheran here and he proceeds cautiously: the threshold has not been

---

56. Ibid., p. 369.
57. Ibid., p. 365.
58. Ibid.

reached clearly yet (September 1933) and it would need a Council of the Church to identify when it had been. However, the basis for his own later costly resistance is clearly being laid.

So far, in many ways so admirable. However, there remain some deeply disturbing aspects to Bonhoeffer's essay. To begin with, although ultimately the essay justifies resistance to the State, it first allows secular government a very large measure of freedom indeed. The echoes of Pius XII, and his reluctance to address political matters which did not impinge upon the essential life of the Church, are clear. The Church:

> has neither to praise nor censure the laws of the state. Instead it has to affirm the state as God's order of preservation in this godless world. It should recognise and understand the state's creation of order – whether good or bad from a humanitarian perspective – as grounded in God's desire for preservation in the midst of the world's chaotic godlessness. … [T]he actions of the state remain free from interference by the church. This is not a schoolmaster-like or peevish objection on the part of the church.[59]

In other words, what the State does might look brutal, but the Church must not presume to judge or scold. If criminals need executing, unions banning, or opposition parties dissolving to secure law and order, the State is justified in doing so. The duty to restrain chaos frees the State from the fussy standards of humanitarian ethics. Quite how Bonhoeffer reconciles all this with the ultimate right of resistance is unclear, but his readers might well feel justified in travelling a long distance with Nazi rule before the question arose.

Even more alarmingly, Bonhoeffer specifically allows great latitude to the State when it comes to the Jews: 'without doubt, one of the historical problems that must be dealt with by our state is the Jewish question, and without doubt the state is entitled to strike new paths in doing so'.[60] Why did Bonhoeffer so readily accept that there was indeed a Jewish question which merited serious attention? Perhaps, whilst helping conservative Lutheran clergy gird themselves for theological resistance to the State, he could not afford to openly doubt widely accepted truths. However, it was still unfortunate to 'give unwitting credence to a conviction widespread

---

59. Ibid., pp. 362-63.
60. Ibid., p. 363.

in his day, namely, that "Jews" were an alien people whose very existence posed a threat to ethnic Germans'.[61] Moreover, even in 1933 – although very few could anticipate the ultimate destination of the Final Solution – it was plainly apparent that the 'new methods' soon to be adopted by a Nazi state towards the Jewish question would be deeply violent and unjust: in that context, to write the state a blank cheque seems morally careless.

Bonhoeffer allows that individual Christians, 'who see themselves called to do so', and those influenced by humanitarian ideals, may well question the State as to the morality of its measures.[62] However, his tone implies that such criticism should be an occasional matter, and always risks being rather airy and idealistic. The State is in the serious, practical business of 'history-making' and, therefore, the Church:

> which lives by the gospel alone and knows the nature of state actions, will never interfere in the functioning of the state in this way, by criticising its history-making actions from the standpoint of any sort of, say, humanitarian ideal. The church knows about the essential necessity for the use of force in this world, and it knows about the 'moral' injustice that is necessarily involved in the use of force in certain concrete state actions.

In other words: one cannot make history without occasionally breaking heads. Thus, 'even today, in the Jewish question, [the Church] cannot address the state directly and demand of it some definite action of a different nature'.[63] So, Bonhoeffer's argument essentially goes: there is a real Jewish question; the State has every right to sort it out; some moral abuses are bound to happen as it does; and the Church is not in the business of scolding, let alone resisting, the State because of those abuses. True, he retained an ultimate right of resistance should the abuses reach an extreme peak, and finally exercised that right at the cost of his life. The Bonhoeffer of 1945 would probably have written a very different essay.[64] However, if even he could think and write like this in

---

61. Stephen R. Haynes, *The Bonhoeffer Legacy: Post-Holocaust Perspectives* (Minneapolis: Fortress Press, 2006), p. 67.
62. Bonhoeffer, 'The Church and the Jewish Question', p. 363.
63. Ibid.
64. This is almost certainly true. However, Stephen Haynes (even while acknowledging some significant shifts in Bonhoeffer's approach) argues

1933, we can appreciate how easily so many other Protestant Christians were swept along by the Nazi surge.

One other feature of Bonhoeffer's essay remains to be noted: he is clear that the Jews can never be, for Christians, just another group of victims: 'The Church of Christ has never lost sight of the thought that the "chosen people", which hung the Redeemer of the world on the cross, must endure the curse for its action in long drawn-out suffering.'[65] With the Gentile executioners of Jesus forgotten, we are back with the blood curse of Matthew 27:25. Admittedly, Bonhoeffer deploys the idea in a nuanced way: it is not just that the Jews suffer for what they did to Christ, but also that this suffering in some way bears a promise within it. God has not destroyed the Jews: He wills that their suffering might end through their repentance and conversion to Christ. Christians do not delight in the destruction of Jews, still less seek to bring it about. They hope, instead, for Israel's turn to Christ. We might read into Bonhoeffer's words a warning to Nazis that the destiny of the Jews is not theirs to control, or to end: 'no state of the world can deal with this enigmatic people, because God has not yet finished with it'.[66] However, one could equally take his words as undermining any moral imperative to end the suffering of the Jews. The Church 'trembles at the sight of the people Israel's history, as God's own free, terrible way with God's own people'.[67] Such language could easily temper the outrage against Jewish suffering and sap the determination to stop it.

Bonhoeffer's comments on the curse are brief and his meaning elusive. What is clear, though, is that he believes that the curse is real and somehow explains Jewish suffering. He attributes theological significance to this suffering, which means that the Church's response to this must rise 'far beyond any sort of cheap moralising'.[68] Even if one accepts Richard Rubenstein's point that the conservative clergy he was writing for would not have been swayed by mere humanitarianism,[69] it is hard not to echo John Bowden's stinging verdict on Karl Barth's equal

---

that the traditional theological assumptions underlying 'The Church and the Jewish Question' were never fully repudiated by Bonhoeffer. See Haynes, *The Bonhoeffer Legacy.*

65. Bonhoeffer, 'The Church and the Jewish Question', p. 367.

66. Ibid.

67. Ibid.

68. Ibid.

69. Richard L. Rubenstein, 'Was Dietrich Bonhoeffer a "Righteous Gentile"?', *International Journal on World Peace* 17, no. 2 (June 2000), pp. 33-46, p. 37.

determination to distance himself from any conventionally ethical response to Nazi terror: 'one longs for him to say, just once, "in the name of mankind, this is wicked", for him to show insight into what other men, women, and children think and feel and suffer as fellow human beings. But this he cannot do.'[70] Instead, at least in 1933, Bonhoeffer theologised terrible Jewish suffering, made it unreal, made it explicable and even justifiable. It invites a terrible last element to our summary of his argument: there is a real Jewish question; the State has every right to sort it out; some moral abuses are bound to happen as it does so; the Church is not in the business of scolding, let alone resisting, the State because of those abuses; and, finally, terribly, the Jews deserve it because of what they did to Christ. If this is how even Bonhoeffer thought, how much more so the others? This is why Stanley Rosenbaum says that, for Jews, Bonhoeffer can only ever be 'the best of a bad lot'.[71]

The Broader Protestant Response

What then of Protestantism more widely? We have already mentioned the emergence of a 'Confessing Church' ready to oppose, in some measure, the total subordination of the Church to the State. However, even many of those brave souls would have vigorously disowned any notion of broader or more fundamental 'resistance' to Hitler. In 1938, the overwhelming majority of Confessing pastors were prepared to swear an oath of allegiance to the Führer. This oath, the authorities made clear, meant 'more than a mere confirmation of the duty enjoined on Christians by the New Testament to be subject to the authorities ... it means the most intimate solidarity with the Third Reich ... and with the man who has created that community and embodies it'.[72] Confessing Church synods attempted to evade this interpretation of the oath. However, the attempts were unconvincing and, at any rate, large numbers of Confessing clergy had sworn even before they were made. This was devastating to Bonhoeffer but should not have been surprising: he knew that many others would have wholeheartedly endorsed the Munich pastor who said in 1937 that 'the Confessing Church had no politics of her own, but rather stood completely and fully behind the Führer, and that her pastors were

---

70. John Bowden, *Karl Barth* (London: SCM, 1971), pp. 74-75.
71. Stanley R. Rosenbaum, 'Dietrich Bonhoeffer: A Jewish View', *Journal of Ecumenical Studies* 18, no. 2 (Spring 1981), pp. 301-7, p. 306.
72. Bethge, *Dietrich Bonhoeffer*, p. 505.

as wholehearted in their support of National Socialism and the Third Reich as they had ever been'.[73]

The critical point to realise is that insofar as the Confessing Church did represent opposition to Nazism, this was only on a very narrow question. Could people of Jewish descent hold office in the Church? The Nazis and their supporters said no: the Church of the German *Volk* must be led by members of that *Volk* and Jews were by definition outsiders. They might be Christians by belief, but they remained biologically Jewish and thus un-German. The Confessing Church stood, by contrast, for the principle that baptism trumps biology and creates a new common identity in Christ. One cannot treat Jews and Gentiles differently within the Church, without denying the reality of that new creation. This is indeed a crucial point but an isolated one. One could be a good Confessing Christian and remain wholly signed up to Nazi militarism, the Führer principle and violent anti-Semitism – and many were. Still more who were not remained hamstrung by the abiding influence of traditional 'two-kingdom' doctrine.

All this explains how the Confessing Church synod in September 1935 was able to affirm with vigorous clarity the necessity of mission to the Jews, that Jews were truly able to become Christian through baptism and that, after baptism, they must be treated as equals within the Church – whilst simultaneously failing even to mention the Nuremburg Laws, promulgated weeks before.[74] Indeed, many Confessing clergy welcomed the Laws. Wilhelm Halfmann, who served as a spiritual director for the Confessing Church in Schleswig-Holstein, wrote: 'we of the church must say, based upon almost two thousand years' experience with the Jews: the state is *right*. It is attempting to protect the German people.'[75] Others willingly allowed their parish registers to be scrutinised to reveal who might have Jewish ancestry. What the State might do with such information was not the Church's concern: it was 'for many pastors almost a relief to be able at least at this point to be obedient in satisfying the requirements of the Nazi Government'.[76] Even *Kristallnacht* was passed over largely in silence. Not even the New Testament injunctions against violence were decisive here: at least some Confessing Christians

---

73. Gutteridge, *Open Thy Mouth for the Dumb*, p. 130.

74. Ibid., p. 158.

75. Cited in Gerlach, *And the Witnesses Were Silent*, p. 105.

76. Heinz Schmidt, cited in Gutteridge, *Open Thy Mouth for the Dumb*, p. 153.

shared the view that 'it was inadmissible to judge or to condemn [anti-Jewish violence] by reference to the Word or to the spirit or thought of the New Testament, since New Testament standards were valid only for the regulating of relations between believing Christians'.[77]

The Confessing Church did not, therefore, represent much threat to Nazism. Insofar as it did, it was gradually worn down by a mixture of harassment, pressure and divide-and-rule tactics by the State and by the mainstream Protestant Church. Bethge writes that by 1941, when the Nazi persecution of the Jews mutated into the full-scale genocide of the Final Solution, 'what was left of the Confessing Church was fully occupied with questions concerning its own existence, and there were only a few brave, isolated actions'.[78] This was not because people did not know what was happening to the Jews in the East. 'Only a modicum of intelligence,' writes Gutteridge:

> ...must surely have been required in order to be pretty certain that the Jews who had been treated with ever increasing barbarity in Germany prior to the outbreak of war were being subjected to something yet worse following deportation. Wholesale and brutal massacre was after all just about the only method for the solution of the Jewish problem left untried.[79]

Nor was it entirely a matter of surmise: eyewitness accounts of the killings were beginning to circulate widely. What was happening was known and the Church – even in its Confessing form – was largely silent.

Silent, that is, until the intervention of Bishop Theophil Wurm of Württemberg in July 1943. Wurm's relationship to the Confessing Church had been ambivalent, but now he wrote as the most senior Bishop in Germany directly to Hitler, calling for a halt to 'the persecution and annihilation to which many men and women under German domination are being subjected, and without judicial trial'.[80] This was:

> in the sharpest contrast to Divine Law and an outrage against the very foundations of western thought and life and against the very God-given right of human existence and human dignity. In invoking this right so absolutely bestowed by God upon

---

77. Ibid., p. 190.
78. Bethge, *Dietrich Bonhoeffer* p.593.
79. Gutteridge, *Open Thy Mouth for the Dumb*, p. 236.
80. The letter is reproduced in ibid., pp. 353-55.

man we solemnly raise our voices in protest against countless
measures that have been adopted in occupied territories.[81]

The letter was forthright, even if the Jewishness of the principal victims
is only briefly touched on. Hitler was enraged, and many senior Nazis
urged that Wurm should be arrested or even executed. Hitler refused:
'this was one of the scores that would be settled once the war was
victoriously over'.[82] Wurm was too popular to proceed against safely:
a recognition which does raise the question of what more forceful
intervention, earlier, from such leaders could have achieved.

Wurm's July 1943 letter stands to the credit of the German Protestant
Church when little else does. However, it was never intended for publication. Wurm intended to make a private appeal to the conscience of
Hitler and other Nazi leaders and was aghast when his letter found its
way into Allied propaganda. He was a loyal German, who did not want
to assist his country's enemies.[83] Moreover, by July 1943 millions had
already been slaughtered. Why did Wurm not protest more promptly
and publicly?

Part of the reason is evident from the letter itself. Wurm writes:

> now that the non-Aryans who have been the victims of the
> German onslaught have been very largely eliminated, it is to
> be feared, in the light of what has already happened in certain
> individual cases, that the so-called 'privileged' non-Aryans
> who have so far been spared are in renewed danger of being
> subjected to the same treatment.[84]

The 'privileged' Jews were those who were married to Aryans and the
children born of such marriages. It is difficult to resist the impression of a
hierarchy of victims: all the murders have been wrong, but to move to this
new class of victim would be even worse. Gutteridge also suggests that
Wurm may have waited until July 1943, because only then was German
defeat beginning to look likely.[85] Perhaps Wurm was writing with an eye
to how things might look after the war (was he really so distressed at
the publication of his letter?) or he may have seen the military disasters

---

81. Ibid., p. 354.
82. Ibid., p. 242.
83. Ibid., p. 242.
84. Ibid., p. 354.
85. Ibid., p. 243.

besetting Germany as a judgement from God inviting, even then, repentance from her leaders. We also cannot discount the dragging influence of Lutheran 'two-kingdom' doctrine and Wurm's own – avowed if 'moderate' – anti-Semitism.[86]

Whatever the reason behind it, Wurm's 1943 intervention was much better than nothing. However, it is not the bright shining light of fierce and timely resistance to Nazism one longs to see. That light never shone. Michael Burleigh's verdict stands for both the Catholic and Protestant traditions:

> [the Church] ... bolted the gates of the innermost sanctum, leaving others to the mercies of the neo-barbarian hordes rampaging outside. Even the notion that they resisted 'reluctantly' probably puts things too strongly, for spasmodic protests over issues directly touching the Church and core Christian teachings were accompanied by silence about terrible crimes against their fellow man and sincere professions of loyalty during times of national crisis.[87]

The record is dire. In the next chapter we examine how Christianity has come to terms with it.

Coda: Christian Nazis?

Are Burleigh's words, damning as they are, too comforting for Christianity? Burleigh contrasts the timorous Church with the neo-barbarian hordes rampaging outside – but there is an even more disturbing possibility. Were the hordes *Christian*? Might they have thought of themselves as carrying out their Christian duty, even to the point of genocide?

Many of those directly involved in the Holocaust certainly thought of themselves as moral beings. Walther Mattner, a Viennese police officer serving in an *Einsatzgruppe* in Belarus wrote home to his wife in October 1941, describing the grim sense of moral duty driving his participation in mass executions of Jews:

---

86. Gerlach, *And the Witnesses Were Silent*, p. 149.
87. Michael Burleigh, *The Third Reich: A New History* (London: Macmillan, 2000), pp. 718-19.

> I aimed calmly and shot with confidence at the women, children, and numerous babies, aware that I have two babies of my own at home, and that these hordes would treat them just the same, or ten times worse perhaps. The death we gave them was nice and quick, compared with the hellish suffering of the thousands and thousands in the GPU jails. The babies flew in great arcs and we shot them to pieces before they fell into the ditch and the water. We need to finish off these brutes who have plunged Europe into war.[88]

Mattner considered his actions justified, even moral. It is not such a great step to considering them as in some sense 'Christian', especially in a culture where that word is treated as largely synonymous with 'decent, upstanding citizen'. That was German culture in the Nazi period: in 1939, 95 per cent of the German population, including a clear majority of Nazi Party members and the Führer himself, officially belonged to either the Roman Catholic or Protestant Church. In this nominal sense at least, it is accurate to describe Nazism as a Christian phenomenon. However, were there Nazis who were more than nominal Christians, for whom Christian faith was an important source for thought and action? Was the Nazi movement as a whole in any real sense Christian?

The foundational Nazi Party Programme of 1920 seems to offer an unambiguous answer. Article 24 stated that:

> the party ... represents the standpoint of a positive Christianity, without tying itself to a particular confession. It fights the spirit of Jewish materialism within us and without us, and is convinced that a lasting recovery of our *Volk* can only take place from within, on the basis of the principle: public need comes before private greed.

'Positive Christianity' was never tightly defined, but its broad contours can be readily identified.[89] It was neither Lutheran nor Reformed. Though Luther himself was hailed as a great German figure, and visionary

---

88. Cited in David Cesarani, *Final Solution: The Fate of the Jews 1933-49* (London: Macmillan, 2016), p. 399.

89. For an overview of 'positive Christianity', see Richard Steigman-Gall, *The Holy Reich: Nazi Conceptions of Christianity 1919-1945* (Cambridge: Cambridge University Press, 2003), ch. 1.

anti-Semite, the Party had no interest in getting bogged down in the ecclesiastical disputes between different strands of Protestantism. It was emphatically not Roman Catholic, given that church's internationalist emphasis and the potent figure of the Pope rivalling the Führer as a focus for allegiance. As the religion of a revolutionary movement, it was sharply anti-sacerdotal and anti-clerical. Its positive passion was for national unity and spiritual renewal, expressed above all in social action through such highly successful Nazi programmes as Winter Relief. Finally, of course, it encouraged hatred and persecution of the Jews. The historic churches, with their Jewish influence in the shape (for instance) of the continued used of the Hebrew Scriptures and with their tired conservatism, their rituals and intellectualism, were largely irrelevant – if not actually obstructions – to the spiritual revival Hitler wanted to bring about.

This did not stop some leading Nazis, however, from being strongly committed (at any rate in the first phase of the Nazi era) to those traditional churches. The *Gauleiter* of East Prussia in 1933, Erich Koch, combined his position with being the elected head of the East Prussian church synod. He was praised by one of its leading theologians for his deep understanding of the Church and his commitment to the central teachings of Christianity. He went on to become *Reichskommissar* of Ukraine, where he unsurprisingly proved a 'brutal, ruthless Nazi of the first order'.[90] Hanns Kerrl, the Nazi *Reichsminister* for Church Affairs from 1935 to 1941, was also 'a truly convinced Protestant, and had made himself by his own efforts well acquainted with all of Luther's writings. He even read deeply in the works of the church fathers'.[91] Clearly, at least in terms of how such men understood themselves, there was such a thing not only as a Christian Nazi, but a thoroughly ecclesiastical one.

Other Nazi leaders, however – Himmler, Rosenberg, Ludendorff and, perhaps above all, Bormann, effectively deputy Leader of the Party after 1941 – were unequivocally anti-Christian. It was Bormann who in 1938 issued the Party regulation which required the likes of Koch to choose between their Nazi Party office and church positions (right down to the level of parish organist), who campaigned for the tightest of restrictions on church activity and who stated with simple bluntness: 'National

---

90. Ibid., p. 2.

91. The observation of the former Finance Minister of the German Reich, Schwerin von Krosigk, cited in John S. Conway, *The Nazi Persecution of the Churches, 1933-1945* (Vancouver: Regents College Publishing, 1992), p. 424, n. 26.

Socialism and Christianity are irreconcilable.'[92] Bormann's hostility to Christianity seems to have been fuelled in part simply by calculations of personal political advantage, combined with the conviction that scientific rationality should have rendered Christianity incredible for modern people. Other anti-Christians, such as Richard Darré, Reich Minister of Agriculture, wanted to replace Christianity by reviving a supposedly ancient and authentically German paganism. In 1935, Darré issued a 'German Farmers' Calendar' from which all Christian festivals had been excised, with Good Friday now devoted to recalling the Saxon victims of Charlemagne and Christmas Eve dedicated to the festival of Baldur, a Norse god of light.[93] For him and others, Article 24 seems to have had little or no meaning.

What of the Führer? Hitler was certainly capable of doing a passing impression of sincere belief. He often held up Jesus as an example of the supreme hero, an Aryan warrior figure in his struggle against the Jews (Hitler, of course, held that Jesus was *not* a Jew). In 1926, he claimed that the Nazi movement aimed 'to translate the ideals of Christ into deeds', to complete 'the work which Christ had begun but could not finish'.[94] Addressing the *Reichstag* for the first time as Chancellor in February 1933, Hitler said his Government would 'take Christianity, as the basis of our collective morality, and the family as the nucleus of our *Volk* and State, under its firm protection'. Three years later, Cardinal Faulhaber (no fool, and often a sharp critic of Nazi ideology and policies) left a three-hour meeting with the Führer convinced that Hitler was a man of deep personal faith: 'the Reich Chancellor undoubtedly believes in God ... he recognises Christianity as the builder of Western culture'.[95]

In private, things may have been different. Within days of the 1933 *Reichstag* address cited above, Hitler allegedly told intimates:

> Neither of the denominations – Catholic or Protestant, they're both the same – has any future left. At least not for the Germans. Fascism may perhaps make its peace with the Church in God's name. I will do it too. Why not? But that

92. The opening sentence of Bormann's 'Circular on the Relationship of National Socialism and Christianity' reproduced in ibid., pp. 383-86.

93. For an overview of Darré's thought and work, see Clifford R. Lovin, '*Blut und Boden*: The Ideological Basis of the Nazi Agricultural Program', *Journal of the History of Ideas* 28, no. 2 (April-June 1967), pp. 279-88.

94. Steigman-Gall, *Holy Reich*, p. 27.

95. Cited in Ian Kershaw, *Hitler* (London: Penguin, 1998), p. 373.

won't stop me from stamping out Christianity in Germany, root and branch. One is either a Christian or a German. You can't be both.[96]

John Conway accepts the quotation as genuine, so proving that the warm words from the Reichstag podium were duplicitous. Richard Steigman-Gall, however, shows good reason for doubting its authenticity.[97] Even aside from the question of possible fabrication by interested parties, however, we need to reckon with the fact that Hitler may have said – and thought – different things at different times. Establishing precisely what his view on Christianity was may be a fool's errand.

One reason for this is that for Hitler the question was not very important. The deepest well-springs of his world view were found elsewhere. What really drove him was a 'simplistic, Manichean view of history as racial struggle, in which the highest racial entity, the Aryan, was being undermined and destroyed by the lowest, the parasitic Jew'.[98] Whilst fabrication or dissimulation may account for some of the apparent inconsistencies in his utterances on Christianity, a more accurate explanation might be that his approach varied according to whether the churches seemed to either support or frustrate his pursuit of that more basic world view.[99] Jesus was a valuable figure, if he could be presented as a great fighter against the Jews. The churches could be of some limited use, if they fell totally in line with Nazi ideology. When the prospects for that happening seemed good, Hitler would speak warmly of Christianity. When they did not (and Scholder suggests that by 1937, infuriated by *Mit brennender Sorge*, on the one hand, and the failure of the Protestant Church to unify enthusiastically under Nazi-aligned control, on the other, the Führer was convinced they never would), his mood darkened, sometimes explosively. Jesus himself was still a heroic figure, but Hitler came to see the religion of Christianity as a Jewish invention, 'the hardest blow which ever hit humanity. Bolshevism is the bastard son of Christianity; both are a monstrous issue of the Jews.'[100]

---

96. Cited in Conway, *The Nazi Persecution of the Churches*, p. 15.

97. Steigman-Gall, *Holy Reich*, pp. 28-29.

98. Kershaw, *Hitler*, p. 148, offers a concise summary of Hitler's world view.

99. This case is argued persuasively in Klaus Scholder, *A Requiem for Hitler and Other New Perspectives on the German Church Struggle*, trans. by John Bowden (London: SCM, 1989), ch. 10.

100. Cited in ibid., p. 180.

Hitler said this in the summer of 1941, by which point a senior Nazi – whatever orthodox Christian belief he may have retained privately – could no longer plausibly remain associated with the Church.

* * *

Nazi policy towards the churches shifted, therefore, from the attempt to suborn, to outright hostility. Caution did need to be employed, even as Hitler's view darkened. The churches retained great influence and affection in Germany throughout the Nazi period, making a full-frontal assault impossible. Even the Protestant Confessing Church, with its (faint) whiff of resistance was never simply annihilated by the regime. Nevertheless, the German Church, both Protestant and Catholic, was increasingly persecuted by the Nazis – Catholics, it must be said, for reasons already traced in this chapter, more so than Protestants. The toll of martyrdom was indeed nothing like that experienced by, for instance, Polish Catholics. Yet there were many deaths and, just below the threshold of lethal violence, a consistent campaign of harassment and restriction. As Conway writes, all this flowed from the:

> nihilistic antipathy felt by the Nazis for all sections of the old social hierarchy and its patterns of thought. Like the Army, and the bureaucracy, the Church was a pillar of the old order, whose standing, though it might be exploited as a temporary measure, was fundamentally resented by leading members of the Party.[101]

The Nazis resented both the place of the churches in German public life and their capacity to be a potential alternative source of meaning and value for the people. As a potential rival for allegiance, the churches needed to be ruthlessly 'co-ordinated' with the vision of the State. If over time that should prove impossible, they should be crushed. Conway goes so far as to claim that, had the Nazis been victorious, Christians would ultimately have followed the Jews to the gas chambers:

> the often-proclaimed determination to wipe out Christianity altogether … would have ended in the persecution of Christians by the same methods as had so effectively 'dealt with' the Jews. If the imagination falters at such a horrendous

---

101. Conway, *The Nazi Persecution of the Churches*, p. 102.

Endlösung, who can doubt that the perpetrators of Auschwitz,
Treblinka, Lidice and Oradour would have hesitated to repeat
their experiments?[102]

This is surely overblown. To reiterate: in 1939, 95 per cent of the
German population considered themselves as in some sense Christian –
including most Nazi Party members. Genocide against the Christians
was inconceivable. Nominal, or politically quiet, Christians had nothing
to fear (and noisily courageous ones could always save their lives by
becoming compliant). Christians posed no existential, biological-racial
threat to the *Volk.* They did not need to be exterminated, but merely
cowed. That is indeed what happened in the Warthegau – that portion
of occupied Poland annexed into Greater Germany – from 1940. Nazi
church policy here was not constrained by the existing laws, conventions
and Concordats in force elsewhere in Germany, which demanded at
least lip-service from the Government. The Warthegau offered a blank
slate for the implementation of Nazi church policy and the result was
indeed brutal. Only a handful of churches were allowed to exist. They
would receive no support from the State – no church tax as in the rest of
Germany. Their meeting times were sharply circumscribed, the content of
their activities even more so. Those choosing to attend found themselves
discriminated against by the State in all sorts of ways. Nobody could
pretend that the Government overseeing all this was in any way friendly
towards the churches.[103] Yet, as Steigman-Gall notes:

> just as noteworthy … is the simple fact that the churches
> were allowed in: they were given a place in the Nazi paradise.
> In contrast to the razing of churches, or their conversion to
> museums of atheism in the neighbouring Soviet Union, [in
> the Warthegau] church life continued, although in greatly
> reduced form and totally separated from the State.[104]

Hitler and other leading Nazis may well by this stage have been content
to see the churches and Christianity vanish permanently from German
public life, but both could be safely left to wither. There was no need for
extermination.

---

102. Ibid., p. 331.
103. For a survey of the Warthegau provisions, see ibid., pp. 311-27.
104. Steigman-Gall, *Holy Reich,* p. 229.

Were the Nazi hordes Christian? The movement was simply too large and diffuse for a simple answer to that question to be given. Throughout the whole Nazi era, most of the rank and file considered themselves Christian, if only in a very nominal sense – like most of the German population. Some, even at very high levels within the movement, had a much stronger personal faith and (until the relationship between the Party and the churches became too fraught) a strong commitment to their church. Others, possibly including the Führer himself, at different times either scorned or loathed the churches, but retained a strong attachment to their particular (generally unorthodox) understandings of Jesus and God – sometimes simply for public consumption but, perhaps, in some cases more deeply. A small minority always held, unequivocally, that Nazism and Christianity were irreconcilable. Would that more Christian leaders had been so clear.

Chapter 3

The Aftermath

'I have done that', says my memory. 'I cannot have done that', says my pride, and remains inexorable. Eventually, memory yields.

Friedrich Nietzsche[1]

We have catalogued the Church's devastating failures before and during the Nazi era. Christianity, Protestant and Catholic, is in the dock. Faced with such an indictment, two questions arise. First, to what extent has the Church confessed and repented of its past? That question provides the agenda for the current chapter, before in the next we address the second: regardless of repentance, has the Church's moral culpability dealt a fatal blow to its credibility, and perhaps even to the truth of the Gospel itself?

As in the previous chapter, we take the two traditions, Catholic and Protestant in turn – and once again, we shall see striking parallels between the two. First, then, to the Protestants.

The Protestants and the Aftermath

No, the real guilt lies on the church, because it alone knew that the way being taken would lead to disaster, and it did not warn our people, it did not unmask the injustice that had occurred, or only when it was too late. And here the

1. Friedrich Nietzsche, *Beyond Good and Evil*, trans. by R.J. Hollingdale (London: Penguin, 2003), p. 146.

Confessing Church bears a particularly large measure of
blame, for it saw most clearly what was developing. It even
spoke out about it, but then became tired and stood more
in fear of human beings than of the living God. It is for this
reason that the catastrophe has broken out over us and we
are now pulled into the whirlpool. We, the church, however,
have to beat our breast and confess: my guilt, my guilt, my
enormous guilt.[2]

The speaker, Martin Niemöller, had almost totemic status in the post-
war German Church. A U-boat commander in World War I, he had
impeccably patriotic credentials – and as a concentration camp inmate
between 1938 and 1945 his anti-Nazism appeared unquestionable. The
reality is more complicated: Niemöller was initially a supporter of Hitler
and shared in the generally anti-Semitic culture of the time.[3] His later
opposition to the Nazis had been driven not primarily by humanitarian
concern for the Jews but, as for so many in the Confessing Church, by a
passion for the Church's own integrity and independence. Nevertheless,
his confession of Christian responsibility for war and Holocaust has
stood the test of time. It offers no excuses; it is unequivocal and heartfelt. As such, it is deeply untypical of the German Protestant Church's
grappling with the past.

It is not difficult to understand why. As James Hawes notes, in 1945:

everyone was looking to the future. But how could [Germany]
move on morally and politically, when any surviving business
must, by definition, at least have made its peace with the
Nazi regime? How could you cure a nation almost half of
whose doctors had been Nazi party members? How could
you re-educate a nation in which, for ten years, all university
lecturers had worked alongside colleagues who taught *racial
theory*? The answer was simple … a veil of forgetfulness was
allowed to settle over all but the very worst offenders.[4]

---

2. Cited in Matthew D. Hockenhos, *A Church Divided: German Protestants
   Confront the Nazi Past* (Bloomington: Indiana University Press, 2004),
   p. 68.
3. Matthew D. Hockenhos, *Then They Came for Me: Martin Niemöller, The
   Pastor Who Defied the Nazis* (New York: Basic Books, 2018), is the most
   recent biography.
4. Hawes, *The Shortest History of Germany*, p. 195. Emphasis in original.

So it was, for instance, that the man responsible for implementing the Nuremburg race laws could become head of the West German civil service in the 1950s and could appoint men deeply implicated in Nazi crimes (including former senior SS officers) to lead several major government departments. To this day, a portrait of Hans Maria Globke hangs in the Chancellery in Berlin.[5] As in government, so in the judiciary, banking, business, the Church and other areas of German national life: 'the men who had dedicated themselves to making sure that the wheels of National Socialism turned smoothly and profitably would not be denied the chance to do the same for the new political dispensation'.[6]

The veil was not entirely undisturbed, however. The Auschwitz trials of 1963-65 in Frankfurt prompted public discussion of the Nazi era, as did the student riots of 1968. Communist East Germany consistently took delight in drawing attention to figures like Globke, whom it tried *in absentia* for war crimes in 1963. In the West, the speech of the President of the then Federal Republic, Richard von Weizsäcker, to the Bundestag in May 1985 has often been regarded as heralding a new willingness to grapple with the past. In today's united Germany, schoolchildren are taught in close detail about the Holocaust and cities feature many memorials to the Jews and other victims. However, as Mary Fulbrook has argued, in some respects forgetfulness still reigns. She identifies a 'sense of diffuse shame without differentiated attribution of guilt': an acknowledgement that something very terrible happened in Germany, without a clear identification of exactly who did what, and what level of individual responsibility different perpetrators bear for their actions.[7] The victims are remembered and honoured; the killers and their accomplices are largely left in merciful obscurity.

As with wider society, so with the Church. For several decades, post-war German Protestantism, while increasingly ready to face the full horror of Nazi crimes, was reluctant to acknowledge its own complicity – let alone to hold individuals to strict account. In the immediate post-war era, of

---

5. Tom Bower, *Blind Eye to Murder: Britain, America and the Purging of Nazi Germany – A Pledge Betrayed* (London: Paladin, 1983), p. 425. See also Oliver Moody, 'Hans Globke, Hitler's henchman, was true architect of modern Germany', *The Times*, 4 March 2021, at: https://www.thetimes .co.uk/article/hans-globke-hitlers-former-henchman-was-true-architect -of-modern-germany-7sw76fvkd (accessed 29 April 2021).

6. Bower, *Blind Eye to Murder*, p. 424.

7. Mary Fulbrook, *Reckonings: Legacies of Nazi Persecution and the Quest for Justice* (Oxford: Oxford University Press, 2018), p. 346.

course, there was very little incentive to do so: there was a desperate need for institutions which could lay at least some claim to symbolising order, tradition and decency. The churches, at local and national level, filled that role. The German people could only take so many of their leaders being exposed, ejected and punished. Equally, the victorious occupying powers needed a credible German civic leadership around whom the nation could be rebuilt. Church leaders themselves, of course, had no interest whatsoever in scrutinising their murky past, and the wider ecumenical world was only too keen to re-embrace old friends from before the Hitler nightmare. Now that the Führer was gone, the good Germany could come to the fore again. Thus, the Archbishop of Canterbury, Geoffrey Fisher, urged the British Government to work closely with 'a number of reliable German leaders and churchmen, e.g. Bishop Wurm of Stuttgart, who have resisted the Nazi regime, whose integrity is known, and with whom we could work to restore authentic Christianity in Germany'.[8] We have already encountered Bishop Wurm. Even when assessed charitably, he is not a heroic resistance figure. However, in late 1945, 'good Germans' were needed – and so they were found.

Of course, a certain number of deeply wicked Germans were also required. For the Church, the German Christian movement therefore proved highly convenient. At its height, this organisation had huge influence, but its 600,000 strong membership was always a small minority within the Church. This made it apt for the role of scapegoat:

> once identified as the sole Protestant collaborators, a few German Christian pastors could be removed from their positions and the rest of the church could consider its hands clean. In that way, the torturous prospect of denazifying the church could be recast as the much simpler task of 'de-German-Christianizing' the clergy.[9]

The German Christians protested vigorously. They had been far from the only Nazis in the Church: 'Why were questionnaires about membership and the party not sent to all pastors in Westphalia, for example, with the embarrassing questions: who had been contact men of the Security Service; who had dedicated party flags, held speeches at

---

8. John S. Conway, 'How Shall the Nations Repent? The Stuttgart Declaration of Guilt, October 1945', *Journal of Ecclesiastical History* 38, no. 4 (October 1987), pp. 596-622, p. 613.
9. Bergen, *Twisted Cross*, p. 209.

party events, and baptised under the flag of war?'[10] Such complaints, however, went nowhere. The net was not going to be cast more widely. However, even the scapegoat was not punished *too* harshly. The focus was always largely on the ordained ministry, and the much larger number of lay German Christians encountered few difficulties in re-integrating into the Church. Meanwhile, nearly all the clergy who were dismissed (on full pensions!) in 1945 for German Christian activities were back in office within five years. The impression given is of a Church more interested in forgiveness than in justice – if, indeed, it acknowledged that there was much to be forgiven.

Which, of course, it did. As early as August 1945, the Treysa Conference of German Protestant leaders admitted the Church's failure to witness effectively against the Nazis:

> when the church took its responsibility seriously, it reminded the population of God's commandments and minced no words when it condemned concentration camps, mistreatment and murder of Jews and the sick, and sought to protect youth from the seduction of National Socialist propaganda. But churchmen were pushed into the remote sanctuaries of the church as if into a prison. Our people were separated from the church. The public was no longer allowed to hear its words; no-one heard what it preached.[11]

This apparently fulsome confession begs important questions. When precisely *had* the Church taken its responsibility seriously? When were no words minced in condemnation of Nazi terror? The more historically accurate picture, as we have seen, is of a Church which generally applauded the Nazi rise to power, whilst tolerating (or even supporting) the associated brutality. Treysa paints a picture of a Church which continued to stand firm against terror, but which the State managed to push back into the sanctuaries, so that none could hear its testimony. There is a small element of truth in this, but it ignores the much larger degree to which the Church simply bought into the State's world view.

---

10. Doris L. Bergen, 'Stormtroopers of Christ: The German Christian Movement and the Ecclesiastical Final Solution', in Ericksen and Heschel (eds), *Betrayal*, pp. 40-67, p. 61.

11. The text of the 'Message to the Congregations' is reproduced in Hockenhos, *A Church Divided*, p. 185.

Treysa was followed swiftly in October 1945 by the Stuttgart Declaration, often known as the 'Declaration of Guilt'. This was issued in response to urgent pleas from international ecumenical colleagues for the leaders of the German Church to acknowledge their nation's guilt, and their Church's guilt, for the war. Only such a statement could clear the way, those colleagues argued, for Germany's rehabilitation. It was a tremendously difficult step for the German leaders to take, reminiscent as it was of the much resented 'war-guilt' clause in the 1919 Versailles Treaty. Nevertheless, they took it and in so doing have rightly been recognised as making a critical contribution to post-war reconciliation.

However, today, the most striking thing about the Stuttgart Declaration is that it does not even mention the Holocaust or the Jews. John Conway has shown that the discussions with World Council of Churches (WCC) representatives immediately preceding the Declaration instead focussed largely on the suffering inflicted on the countries attacked by Germany. Even in the briefing notes for the WCC representatives, the Jews appear almost as an afterthought: 'and also the Jews'.[12] We might, charitably, allow that in the immediate aftermath of the war the full scale of the Holocaust was not yet fully comprehended, nor was the genocide generally seen as a discrete horror, clearly distinguishable from the more general slaughter. Equally, it is true that the Stuttgart Declaration was aimed primarily at the countries with which Germany had been at war – at the victims of the international conflict, rather than the genocide. However, charity is really over-stretching here: after all, the Jews slaughtered by Hitler were overwhelmingly the civilians of other attacked and occupied nations. The most plausible reason for the absence of the Jews in the Stuttgart Declaration is that their fate was not uppermost in anyone's conscience. As Tony Judt has observed, that remained true for decades and well beyond Germany: 'except in the minds of a handful of senior Nazis – World War Two was not about the Jews'.[13]

Like Treysa, the Stuttgart Declaration said both too much and too little about the Church's recent past. The claim that 'we have for many years struggled in the name of Jesus Christ against the spirit which found its terrible expression in the National Socialist regime of tyranny' exaggerates heroically.[14] Set against this, however, is confession of failure:

---

12. Conway, 'How Shall the Nations Repent', p. 615.
13. Tony Judt, *Postwar: A History of Europe Since 1945* (London: Pimlico, 2007), p. 821.
14. The text of the Stuttgart Declaration is reproduced in Hockenhos, *A Church Divided*, p. 187.

'we accuse ourselves for not witnessing more courageously, for not praying more faithfully, for not believing more joyously, for not loving more ardently'.[15] Yet, these are all sins of *omission*. There is no facing the sins of *commission*: the Church's positive welcome of much in the Nazi programme and the direct involvement of some Christians in genocide. Matthew Hockenhos describes what is being constructed here as a myth of conservative churchly resistance: 'a myth created, in part, to assuage their consciences and cleanse an unimpressive resistance record ... one-part fact and many parts fiction'.[16]

This myth endured till at least the 1960s. As John Conway puts it:

> Protestant church historians [then] began to accept the need
> to look more closely at the church's failings during the Nazi
> period, from the early acclaim given to Hitler in 1933, to
> the enthusiastic support for his aggressive foreign policy, to
> their applause for Germany's military victories in 1940, and
> most shamefully of all, to their silence at the Nazi's ruthless
> degradation and later annihilation of the Jewish people.[17]

The works of Richard Gutteridge and Wolfgang Gerlach, used extensively in our last chapter, were part of that re-appraisal. The latter in particular, *And the Witnesses Were Silent*, first published in 1987, shows how even the Confessing Church – the subject of much hagiography in the post-war era – was, in fact, deeply compromised by Nazi sympathies. Gerlach's work (although met, unsurprisingly, with some initial resistance) must be recognised as evidence that within five decades German Protestantism developed a truly self-critical approach towards its past.

If there was initial reluctance to face the depth of collaboration during the killing years, there was still more to addressing the deep roots of the Holocaust in Christian tradition. As we saw in chapter one, whilst the Nazi genocide was not directly caused by Christianity, it is foolish to ignore how centuries of Christian anti-Jewish teaching, practice and violence paved the way for it. Indeed, it has not been ignored: the German Protestant churches have been prominent amongst those

---

15. Ibid.
16. Ibid., p. 47.
17. John S. Conway, 'Coming to Terms with the Past: Interpreting the German Church Struggles 1933-1990', *German History* 16, no. 3 (1998), pp. 377-96, p. 380.

calling for a re-examination of traditional doctrine and, in particular, for the renunciation of 'supersessionism': the claim that Christianity has replaced Judaism in the purposes of God and that the old covenant is accordingly now bankrupt.[18] We trace this important development, and the theological questions raised by it, in chapter five. Nonetheless, for several decades after the Holocaust, Protestants were at least as keen to place the historical blame squarely elsewhere.

Bishop Wurm, for instance, argued that both war and Holocaust were the long-term consequences of the general estrangement from God which had marked European culture since the Enlightenment. The fundamental reason for the slaughter was rejection of the divine law. The Nazis were the example *par excellence* of Enlightenment radicals trusting in their own strength, intellect and power: they were like the Jacobins, the most radical and violent element in the French Revolution. 'By associating the Nazis with the Jacobins', Hockenhos writes, Wurm 'uncoupled Nazism from Germany's conservative traditions and tied it to mass politics and secularisation, two trends conservative Lutherans found highly objectionable.'[19] It was not necessary to radically re-examine either the behaviour of contemporary German Protestants or the consequences of their traditional theology. Instead, the Protestant Church must be swiftly restored as a bastion of conservative values at the heart of a renewed Germany, once again on the West's front-line against Soviet communism.

If Nazi crimes were the responsibility of a small group of Jacobin extremists, it was of course unjust for the vast majority of Germans to be held accountable and punished for them. Indeed, even when there was strong evidence that individuals *had* been responsible for war crimes, Wurm showed little interest in investigating further: he was a prominent and uncritical advocate for all those under Allied investigation, regardless of the circumstances of their case. He also engaged in a sustained political campaign against those leading war-crimes investigations.[20] He was far

---

18. There is a useful survey of corporate ecclesiastical appeals for this reappraisal in Jeremy M. Bergen, *Ecclesial Repentance: The Churches Confront Their Sinful Pasts* (London: T. & T. Clark, 2011), ch. 1.

19. Hockenhos, *A Church Divided*, p. 51.

20. For an account of this campaign, see Jon David K. Wyneken, 'Memory as Diplomatic Leverage: Evangelical Bishop Theophil Wurm and War Crimes Trials, 1948-52', *Kirchliche Zeitgeschichte* 19, no. 2, *Neue amerikanische Perspektiven auf die Geschichte der Kirchen in Deutschland im ausgehenden 19. und 20. Jahrhundert* (2006), pp. 368-88.

from a lone voice in this, or in his opposition to the wider 'denazification' attempt to remove Nazis from public life. In 1948, Martin Niemöller called on all Protestants to refuse to serve as prosecutors, assessors or witnesses in denazification cases. He declared that clergy were 'forbidden for the sake of their position and the welfare of the community to help justify this scandal any longer by doing any work in connection with denazification'.[21]

The 'scandal' was that the innocent German people were being victimised and, indeed, subjected to precisely the kind of abuses of which they stood accused. In an open letter to the Archbishop of Canterbury, Wurm claimed that 'the military conquest and occupation of our country was accompanied *by the very same acts of violence* against the civilian population about which such just complaint has been made in the countries of the Allies'.[22] He also protested against the forced deportations of ethnic Germans living in other countries back to Germany and the stripping of German industrial resources: 'to pack the German people into a still more narrow space, to cut off as far as possible the material basis of their very existence, is no different, in essentials, from Hitler's plan to stamp out the existence of the Jewish race'.[23] Even allowing for the fact that Stalin's policies and troops were vengefully destructive, for the recognised leader of German Protestantism to equate such measures with the Final Solution shows conclusively that he had not yet faced the magnitude of the latter. Wurm – like many – preferred to emphasise German victimhood.

Victims, of course, need someone to blame. Much blame could be directed against the occupying powers but behind them a traditional suspect soon loomed into view: the Jews. Anti-Semitism in Germany had not vanished with the Nazi regime. Between 1945 and 1950, many Germans believed that the Jews enjoyed a better standard of living than the average German and that they were preferentially treated by the Allies. Wurm bought wholeheartedly into this resentful way of looking at the world. In April 1948, when invited to endorse a church statement condemning anti-Semitism, he responded caustically:

> Can one issue a statement on the Jewish question in Germany without mentioning the way Jewish literati, since the days of Heinrich Heine, sinned against the German people by

---

21. Hockenhos, *Then They Came for Me*, p. 219.
22. Hockenhos, *A Church Divided*, p. 108 (his emphasis).
23. Ibid.

mocking all that is sacred and how in many areas the peasants suffered as a result of Jewish profiteers? And if one wants to take action against today's rising anti-Semitism, can one be silent about the misfortune that the occupying powers have handed the reins of power to Jews who have returned in order to placate their understandable bitter resentment?[24]

Niemöller, meanwhile, claimed that Jews in the occupying forces, motivated by 'an understandable spirit of hatred and revenge', were content to see Germany starve.[25] Bitter, greedy, vengeful Jews lording it over the battered Germans: the same old anti-Semitism as before – voiced not by street hoodlums, but the very top levels of the German Protestant leadership.

If Jews were in part to blame for German suffering after the war, they could also be blamed for their own during it. The April 1948 statement on anti-Semitism, which Wurm declined to endorse, was written primarily to challenge Christian anti-Semitism, but itself perpetuated some of the same poison. Admittedly, there is nothing unique to German Protestantism here: it simply restated the Augustinian 'witness people' doctrine. However, there is something chilling about a document written in Germany shortly after the Holocaust which states that: 'the fate of the Jews is a silent sermon, reminding us that God will not allow himself to be mocked. It is a warning to us, and an admonition to the Jews to be converted to Him, who is their sole hope of salvation.'[26]

* * *

How did German Protestants come to terms with the Holocaust? For several decades, largely by forgetfulness and by casting blame onto others: onto Hitler and his small band of extremists who ruled the nation by terror; and onto the German Christians who had tried to synthesise Christianity and Nazism. By re-telling (and largely falsifying) the history

---

24. Wurm cited in ibid., p. 151.
25. Hockenhos, *Then They Came for Me*, p. 213.
26. Hockenhos, *A Church Divided*, p. 196. In fairness, one should note that by 1980 German Lutheranism had performed a theological *volte-face* on this question comparable to that represented by *Nostra Aetate* in Roman Catholic thought (see chapter five). The 1980 statement of the Rhineland synod of the Evangelische Kirche in Deutschland (EKD), 'Towards the Renewal of the Relationship of Christians and Jews', is the landmark document in this respect.

of 1933-45 as one where the Church did all it could to resist Nazism and was only quelled through the threat of violence. By never owning what the Church had actually *done*, whether through its enthusiastic welcome for Hitler or its members' support for and participation in the implementation of his programme. By refusing to face the true magnitude of what the Nazis, supported by most German Protestants, did. By emphasising their own victimhood and, perhaps most grimly of all, by blaming the Jews.

Did the Roman Catholics do any better?

The Catholics and the Aftermath: *We Remember* Assessed

> The centrepiece of Pius XII's post-war apologia was that Catholics in Germany and in all of Nazi-occupied Europe – and clergy in particular – had 'endured indescribable sufferings for their faith and their vocation'. It was as if Nazism's greatest crime was that it had declared an unholy war against Christianity.
>
> Robert Ventresca[27]

Even if this is fair comment on Pius XII's reactions in the immediate aftermath of war and Holocaust, it cannot be taken as representative of how the Roman Catholic Church has faced the question of its complicity in the Holocaust since. For one thing, there has been a sea-change in the Church's official teaching about Judaism, heralded above all by the document of the Second Vatican Council, *Nostra Aetate*. Enjoying the highest possible level of authority in Roman Catholic teaching, this decree ended the tradition of contempt we traced in our first chapter. It denied that Jews today could be held responsible for the death of Christ and it rejected all anti-Semitism as a grave sin. We trace the story of this 'Copernican revolution' in chapter five. Here, our focus is more specifically on how the Church confronted its involvement in the Holocaust itself. How does the Church tell itself the story of those terrible years?

The key document in assessing the response is *We Remember: A Reflection on the Shoah* issued by the Holy See's Commission for Religious Relations with the Jews in March 1998. It was in preparation for more than a decade and was preceded by notable statements from Catholic

---

27. Ventresca, *Soldier of Christ*, p. 222.

Bishops in Germany, France, Poland, Italy and the United States, amongst others.[28] The French statement, in particular, was regarded by many as a startlingly frank admission of Christian complicity in the Holocaust, reflecting deeply on its roots in Christian culture and history and facing the Church's passivity or active collaboration during the killing head-on.[29] *We Remember* was thus awaited with keen anticipation. As Cardinal Edward Cassidy, the man initially charged with developing the document, said: 'we set out with the idea that one single document would cover all that the Catholic Church might wish to state on this great tragedy of the twentieth century'.[30]

Cassidy went on to observe, however, that that aspiration proved unrealisable. What the Church in Germany needed to say and hear was very different from the Church in Poland, or the Church in America: to say *everything* would have produced a huge and unwieldy document. Furthermore, the Catholic Church is universal, with hundreds of millions of believers living in countries with no involvement whatsoever in the Holocaust. A universally useful and binding document had to avoid not seeming wholly obsessed with European history. Close engagement with the specifics of, say, how French Bishops had or had not opposed Vichy collaboration with the genocide would not have been helpful to Catholics in Korea. *We Remember* 'had by its very nature to attract the attention of and not alienate those to whom it was addressed'.[31]

Obvious relevance was not the only guiding principle in producing *We Remember*. Cardinal Avery Dulles adds that:

> while seeking to make its readers aware of the inadequacies of the Catholic response to the challenge of Nazi racism, the document had to be composed in a way that would not play into the hands of anti-Catholic propagandists who seek to establish that the Christian faith itself is a source of

---

28. These, along with *We Remember*, are collected together in Secretariat for Ecumenical and Interreligious Affairs (SEIA), *Catholics Remember the Holocaust* (Washington, DC: United States Catholic Conference, May 1998).
29. For a full treatment of the French bishops' statement, see Patrick Henry, 'The French Catholic Church's Apology', *The French Review* 72, no. 6 (May 1999), pp. 1099-1105.
30. Edward Idris Cardinal Cassidy, 'Reflections Regarding the Vatican's Statement on the Shoah', in SEIA, *Catholics Remember the Holocaust*, pp. 61-76, p. 62.
31. Ibid., p. 63.

anti-Semitism, and that the Catholic Church is by its very nature hostile to Judaism. This twofold objective accounts for a certain ambivalence that some have sensed in the document. While some sections sound a penitential note, others are more defensive in tone.[32]

Such comments reflect the fact that *We Remember* ultimately disappointed many expectations. To critics, it recalled 'in its feebleness and vagueness an expression of diplomatic hesitation, equivocation and timidity all too painfully redolent of papal attitudes towards Nazi policy during the war'.[33] It read, some said, as if 'crafted by a cadre of lawyers whose job it was protect Catholicism from the theological equivalent of civil suits'.[34] What had gone wrong? Why did the document succeed 'largely in reopening, if not actually deepening, old wounds'?[35]

First, the case for the defence. At the most basic level, as Judith Banki notes, the statement

affirms 'as a major fact of the history of this century' the murder of millions of Jews. ... It stands as a forthright rebuttal to what has become an entire industry of Holocaust denial and revision. To some eight hundred million Catholic faithful and to the world at large, the Church says: 'it happened!'[36]

Given that some on the wilder fringes of ultra-'Catholic' opposition to the reforms of Vatican II seem prone to Holocaust denial, the importance of such unequivocal teaching cannot be gainsaid.[37]

---

32. Avery Cardinal Dulles SJ, 'Commentary', in Avery Dulles SJ and Rabbi Leon Klenicki, *The Holocaust, Never to Be Forgotten: Reflections on the Holy See's Document* We Remember: *Commentaries by Avery Dulles SJ and Rabbi Leon Klenicki, with an Address by Edward Idris Cardinal Cassidy* (New York: Paulist Press, 2001), pp. 47-72, p. 56.
33. Kevin Madigan, 'A Survey of Jewish Reaction to the Vatican Statement on the Holocaust', *Cross Currents* 50, no. 4 (Winter 2001), pp. 488-505, p. 495.
34. Ibid., p. 500.
35. Ibid., p. 488.
36. Judith H. Banki, 'Appendix B: Vatican II Revisited', in Banki and Pawlikowski (eds), *Ethics in the Shadow of the Holocaust*, pp. 211-14, p. 213.
37. The schismatic, ultra-conservative, 'bishop' Richard Williamson caused serious problems in Catholic-Jewish relations in 2009, when statements he

Furthermore, *We Remember* clearly admits that Christians bear much responsibility for the Holocaust. Precisely how that responsibility is understood is one of the perceived failings of the document, but its existence is freely acknowledged. The document quotes John Paul II: 'In the Christian world – I do not say on the part of the Church as such – erroneous and unjust interpretations of the New Testament regarding the Jewish people and their alleged culpability have circulated for far too long, engendering feelings of hostility towards this people.'[38] Such interpretations, the document notes, have been 'totally and definitively rejected by the Second Vatican Council'.[39] However, they left a deep stamp on Christian attitudes to Jews. It is reasonable to speak of 'long-standing sentiments of mistrust and hostility' constituting an 'anti-Judaism' of which many Christians have been guilty throughout history.[40] *We Remember* then faces the obvious question: 'whether the Nazi persecution of the Jews was not made easier by the anti-Jewish prejudices imbedded in some Christian minds and hearts. Did anti-Jewish sentiment among Christians make them less sensitive, or even indifferent, to the persecutions launched against the Jews by National Socialism when it reached power?'[41]

The document warns against too simplistic or sweeping an answer to this question (and is reluctant to offer even a more nuanced one). There might be many reasons why Christians failed to resist as they should have done, such as straightforward fear of the consequences. It also wants to remember those Christians who *did* stand heroically with the Jews. However:

> alongside such courageous men and women, the spiritual resistance and concrete action of other Christians was not that which might have been expected from Christ's followers. ... [F]or Christians, this heavy burden of conscience of their brothers and sisters during the Second World War must be a

---

had made, widely understood as constituting Holocaust denial, came to light on the same day he was re-admitted to communion with the Pope. He has subsequently once again incurred excommunication (although not on the grounds of these comments).

38. *We Remember*, III.
39. Ibid.
40. Ibid., IV.
41. Ibid.

call to penitence. We deeply regret the errors and failures of those sons and daughters of the Church.[42]

Though such statements in themselves are welcome, we shall see there has been much controversy about precisely how they are to be understood – which has perhaps eclipsed another very positive feature of *We Remember*. In chapter one, we noted Augustine's doctrine of the Jews as 'a witness people': they must survive and indeed be protected, but only to serve as an example to Christians of what happens when a people reject God. They are left spiritually adrift, materially and morally bereft, subjugated and miserable. *We Remember*, following the lead of *Nostra Aetate*, understands contemporary Jewish life quite differently. Christians should live with Jews in mutual respect 'as befits those who adore the one Creator and Lord and have a common father in faith, Abraham'.[43] The Jews offer a 'unique witness to the Holy One of Israel and the Torah' and have suffered much for doing so;[44] and Christians and Jews are now called to work together for a world of 'true respect for the life and dignity of every human being, for all have been created in the image and likeness of God'.[45] John Morley notes, 'what is so beautiful and touching about this recognition of Jewish witness in such a positive way is the realisation of what a quantum leap it is from the traditional notion of the Jews as a "witness people"'.[46] What for centuries had been a deeply anti-Jewish trope is now being deployed, by the Pope, to exhort Christians to celebrate and emulate Jewish faithfulness.

So why then has *We Remember* seemed so inadequate to so many?

The problems begin with the document's representation of history. As noted above, *We Remember* acknowledges that many Christians failed to show the kind of resistance to the Nazis and their genocide one might expect of Jesus' followers. However, the context of this admission is fascinating and revealing. Having described the rise to power of the Nazis and the willingness of wider German society to see in Hitler a solution

---

42. Ibid.

43. Ibid., V.

44. Ibid., II.

45. Letter of Pope John Paul II to Cardinal Cassidy, serving as preface to *We Remember*. Reproduced in SEIA, *Catholics Remember the Holocaust*, p. 42.

46. John F. Morley, 'Reaction of a Catholic Theologian to the Vatican's We Remember Document', in Randolph A. Braham (ed.), *The Vatican and the Holocaust: The Catholic Church and the Jews during the Nazi Era* (New York: Rosenthal Institute for Holocaust Studies, distributed by Columbia University Press, 2000), pp. 47-67, p. 57.

to their country's problems, *We Remember* states that 'the Church in Germany responded by condemning racism'.[47] This claim is supported by reference to the statements of bishops and clergy and influential lay Catholics, as well as the papal encylicals, *Mit brennender Sorge* (Pius XI, 1937) and *Summi Pontificatus* (Pius XII, 1939). Turning then to the grassroots, *We Remember* asks whether Christians gave 'every possible assistance to those being persecuted, and in particular to the persecuted Jews?'[48] It answers its own question: 'Many did, but others did not.'[49]

There are several issues here revealing what Kevin Madigan has called the document's 'shockingly selective and partial' treatment of historical evidence.[50] Firstly, if one only knew *We Remember*, one would assume that the only sins committed by Christians during the Holocaust were those of omission – of failing to prevent or speak out against what the Nazis were doing to the Jews and their other victims, perhaps out of fear or even complacency. However, as in the case of German Protestantism, the reality is darker. Unless we are to circumscribe drastically the meaning of the word Christian and accept that there were *far* fewer Christians in twentieth-century Europe than the Church would usually like to claim, we have to face the fact that the principal sins were ones of *commission*. Christians were directly involved in and responsible for the genocide: drawing up lists, teaching anti-Semitic school lessons, confiscating property, making arrests, driving trains, forming shooting parties, and guarding camps. The Holocaust was not something done by powerful and wicked pagans whilst Christians timorously stood by.

Secondly, to say in response to the question of whether Christians aided Jews 'many did, but others did not' seems to suggest that the numbers in both groups were comparable – or even that the 'others' were exceptions to the rule. The reverse is true. Had *most* Christians, or even a large proportion of them, done their best to frustrate the Holocaust, it would have been almost impossible for the Nazis to succeed. In fact, what happened was that the genocidal operation ran very smoothly – in part, because, as Patrick Henry points out, 'only an exceedingly small fraction of Christians did anything at all to help Jews'.[51]

---

47. *We Remember*, III.
48. Ibid., IV.
49. Ibid.
50. Madigan, 'A Survey of Jewish Reaction', p. 501.
51. Patrick Henry, 'The Art of Christian Apology: Comparing the French Catholic Church's Apology to the Jews and the Vatican's *We Remember*', *Shofar* 26, no. 3 (Spring 2008), pp. 87-104, p. 92.

This grassroots failure went alongside an equal failure at the level of church leadership. The episcopal statements cited by *We Remember* quickly dried up as Hitler secured his hold on power, partly because of the threat of repression but, equally, as Randolph Braham notes, because the bishops 'like the nation as a whole … were swept along by the wave of nationalism and patriotism that had engulfed the Third Reich'.[52] *We Remember*, Braham complains, 'overlooks the enthusiasm with which most [bishops] supported the domestic and foreign policies of the Führer during almost the entire National Socialist era'.[53] No bishop offered clear, consistent and public opposition to the anti-Jewish policies as they escalated in murderous intent. There may indeed be a case, explored in the last chapter, for saying that this discretion was the better part of valour during the height of the killing. However, that does not hold for the years before the escalation to full-scale genocide. Throughout that period, the Church largely either stayed silent or applauded the persecution. *We Remember* whitewashes a very dirty past.

This is perhaps most evident in how *We Remember* treats Pius XII. As we have seen, Pius is a deeply ambiguous character, and any sound judgement of his war-time role must be very nuanced. Such caution is not welcome in many Catholic circles, including – it seems – in the Vatican; instead, for many years there has been a vigorous campaign for his canonisation. In 2009, one vital preliminary stage was accomplished when Pope Benedict XVI declared his predecessor to have lived a life of 'heroic virtue'; full canonisation now awaits official confirmation of two miracles attributable to Pius' heavenly intercession. *We Remember* can be viewed as an important landmark in this campaign. It presents Pius as a tirelessly courageous champion of the menaced Jews. However, as Kevin Madigan notes, many Jews find this depiction 'wildly exaggerated and even false'.[54]

We have traced some of the complexities in assessing Pius' actions in our last chapter, and the judgement *is* complex – though not according to *We Remember*. As the Catholic theologian John Morley observes, 'to read this praise of Pius XII without any reference to the controversy that surrounds his reaction to the Holocaust appears almost surrealistic'.[55] It

---

52. Randolph L. Braham, 'Remembering and Forgetting', in Braham (ed.), *The Vatican and the Holocaust*, pp. 13-46, p. 24.

53. Ibid., p. 20.

54. Madigan, 'A Survey of Jewish Reaction', p. 497.

55. Morley, 'Reaction of a Catholic Theologian', in Braham (ed.), *The Vatican and the Holocaust*, p. 64.

is also revealing how the document's defenders react to such criticism. Cardinal Avery Dulles has spoken of a 'campaign of defamation' against Pius XII;[56] whilst Cardinal Cassidy identifies 'monstrous calumnies regarding Pius XII and the period of the Second World War [which] have gradually become accepted facts, especially within the Jewish community'.[57] Whilst he argues that *We Remember* did not seek 'to close the historical discussion on the role of Pius XII. … [W]e did, indeed, intend to keep the question open for further study, in the face of a growing tendency on the part of Jewish organisations to condemn Pius XII on emotional judgements with no historical foundation'.[58] No doubt there have been some scurrilous attacks on Pius, but it does not look good for the Church to defend its hagiographical approach by implying that only a Jewish campaign against Christianity could see things differently.

This casting of Christians in the role of victim is related to two further troubling aspects of *We Remember*. First, it emphasises the persecution of the Church by the Nazi regime. Many Nazis, we are told:

> gave proof of a definite hatred directed against God Himself. Logically, such an attitude also led to a rejection of Christianity, and a desire to see the Church destroyed or at least subjected to the Nazi State. … [I]n pursuing its aims, [Nazism] did not hesitate to oppose the Church and persecute her members also.[59]

There is of course some truth in this: in Poland thousands of Catholic priests were slaughtered. However, this probably had at least as much to do with Catholic clergy being potential leaders of national resistance to German occupation as with any anti-Christian hatred. Whilst the Church in Germany was certainly harassed, and whilst it probably is true to say that in the long run the Nazis would have turned on it more fiercely, the obvious fact remains that it was not subjected to Nazi terror in remotely the same way as the Jews. There is no evidence that any

---

56. Dulles, 'Commentary', in Dulles and Klenicki, *The Holocaust, Never to Be Forgotten*, p. 62.
57. Edward Idris Cardinal Cassidy, 'Address', in ibid., pp. 73-91, p. 87.
58. Edward Idris Cardinal Cassidy, 'The Vatican Document on the Holocaust: Reflections towards a New Millennium', in Banki and Pawlikowski (eds), *Ethics in the Shadow of the Holocaust*, pp. 5-22, p. 6.
59. *We Remember*, IV.

Nazi ever seriously planned the extermination of all Christians. To call attention to Nazi hostility towards Christianity whilst directing it away from Christian enthusiasm for Nazism is therefore suspicious.

Those suspicions are heightened when one examines how the document traces the roots of tension between Christians and Jews back to 'disputes between the early Church and the Jewish leaders and people who, in their devotion to the Law, on occasion violently opposed the preachers of the Gospel and the first Christians'.[60] Its conclusion also contains the aspiration that, as there will be no more anti-Judaism among Christians, so also there will be no more 'anti-Christian sentiment among Jews'.[61] While it would be futile to deny that Jews had ever held prejudices against Christians, the risk here is that, as noted by James Rudin, *We Remember* 'transmits the not-so-subtle message of a moral equivalency between historic, often deadly, Christian persecution and denigration of Jews and Judaism and the anti-Christian attitudes and behaviour of some Jews. It is an equation that has no historic basis.'[62] That Rudin is not mistaken here is made evident by Cardinal Dulles, who writes that 'to some degree Christian antipathy towards Jews is explicable in terms of Christian recollection of persecution by Jews in the first century, which have left a deep trauma on the Christian imagination, just as the ghettos, pogroms and forced conversion of the Middle Ages have continued to shape Jewish sensitivities'.[63] As Leon Klenicki notes, however, Jewish anti-Christian sentiment 'has never produced Jewish Crusades, persecutions, discrimination and even murder of whole Christian communities'.[64] In a document which should be wholly about owning Christian responsibility for the Holocaust, the tendency to claim Christian victimhood is deeply unattractive as well as historically implausible.

Such surprising tone-deafness is also apparent in how *We Remember* broadens its focus to emphasise the Church's present determination to reject 'every persecution against a people or human group anywhere, at any time'.[65] No doubt this was part of what Cardinal Cassidy meant when

---

60. Ibid., III.

61. Ibid., V.

62. A. James Rudin, 'Reflections on the Vatican's "Reflection on the Shoah"', *CrossCurrents* 48, no. 4 (Winter 1998/1999), pp. 518-29, p. 522.

63. Dulles, 'Commentary', in Dulles and Klenicki, *The Holocaust, Never to Be Forgotten*, p. 60.

64. Leon Klenicki, 'Commentary', in ibid., pp. 23-46, p. 42.

65. *We Remember*, IV.

he emphasised that *We Remember* had to speak to the universal Church, to Christians in countries not directly implicated in the Holocaust. So, the genocide of the Armenians is recalled, as are a series of other horrendous slaughters. Then, however, the document states: 'Nor can we forget the drama of the Middle East, the elements of which are well known.'[66] This appears to be an oblique reference to the Israel-Palestine question and to imply a parallel between the plight of the Palestinian people and the fate of the Jews in Nazi Germany. One does not have to approve of every Israeli Government policy to see that this is not a sensible comparison. For a Church seeking to show it has expunged anti-Semitism from its ranks, such a cavalier condemnation of Israel would be strange. Nevertheless, the reference is there, in all its opacity.

There is one remaining aspect of *We Remember* which has been of much concern to critics. As we have seen, the document acknowledges that there has been a strain of anti-Judaism within the Church which may have contributed to the failure of some Christians to resist the Nazi genocide. However, we are told that this anti-Judaism was quite distinct from Nazi anti-Semitism. Anti-Judaism, whilst pernicious, had not stood in strict contradiction to 'the constant teaching of the Church on the equal dignity of all races and peoples'.[67] It had always been possible for a Jew to convert to Christianity and thus escape Christian anti-Judaism. Nazi anti-Semitism, however, was based upon race and biology: there was a great chasm fixed between Jew and Gentile which no baptism could expunge. It was this, fused with an equally modern emphasis on the nation state, which fuelled the Holocaust: 'The Shoah was the work of a thoroughly modern neo-pagan regime. Its anti-Semitism had its roots outside Christianity, and in pursuing its aims, it did not hesitate to oppose the Church and persecute her members also.'[68] It is not the Church which is to blame for the Holocaust, but the Nazi version of modernity.

As we have seen, the genesis of the Holocaust is indeed complex. Christianity was not either its sole or sufficient cause. It is indisputable that other factors played crucial roles. Indeed, one factor in the Holocaust was actually the *weakness* of the Church: for all its anti-Judaism had been appalling, it had been restrained both by the Augustinian doctrine of 'the witness people' and the traditional Christian prohibition of murder. As Christianity lost its power, so all restraint was lifted from

66. Ibid.
67. Ibid.
68. Ibid.

Jew hatred. To that significant extent, *We Remember*'s insistence that one cannot simply blame Christianity for the Holocaust is correct.

However, it also excuses Christianity too quickly. Neither people nor cultures are rigidly compartmentalised in the way that they think and behave. Whilst it is true that Nazi anti-Semitism owed much to modern theories of race and biology, it also drew upon centuries of Christian practice, doctrine and culture. That older tradition also had its own quasi-biological elements: sixteenth-century Spanish Catholicism, for instance, had been marked by a concern for 'purity of blood', the lack of which justified discrimination and violence against the baptised descendants of Jewish converts to Christianity. There has been, as a recent Church of England report puts it, an 'open border between religious anti-Judaism and racist anti-Semitism'.[69] At the very least, the ease with which 'pagan' modernity could identify the Jew as its principal enemy is most readily explained by the fact that it sprang from a Europe shaped by Christianity. The consistent identity of the victim was no mere coincidence. As the Catholic critic of *We Remember* John Pawlikowski puts it, Christian anti-Judaism provided an 'indispensable seed-bed' for Nazism.[70] Nazism is not the same thing as Christianity, nor inevitably produced by it – but, equally, you could not have the former without the latter. The worrying tendency of the Vatican document is to minimise this grim continuity.

It is salutary to compare the approach of the French Bishops in their Drancy Statement, issued a year before *We Remember*. Whilst insisting, like the Vatican, that Nazi anti-Semitism had roots outside the Christian tradition, the Bishops are much franker in identifying the poisonous elements in the latter:

> it is a well proven fact that for centuries, up until Vatican Council II, an anti-Jewish tradition stamped its mark in different ways on Christian doctrine and preaching, in theology, apologetics, preaching and in the liturgy. It was on such ground that the venomous plant of hatred for the Jews was able to flourish.[71]

---

69. Faith and Order Commission of the Church of England, *God's Unfailing Word: Theological and Practical Perspectives on Christian-Jewish Relations* (London: Church House Publishing, 2019), p. 13.
70. John T. Pawlikowski, 'Appendix C: The Vatican and the Holocaust: Putting *We Remember* in Context', in Banki and Pawlikowski (eds), *Ethics in the Shadow of the Holocaust*, pp. 215-26, p. 223.
71. The Drancy Statement is reproduced in SEIA, *Catholics Remember the Holocaust*, pp. 31-37, p. 34.

Moreover, they admit that all this was largely due to the failure of those in authority in the Church, who 'let such a teaching of disdain [for Judaism and Jews] develop for so long, along with an underlying basic religious culture among Christian communities which shaped and deformed people's attitudes'.[72] Christianity, the French Bishops confess, helped pave the way for the Holocaust and this was in large measure due to the failure not just of individual 'grassroots' Christians but of those charged with teaching and leadership in the Church.

We Remember is much more cautious. We have already noted Pope John Paul II's acknowledgement that false interpretations of the New Testament had fuelled Christian anti-Judaism, but we did not mark his caveat – 'I do not say on the part of the Church as such.'[73] That is, many individual Christian teachers may have given this false teaching – but not the Church itself. In a similar fashion, *We Remember* cautiously speaks of the 'errors and failures of [the] sons and daughters of the Church', rather than of the Church itself.[74] The impression is given that Christian anti-Judaism, or the failure to resist Nazism (or, as we would insist, active enthusiasm for and collaboration with Nazism), was the fault of individual Christians, rather than of the Church considered corporately or institutionally. It was a case of a few bad apples, rather than a rotten tree.

It did not help, of course, that this insistence was accompanied by a vigorous defence of Pius XII and other senior episcopal figures. To those unfamiliar with Catholic theology, this was bound to give the impression that 'the sons and daughters of the Church' were the laity, while the Church itself was represented by the hierarchy – and, because the latter had (allegedly) acquitted itself well, the Church *per se* could therefore be untainted by complicity in the Holocaust. However, this is not the intention of the document. As Cardinal Dulles writes, 'When the Pope and the document *We Remember* speak of the "members" or "children" of the Church, they are not referring to the laity alone. These terms apply to all members, including popes, cardinals, bishops, priests, religious and laity. All of them can sin and err.'[75] However, the Cardinal goes on instantly to make the point that, even so, *the Church itself* cannot strictly be said to have sinned. There may be some very bad apples on some very high branches, but the tree itself is still fundamentally good.

---

72. Ibid.

73. *We Remember*, III.

74. Ibid., IV.

75. Dulles, 'Commentary', in Dulles and Klenicki, *The Holocaust, Never to Be Forgotten*, p. 58.

Which instantly raises the question: can this judgement be searching enough? The tree has not produced just a few bad apples, but season after season of corruption. As Franklin Littell asks: 'where did these sons and daughters come from? By whom were they catechized? The painful truth is that they absorbed the religious and cultural anti-Semitism by which they were corrupted from the Church and its teaching across centuries.'[76] If this is really faced squarely, can fundamental ecclesiology remain untouched? Could it be that the sinfulness of the Church's members is so extensive and consistent, so overwhelming and catastrophic, that the Church's claim to be a community of moral and spiritual renewal is wholly discredited? Put pugnaciously: has the Church disproved the Gospel? That is the question to which we turn in the next chapter.

---

76. Franklin H. Littell, 'Reaction of a Protestant Theologian to the Vatican's *We Remember* Document', in Braham (ed.), *The Vatican and the Holocaust*, pp. 71-87, p. 83.

Chapter 4

Has the Church Disproved the Gospel?

You are the salt of the earth; but if salt has lost its taste, how can its saltiness be restored? It is no longer good for anything, but is thrown out and trampled underfoot.

Matthew 5:13

Why Is There a Problem at All?

It may be difficult to understand why the question this chapter poses should even be asked. Even if the case developed so far is broadly correct – that the Church paved the way for the Holocaust over the centuries, failed lamentably to resist during the killing years and subsequently demonstrated a very inadequate level of repentance – why should that dismal record undermine the Gospel itself? How does the awful behaviour of some believers – even many believers – change the fact that God so loved the world that He gave His only Son to die and rise again for its salvation? These questions (and those explored in subsequent chapters) are of a different nature to those we have explored so far: from the historical focus of the first section, our investigation now becomes primarily *theological*.

Puzzlement at our question is due, primarily, to an understanding of the Church far removed from that assumed by the New Testament and the earliest Christian theology. Christians and others today often operate with a quite unexamined model of the Church as something akin to a movement dedicated to following and spreading the teachings of its founder. Like all such movements, its success in this task has been decidedly patchy. However, the essential truth of the message is understood as floating independently of its bearers: just as some apologists for Marxism are keen to disassociate themselves from the record of 'actually existing socialism', so on this account 'actually existing Christianity' has little to do with the truth or otherwise of the Gospel.

This is not an approach the theological consensus of the early Christian centuries would have endorsed. Christians, says this tradition, are not just Jesus' supporters: in St Paul's famous metaphor, they are his *body*. A distinction can no more easily be drawn between Christ and his Church than it can between my body and me. We shall see that it is a distinctive development of this fundamental early Christian conviction which underlies the contemporary Roman Catholic refusal, observed in the last chapter, to allow that the Church *per se* might have sinned dreadfully in the matter of responsibility for the Holocaust.

Paul used the idea of the Church as Christ's body above all in his correspondence with the Christians in Corinth, as he pleaded with them to maintain unity and high moral standards. Stoic philosophers had frequently used the metaphor to emphasise the proper interdependence of individuals within society. However, as Richard Hays notes, Paul gives it 'a surprising twist'. Commenting on 1 Corinthians 12:12, 'Just as the body is one and has many members ... so it is with Christ', Hays writes: 'We expect Paul to say "so it is with *the church*." Instead, by identifying the many members of the Church directly with Christ, Paul seems to press beyond mere analogy to make an ontological equation of the Church with Christ.'[1]

This is no slip of the pen. Whilst (as we shall shortly note) the iden-tification of the Church with Christ is indeed qualified by Paul, its fundamental reality is a consistent emphasis in his thought. It features even in contexts which militate against it, as when Paul condemns believers who have been visiting prostitutes (1 Corinthians 6:12-20). He is scandalised not just at the breach of an obvious moral rule, but because such Christians have, somehow, implicated Christ Himself in union with the prostitute: 'Do you not know that your bodies are members of Christ? Should I therefore take the members of Christ and make them members of a prostitute? Never!' (6:15). He then goes on to use the same verb – *kollaō* – to denote sexual union with the prostitute (6:16) and spiritual union with Christ (6:17). Hays comments, 'those who are in Christ have been united with him in a relationship of intimate union ... that

---

1. Richard B. Hays, *First Corinthians: Interpretation: A Bible Commentary for Teaching and Preaching* (Louisville, KY: John Knox Press, 1997), p. 213 (emphasis in the original).

is analogous to – but even deeper than – sexual union'.[2] Christians have become one flesh, one spiritual being, with their risen Lord: that is why fornication is unthinkable for Christians. (Unthinkable, but not evidently unheard of – we shall see shortly how Paul resolves this paradox.)

The sexual analogy is picked up again, by Paul or an author deeply influenced by him, in Ephesians 5:22-33. Once again, a fairly conventional idea in ancient society – that the husband is the head of the wife – is given a twist: male headship in Christian marriage is to be modelled after the pattern of Christ who is the head of his body, the Church. This offers no pattern of dominance, because Christ loved the Church and gave himself up for her, 'to present the Church to himself in splendour, without a spot or wrinkle or anything of the kind – yes, so that she might be holy and without blemish.' (5:27) The picture is of Christ gently washing, feeding and tending his spouse (5:29), pouring Himself into her so that she may be transformed into beauty. She belongs to his life, just as woman belongs to man in marriage: 'This is a great mystery, and I am applying it to Christ and the Church.' (5:32).

A similar idea is found in the Johannine tradition. Whereas for Paul the key image was that of the body, in John a similar purpose is served by the vine – above all, in John 15:1-11, described by Barrett as symbolically summarising John's doctrine of the Church.[3] The relationship pictured between Christ and the Church here is even closer than that between the stem of the vine and its branches. Christ is the true vine, not just the stem. The branches are *in* Him, not just connected *to* Him or associated *with* Him. All their life and fruitfulness is utterly derived from his : he fills them with His own fruitfulness. As Raymond Brown comments (on a different, though related passage): 'one might have liked a sharper differentiation than John provides between God's incarnation in Jesus, and God's indwelling in the Christians'.[4]

The ground is thus laid for some of the most troubling statements in the New Testament – supremely troubling in the light of our first three chapters. The author of the First Letter of John understood the moral implications of Johannine ecclesiology thus: 'Little children, let no-one deceive you ... those who have been born of God do not sin, because

---

2. Ibid., p. 104.
3. C.K. Barrett, *The Gospel According to St John: An Introduction with Commentary and Notes on the Greek Text*, 2nd edn (London: SPCK, 1975), p. 96.
4. Raymond E. Brown, *The Anchor Bible: The Gospel According to John*, 2 vols (London: Geoffrey Chapman, 1971), vol. 2, p. 778-79.

God's seed abides in them; they cannot sin, because they have been born of God.' (1 John 3:7, 9). A Christian is someone filled with Christ, whom Christ is loving and transforming into beauty. Before union with Christ, they may have been the very worst of sinners. Now, however, it is no longer they who live, but Christ who lives in them. Sin, therefore, is simply impossible in the Christian life.

The point is, of course immediately qualified: 1 John 1:8-10 allows that Christians may indeed sin and, having once repented, can trust in forgiveness through Christ; 1 John 5:16 says that we should pray for fellow Christians who fall into sin and that God will restore them to life (although this concession is restricted to those sins which are 'not mortal' – traditionally understood as excluding murder, idolatry and fornication). Although the logic of what might be called the 'perfectionist' tradition is indeed simple, the testimony of experience was overwhelming: Christians sin. That Christians visit prostitutes may indeed be unthinkable for Paul – but it still happened.

The New Testament writers never wholly resolve this paradox. To do so would defuse its scandal and this they are determined not to do. Life in Christ and sin are an intolerable contradiction, and no quarter must be given to complacent acquiescence. At another level, both John and Paul maintain that there must be a 'not yet' element to Christian experience: that, though Christ is indeed the deepest reality of the Christian's life, this is not yet fully realised. As 1 John 3:1-2 also puts it, beautifully:

> See what love the Father has given us, that we should be called children of God; and that is what we are. ... Beloved, we are God's children now; what we will be has not yet been revealed. What we do know is this: when he is revealed, we will be like him, for we will see him as he is.

The same sense of yearning expectancy is present in Paul: 'The creation waits with eager longing for the revealing of the children of God ... [so that] the creation itself will be set free from its bondage to decay and obtain the freedom of the glory of the children of God.' (Romans 8:19-21). John and Paul concur: we have not yet arrived at our destiny. Everything changed when we were united to Christ but for now we are still teetering on the edge of glory, longing for fullness.

For now, however, the Christian life is still marred by the remnants of sin. If nothing else, we remain subject to 'the wages of sin', our common mortality (Romans 6:23) – though some early Christians may have been startled even by this discovery (Paul seems to be responding to a flurry of concern about this in 1 Corinthians 15). The New Testament can understand, if not quite accept, the presence of sin in the Christian life in this way: these are the remnants of the old life, which still have some limited purchase on us. They are to be struggled against and thrown off, before being removed decisively and forever at the final coming of the Lord Jesus.

However, this acknowledgement of sin within the Christian life was very limited. 1 John, we've seen, holds certain sins to be 'mortal': once committed they kill the Christian life so definitively that there is no point in praying for forgiveness. The Letter to the Hebrews teaches:

> It is impossible to restore again to repentance those who have once been enlightened, and have tasted the heavenly gift, and have shared in the Holy Spirit, and have tasted the goodness of the word of God and the powers of the age to come and then have fallen away, since on their own they are crucifying again the Son of God and are holding him up to contempt. Ground that drinks up the rain falling on it repeatedly, and that produces a crop useful to those for whom it is cultivated, receives a blessing from God. But if it produces thorns and thistles, it is worthless and on the verge of being cursed; its end is to be burned over.
>
> Hebrews 6:4-8

As Howard Marshall notes, 'the early Church took much more seriously than we do the possibility that a person may sin beyond hope of redemption.'[5]

Unsurprisingly, this line proved difficult to hold. Within a couple of generations, there were many Christian voices saying that even the dreaded mortal sins could perhaps be forgiven: albeit only after a lifetime of penitence, and only once. However, in the first three Christian centuries, that is as far as indulgence went. The idea that serious sin might become a general and settled condition in the Church remained anathema. There were indeed some attempts, especially associated with the theological school of Alexandria, to distinguish between a Platonic 'ideal' of the Church and the messy, compromised Church of history – but this move was not generally accepted. For all the tension it had to bear, the mainstream position insisted on the actual moral transformation of believers and the believing community.

'Community' is indeed where a properly biblical focus directs us. Right from the grand sweep of the introduction to the Letter to the Ephesians, for instance, the author's focus is on God's plan set forth in Christ: 'a plan

---

5. I. Howard Marshall, *The Epistles of John* (Grand Rapids, MI: William B. Eerdmans, 1978), p. 249.

for the fullness of time, to gather up all things in him, things in heaven and things on earth' (1:10). God's purpose is for reconciliation: to bring not just individuals but all things back into right relationship with Him and with each other. It is through its existence as a reconciled and reconciling community that the Church makes known the purposes of God before 'the rulers and authorities in the heavenly places' (Ephesians 3:10). It is bitterly ironic in a book about the Holocaust to note that, for Ephesians, the prime instance of this reconciliation is that between Jew and Gentile. Look, the Apostle is saying: the purposes of God are at last most plainly revealed in the fact that Jew and Gentile are at peace. Where once two peoples were bitterly divided, now there is a community of mutual service and love.

Luke's vision is similar. The Acts of the Apostles is most naturally read as the story of one division after another being ended by the reconciled and reconciling community. From the Pentecostal miracle of strangers being able to understand each other's languages (Acts 2:5-11); the sharing of wealth between rich and poor (2:43-47); the prominence given to women in the church; the inclusion of a persecutor as an apostle; and running through it all the master-narrative of Gentiles being brought into the renewed people of God: the point is that the Church is where divisions come crashing down. For the Acts of the Apostles (and the letter to the Ephesians), the quality of 'actually existing Christianity' is essential. If all the old enmities and exclusions are not actually overcome in the Church, if humanity is still carved up against itself, then the principalities and powers are not in fact overthrown.

This was an abiding emphasis in early Christianity. The highly influential fourth-century bishop of Alexandria, Athanasius, provides just one instance. Not coincidentally, his soteriology – famously summarised in the saying, 'God became human, so that we might become divine' – emphasised Christ's sharing of life with the Christians, and the Church's participation in Christ. Athanasius spells out why this is truly good news:

> the barbarians of the present day are naturally savage in their habits, and as long as they sacrifice to their idols they rage furiously against each other and cannot bear to be a single hour without weapons. But when they hear the teaching of Christ, forthwith they turn from fighting, and instead of arming themselves with swords, extend their hands in prayer. In a word, instead of fighting each other, they take up arms against the devil and the demons.[6]

---

6. Athanasius, *De Incarnatione*, 52.

This, for Athanasius, is a powerful argument for the truth of the Gospel: the reconciled community itself embodies and brings reconciliation. If it did not, its message would lack all credibility.

This, of course, is our problem. Nicholas Lash puts it in hypothetical form: 'If it could be shown that Christianity had not, in fact, effectively contributed to the liberating transformation of human structures and relationships, the legitimacy of Christian hope would already have been deprived of one of its necessary conditions.'[7] Our argument in the previous three chapters has been that the case is proven. Through the long history of violent anti-Semitism, culminating in the Holocaust, Christianity has *not* been a transformative factor for the good. In the best case, it provided the seedbed for genocide; in the worst, it collaborated; in neither has it adequately repented. Paul hailed peace between Jew and Gentile as decisive proof of the Gospel: our question is whether the slaughter of Jews by baptised Gentiles does not then *disprove* the Gospel. As Doris Bergen puts it, sharply: 'What is the value ... of Christianity, if it provides no defence against brutality and can even become a willing participant in genocide?'[8]

The Usual Defence: Augustine and the Donatists

Moral scandal, of course, is not a new problem in the Church. We have already traced how the New Testament, with difficulty, acknowledged the reality of Christian sin. Nor was the question of what this undoubted fact meant for the nature of the Church ignored. In the early development of doctrine, the closest analogue to our problem – though in some important respects, *not* an exact one – comes in the fourth-century 'Donatist crisis' in North Africa.[9]

The Donatist crisis had its origins in the persecutions of Diocletian, Roman emperor between 284 and 305. Christians at this time were often required to hand over their sacred books and liturgical vessels on pain of execution. Many resisted and suffered the consequences: others did not and handed over the books – becoming known as *traditores* (those who hand over). Unsurprisingly, the *traditores* were often viewed by those who had resisted as traitors. Their action was viewed as apostasy,

---

7. Nicholas Lash, *A Matter of Hope: A Theologian's Reflections on the Thoughts of Karl Marx* (London: Darton, Longman & Todd, 1981), pp. 278-79.

8. Bergen, *Twisted Cross*, p. xi.

9. W.H.C. Frend, *The Donatist Church: A Movement of Protest in Roman North Africa* (Oxford: Clarendon Press, 1951), remains in many respects the standard account of the crisis.

a mortal sin from which there could be little, if any, hope of restoration. For rigorists, the holiness of the Church required the *traditores* to be banished from its life.

However, this was not the policy most of the bishops of North Africa chose to pursue. In 312, a new bishop of Carthage was consecrated and, to the horror of the rigorist party, one of the other bishops chosen to consecrate him was a *traditore*. Far from being excluded, he had been allowed to continue at the very centre of church life – thus, to purist eyes, polluting that whole life. The new bishop of Carthage was no real bishop if he was associated with such a man; the Church was no longer really the Church if it tolerated such wickedness at its heart. It would indeed disprove the Gospel, insofar as it could no longer be the new humanity, the Spirit-filled Body of Christ, which the New Testament envisaged. The only solution for faithful Christians was to abandon the shipwreck of the old Catholic Church and begin again. Thus, came the Donatist schism, named for its leader Donatus. The schismatics were numerous and powerful, and it was by no means a foregone conclusion that in the long historical run they would come to be viewed as heretics by triumphant Catholicism.

It is not quite accurate to describe the Donatists as insisting upon a morally pure Church. Their principal opponent, Augustine, took great delight in pointing out how they themselves would fail such a test.[10] The jibe, whilst effective, is not wholly fair:

> The Donatists were not 'Puritans' in the Northern European sense ... the Donatist Church was 'pure' in an obvious and not particularly exacting sense: it had kept itself from a single, unspeakable crime, from *traditio*, the sacrificing of the Christian 'Law'; that is, from a crime committed by total strangers in a conveniently distant past.[11]

However, albeit in this nuanced sense, the Donatists did make the reality of the Church dependent upon the moral performance of its members, and especially of its bishops. A similar understanding prompts our current question, as to whether the Church's historic complicity in the violent anti-Semitism which culminated in the Holocaust disproves its

---

10. Peter Brown, *Augustine of Hippo: A Biography* (London: Faber & Faber, 1967), p. 218.
11. Ibid., pp. 218-20.

claim to be the Church, the Spirit-filled Body of Christ. So, might the orthodox response to Donatism also answer our question?

The Donatists' central point was that the Catholic episcopate was compromised beyond repair: because of the clergy's apostasy the Spirit had abandoned them and they could minister no real sacraments. Augustine offered a response which became normative for all subsequent Catholic theology, which radically relativised the importance of the personal qualities of the human minister of the sacrament. Bishops and priests might indeed be radically sinful. However, the real minister of any sacrament is not them, but the risen Jesus – who is perfectly capable of using deeply flawed human instruments for His purposes. On the Augustinian view, later classically expressed in Article 26 of the Church of England's Articles of Religion, 'the unworthiness of the ministers ... hinders not the effect of the Sacrament'.

The point is not narrowly restricted to bishops and priests and the validity of sacramental actions. What Augustine was rejecting was the idea that the Church needs to jealously guard its purity in the way that the Donatists did. The union of Christ and the Church does not depend upon the highly questionable merits of its members. It flows solely from the faithfulness of the risen Christ, who has promised to work with and through ordinary, fallible, sinful human beings. The Church is indeed holy, but not considered in itself – only because the deepest reality of her life is Christ, breathing Himself ever anew into human lives.

This breathing takes time, can be resisted and has to win through against the stubbornness and stupidity of those in whom it is taking place. So, there will be plenty of sin and failure in the Church. However, it does not, as it were, go all the way down: it does not express the Church's true identity, it is a miscarrying of what the Church truly is. In God's good time, His breathing will bear its full fruit and the Church will be made perfect. Until then, however, it is not for those who are themselves morally fallible to start carving out morally pure communities. The parable of the Wheat and the Tares (Matthew 13:24-30) was, unsurprisingly, a central feature of anti-Donatist polemic: 'in gathering the weeds you would uproot the wheat along with them. Let both of them grow until the harvest.'

Augustine's response to Donatism has formed the principal resource for Christian theology when faced with gross moral failure in the Church. How might it help address the scandal of the Church's complicity in the Holocaust? Those shaped by Augustine might readily admit that the Church from top to bottom has been radically implicated in guilt: that laity and clergy and even the Pope failed to act as they should have done. They might agree that corporate repentance is desperately needed. However, they would *not* agree that this moral failure in any way disproves the Gospel, or invalidates the claim of the Church to really be the Church. What if some believers have been faithless? The risen Jesus remains faithful, and He has bound Himself to the Church in all its fallibility and guilt.

Avery Dulles provides a good example of such a response. Commenting on proposals that the Church should acknowledge and repent for its role in the Holocaust, he argues that a careful distinction must be drawn between the sins of believers, and the sin of the Church *per se*.[12] Individual believers, be they laypeople or popes, certainly sin. However, the Church itself 'is not related in the same way to holiness and sin'.[13] Holiness is the ontologically fundamental reality of the Church, because the deepest reality of the Church is Christ sharing his life with humanity. When believers show forth this reality, they are most at one with the Church: the vine is bearing its fruit. When they do not, it is because they have become alienated from that belonging: 'affected as they are by the secular culture of their day and by the weight of their own fallen humanity, the members resist the truth and goodness that the Church by her nature tends to instil in them'.[14] The ultimate end of such alienation would be excommunication: however, short of that, the members of the Church are called to constant penance and renewal.

So, take, for instance, the ambiguous record of Pius XII in relation to the Holocaust. Dulles reads the record more favourably than many – but, even if his verdict was harsher, he could still say that *the Church itself* remains holy and pure, because the Christ at its heart remains holy and pure. Insofar as even a Pope falls away from that holiness and purity, to just that degree he is becoming detached from the fundamental, theological reality of the Church – even though serving at its institutional heart. His wicked behaviour in no way dissolves or negates the bond between Christ and humanity which is the ultimate truth of the Church. It follows that the right response for Christians scandalised by wickedness in the Church can *never* be to leave, as the Donatists did. The treasure of the union of God with humanity may be mediated in very obviously fragile clay jars, but it is *only* in these jars

---

12. Avery Cardinal Dulles SJ, 'Should the Church Repent?', in Avery Cardinal Dulles SJ, *Church and Society: The Laurence J. McGinley Lectures, 1988-2007* (New York: Fordham University Press, 2008), pp. 262-75, pp. 266-67.
13. Ibid.
14. Ibid.

that it will be found at all. This community is where God has promised to give Himself and, thus, as St Cyprian once said: 'You cannot have God for your Father, if you have not the Church for your mother.'[15]

There is much that is deeply attractive about all this. The anti-Donatist position insists upon identifying a real community, made up of actual people, as God's Church, rather than taking flight into some abstract or invisible ideal. It has a keen sense of what the Church truly is already, and the holiness of life it must still struggle towards, which will only be finally and fully manifest in the eschaton. It is realistic about the frailties and worse of even the most 'senior' Christian leaders and will not make anything of decisive theological importance hang upon the quality of their moral performance. Accordingly, it resists the urge to fly into ever smaller and more fanatical communities of the pure. Augustine's doctrine prevailed for very good reasons.

However, it is not at all clear that it provides a sufficient answer to our post-Holocaust problem. It is hard to resist the impression when reading Augustine – and certainly Dulles – that what really troubles them is 'a few bad apples'. The problem addressed is the moral failure of individual Christians. Our problem, though, is one of Christian *culture*. As noted above, Dulles writes that believers sin when they are unduly influenced by secular culture, making them resistant to the 'truth and goodness the Church by her nature tends to instil in them'. But truth and goodness are not all that the Church instils. It was never just *secular* culture which dripped poison against the Jews. It was *church* culture, *church* teaching. The problem is not a few bad apples but a suspect tree.

Peter Brown suggests that Augustine's anti-Donatist teaching 'reflects the attitude of a group confident of its powers to absorb the world without losing its identity'.[16] The Donatists lacked confidence: they were driven by anxiety to preserve purity, by expelling *traditores*. Their church was a citadel under siege in a darkening world; their task was simply to endure: 'Ultimately, the Donatists regarded their church as an alternative to society, as a place of refuge, like the Ark. Augustine believed that the Church might become co-extensive with human society as a whole: that it might absorb, transform and perfect, the existing bonds of human relations.'[17] Augustine's vision won through in fourth-century North Africa but our study so far suggests that, as the centuries unfolded,

---

15. Cyprian, *The Lapsed; Unity of the Catholic Church*, trans. by Maurice Bévenot SJ (New York: Newman Press, 1957), pp. 48-49.

16. Brown, *Augustine of Hippo*, p. 214.

17. Ibid., p. 224.

his confidence proved misplaced. In respect of the Jews, far from transforming and perfecting the bonds of human relations, the Church absorbed and reproduced and magnified the hatreds of the world. If the deepest identity of the Church is indeed Jesus Christ, the all-holy, then this now needs to be articulated in a way which recognises that, nevertheless, unholiness has somehow penetrated to the very core of the Church's existence. The Church might not – perhaps – have disproved the Gospel: but it certainly has disproved any but the most radically self-critical accounts of its own existence.

A Broken Church

What then might a radically self-critical ecclesiology look like?

The work of Dietrich Bonhoeffer offers some suggestive leads. Bonhoeffer, of course, starts in a different place from Dulles. He believed the Church to which he belonged had become so corrupted, above all, through its adoption of the Aryan Paragraph (see chapter two), that for the sake of the Gospel it had to be abandoned. Dulles holds that one should *never* abandon the Church: whatever the abuses inside it, whoever they are committed by, they can never nullify the ultimate truth of its life – the union of God with humanity in Jesus Christ. In this fundamental divergence, Dulles represents the Roman Catholic appropriation of Augustine, and Bonhoeffer the Protestant. The Protestant Reformation can indeed be understood as a thoroughly Augustinian debate, as Benjamin Warfield observes: 'The Reformation, inwardly considered, was just the ultimate triumph of Augustine's doctrine of grace over Augustine's doctrine of the Church.'[18]

To clarify that thought: what provoked the Reformation was, in Martin Luther's eyes, something much worse than mere moral scandal. There were, of course, scandals and Luther was appalled by them – but Augustine's arguments against the Donatists justified good Christians, nonetheless, remaining within the morally compromised Church. What was decisively different in the sixteenth century was that the authorities of the Church – above all, the papacy – had explicitly committed themselves to a contradiction of the Gospel (over the issue of indulgences, which Luther took to mean that salvation could be bought or merited and was, accordingly, not a free gift of grace). The problem was not the traditional one of Christians failing to live up to the Gospel, but of the Gospel being

18. Benjamin B. Warfield, *Calvin and Augustine* (Phillipsburg, NJ: Presbyterian & Reformed Publishing Co., 1954), pp. 321-22.

replaced. This drove Luther to affirm that the Church existed only where the Gospel was truly preached – and that this was no longer the case in the Pope's church. A church should, indeed, never be abandoned *lightly*. To that extent, Luther still shared Augustine's anti-Donatism. However, a time could come, and now had, when what was once a church no longer was – and then departure was the only obedient option.

Bonhoeffer was Luther's heir in this relativisation of the institutional forms of the Church. He emphasised, of course, that that such forms should never be held cheap or despised. They are not just the product of sinful history, and the institutional Church is not solely a human organisation. Like the New Testament and the Fathers, Bonhoeffer's fundamental ecclesiological conviction was that the risen Jesus shared his life with men and women – his favoured way of putting this was to speak of 'Christ-existing-as-community'.[19] The institutional forms which spring up to give coherence and continuity to this corporate life – like the ordained ministry, like the great Roman communion itself – are indeed energised by the life of Christ at their heart. As Bonhoeffer wrote in his earliest work, the actually existing forms of the Church are sanctified by what they bear: 'It carries it in its heart.'[20] The allusion is to Luke 2:51, suggesting a parallel between the Church and Mary: both are truly blessed and truly holy. Yet, the key point from the Protestant perspective is that they are both also vulnerable to sin.

The Roman Catholic teaching on Mary is, of course, significantly different: the dogma of the Immaculate Conception holds that she was, from the very beginning of her existence, preserved from all taint of original or actual sin.[21] Admittedly, this is true only in virtue of her relationship to Jesus, but the key point remains: grace makes it possible for her to be utterly without sin. What 1 John 3:2-3 promises for all Christians eschatologically is thus affirmed of Mary historically. This

---

19. The theme runs throughout Bonhoeffer's work, beginning with his *Sanctorum Communio: A Theological Study of the Sociology of the Church: Dietrich Bonhoeffer Works, Volume 1*, ed. by Clifford J. Green, trans. by Richard Krauss and Nancy Lukens (Minneapolis: Fortress Press, 1998). A useful essay on the topic is Clifford Green, 'Human Sociality and Christian Community', in John W. de Gruchy (ed.), *The Cambridge Companion to Dietrich Bonhoeffer* (Cambridge: Cambridge University Press, 1999), pp. 113-33.

20. Bonhoeffer, *Sanctorum Communio*, p. 216.

21. This doctrine was defined as a dogma of the faith by Pope Pius IX in his *Ineffabilis Deus* of 8 December 1854, making assent to it binding on Roman Catholics.

matters for our purposes because Roman Catholicism also makes a parallel ecclesiological move – saying of certain features of the Church that they are not only holy and blessed, but somehow (like immaculate Mary) hermetically sealed from the frailty and sin of the world. The move can be seen in various areas of doctrine: the bread of the eucharist is no longer bread, but replaced by the body of Christ. The marriage bond is (save by death) *utterly* indissoluble, because the frailty of human commitment is now taken up and transformed in the indestructible union of Christ with the Church. The magisterium of the Church in general, and on occasion of Peter's successor in particular, is preserved from all error. At each point, the fallible is made infallible: the righteousness of Christ is seen as invested or infused into human beings, their history and their institutions in such a way as to make them – as Bonhoeffer did not put it, but could have done – Jesus rather than Mary.

This is why John Paul II entered his caveat – 'I do not say the Church as such' – when he spoke of Christians misinterpreting New Testament texts in an anti-Jewish fashion. It is why Dulles must identify Christian anti-Semitism as due to external, secular influence. It is why we observed a tendency in *We Remember* to minimise the culpability of the Church and to lionise Pius XII. It is the same basic motive as Michael Marrus sees underlying the Vatican's conduct throughout the Nazi era: 'foremost among these priorities, understood as a supreme value in its own right, was the safeguarding and promotion of the institutions, integrity and the mission of the Church in a turbulent and dangerous world'.[22] Whether through diplomacy or theology, the honour and interests of the Church must be vigorously asserted, because they are the honour and interests of Christ. Such a stance makes radical self-critique almost impossible.

Yet, such critique is abundantly necessary. To take just one instance: where did the teaching of contempt for the Jews – which all acknowledge deformed the Christian response to the Holocaust – come from, if not from the teaching office of the Church across the centuries? As we shall shortly see, the claim that the Second Vatican Council's radically new teaching on the theology of Judaism represents anything other than *rupture* with this past strains credulity. Those who, nonetheless, make it do so because anything else would involve the admission that the Christian tradition has been disastrously wrong. A Protestant can do that, because it is of the essence of Protestantism that even General

---

22. Michael R. Marrus, 'The Role of the Holy See during the Holocaust', in Rittner and Roth (eds), *Pope Pius XII and the Holocaust*, pp. 43-55, p. 45.

Councils (never mind Popes) 'may err, and sometimes have erred, even in things pertaining to God'.[23] An orthodox Roman Catholic cannot.

If it is true that Popes and bishops and general councils have behaved and taught in error, in ways that directly harmed Jews, and which paved the way for the Holocaust, what follows? Not so much that the Church has disproved the Gospel, but it certainly has discredited any version of the faith which sees that magisterium as invested with Christ's authority, as being, in fact, Christ's living voice. Cardinal Newman's lines, 'And I hold in veneration / for the sake of Christ alone / Holy Church as His creation / and her teaching as His own', should now stick in the throat.[24] The Church's complicity in the Holocaust – both during the killing years and in the long historical build-up to them – may not have disproved the Gospel, but it has certainly discredited infallibilist ecclesiological fantasies. The Church is not, as Vatican II's *Lumen Gentium* exults, the 'initial budding forth on earth' of God's Kingdom.[25]

Nothing said so far, however, should be taken as suggesting that somehow Protestantism's record in resisting Nazism is better than that of Catholicism. If anything, the Protestant failure during the Nazi era was more abject still. Already in 1927 Dietrich Bonhoeffer was reflecting gloomily on the cultural captivity of German Protestantism and wondering whether the Gospel could indeed still be preached faithfully within the existing Evangelical Church: '[We have] reached a point where questions such as these must find their answer. ... [W]e are also more than ever attentive to the danger of [the Church's] complete desecration.'[26] Spoken like a true Donatist, but Bonhoeffer had no illusions about the new church that would emerge from the wreckage of the EKD: the Confessing Church. He did not view the schism as creating a brave band of true Christians, vigorous in moral splendour. Indeed, he would have considered such a perspective as, ironically, almost papal in its confusion of the actuality and the reality of the Church. The reality of the Church – as the New Testament and the Fathers teach – is Christ-existing-as-community. The actuality of the Church, including the Confessing Church, is to a greater or lesser degree shaped by sin, and in early twentieth-century Germany shaped thus to a very high degree.

---

23. Article 21 of the Church of England's Articles of Religion.
24. The lines are from his hymn, 'Firmly I believe and truly'.
25. *Lumen Gentium*, promulgated by Pope Paul VI, 21 November 1964, 'The Mystery of the Church', ch. 1, para. 5.
26. Bonhoeffer, *Sanctorum Communio*, p. 271, n. 429.

None, save Jesus Christ, is truly holy. None, save Jesus Christ, has a claim to moral brilliance, or to infallibility in doctrine.

What makes the Church the Church, for Bonhoeffer, is not its institutional pedigree, its teaching authority or its moral brilliance. Such things may flow from – and sometimes they may choke – what really is the essence of the Church: Christ-existing-as-community, the risen Jesus drawing men and women into communion with himself. In the seminal essay 'Ethics and Formation', Bonhoeffer works this out in terms of 'the form' of Jesus Christ; the risen Jesus is understood as conforming His disciples to the pattern and energy of his life. It is not so much that believers try very hard to imitate Christ, as that through the ministry of word and sacrament they find themselves changed *by* him. Precisely what this change looks like varies in every situation, but the template is always the same: the life of Jesus, poured out to death so that others might live – the pattern of crucifixion and resurrection.[27]

Bonhoeffer finds it easier to explore the first movement in that pattern than the second. Our risen life, as the first letter of John suggests, lies hidden with God in Christ, waiting to be revealed and now only gleaming through on occasion. For now, the Church is marked, above all, by its sharing in the movement of crucifixion. The Christian, and the Church, die to worldly standards of success, self-preservation, to concepts of public honour and shame, even to their own ideals of righteousness. So, for instance, a respectable German pastor might incur the shame of a traitor's death and even assume the guilt of involvement in a plot to murder the Führer (against his own pacifically inclined conscience, and the finest traditions of his church and class). The Christian, and the Church, might have to become the condemned prisoner and even – this is the supreme paradox – the sinner, abandoning his own righteousness for the sake of loving his neighbour. That is what Jesus did; that is what he still does through his people.

The Church, then, will be utterly unconcerned about its own status – whether it is seen as the possessor of an impeccable teaching authority, or as being morally heroic. Its most obvious mark will be humility. Bonhoeffer wrote in May 1944 that even the Confessing Church had been fighting 'only for its self-preservation, as though that were an end in itself. ... So the words we used before must lose their power, be

---

27. Dietrich Bonhoeffer, 'Ethics as Formation', in Dietrich Bonhoeffer, *Ethics: Dietrich Bonhoeffer Works, Volume 6*, ed. by Clifford J. Green, trans. by Reinhard Krauss, Charles C. West and Douglas W. Stott (Minneapolis: Fortress Press, 2005), pp. 76-102.

silenced, and we can be Christians today in only two ways, through prayer and in doing justice among human beings.'[28] All else might fall away: every effort to promote the cause of the Church, to present it in the best light, to struggle for its existence and place in society. The moral failings of such a Church would not disprove the Gospel, because such a Church never thought the Gospel involved making it anything other than what it is: a rag-tag of deeply sinful people, gradually being formed into the image of Christ – which means, simply, into loving service for others. Such a Church would not be surprised by its failures, though it would be humbled. It would not exalt its leaders as spiritual heroes, but love them as fellow-sinners. It would not be interested in proving the correctness of all its teachings, or in claiming that its teachers never made mistakes – even terrible mistakes. 'Prayer and doing justice': that would be its one focus.

All this means, as Rowan Williams puts it, that: 'A Christian community doing its job is a community where people expect to be repenting quite a lot, and where the confident calling of others to repentance, which Christians enjoy so much, needs to be silenced by self-scrutiny and self-questioning before God.'[29] Yet in all this dispossession and stripping away lies the good news:

> a repentant community, a community of people who are daily aware of their own untruthfulness and lack of love and are not afraid to face their failures, is a community that speaks profoundly of hope. The Church does not communicate the good news by consistent success and virtue ... but in its willingness to point to God; and repentance, which says that you do not have to be paralysed by failure, is thus one of the most effective signs of the Church's appeal to something more than human competence and resource. Perhaps we should add a fifth mark of the Church to the four in the Creed – a Church that is one, holy, catholic, apostolic and repentant.'[30]

---

28. Dietrich Bonhoeffer, 'Thoughts on the Day of Baptism of Dietrich Wilhelm Rüdiger Bethge', in Bonhoeffer, *Letters and Papers from Prison: Dietrich Bonhoeffer Works, Volume 8*, ed. by John W. de Gruchy, trans. by Isabel Best, Lisa E. Dahill Reinhard Krauss and Nancy Lukens (Minneapolis: Fortress, 2010), pp. 383-90, p. 389.
29. Rowan Williams, *Tokens of Trust: An Introduction to Christian Belief* (Norwich: Canterbury Press, 2007), p. 152.
30. Ibid.

A Church which comes out of the experience of the Holocaust in any other condition would indeed betray the Gospel. And if such betrayal were to become the settled state of the Church, we would indeed be well on the way to disproving the Gospel. Our question hangs in the balance. One hopeful sign of repentance, however, is the astonishingly swift and radical revision of Christian teaching and practice concerning Jews and Judaism which has taken place since 1945. We turn to that now.

Chapter 5

Christians, Jews and Israel

For mine eyes have seen thy salvation, Which thou hast prepared before the face of all people; A light to lighten the Gentiles, and the glory of thy people Israel.
      Simeon, before the infant Jesus – Luke 2:30-32 (KJV)

The *Nostra Aetate* Revolution

For most of Christian history, a Jew was fortunate only to encounter Christians who held Augustine's doctrine of the 'witness people'. By this account, Jews were pathetic figures, doomed to misery and decay and embodying what it meant to be cut off from the life of God. In the second millennium, the view was often much darker: the Jew was now an actively malevolent, even demonic, agent against whom no slander was too outrageous. They were not to be tolerated, but expelled or exterminated. As we have seen, it is too simplistic to say that such beliefs caused the Holocaust. Yet, without them, the Holocaust would not have happened.

What followed was the swiftest and most thorough doctrinal revolution in the history of Christianity. Oddly, it came from the top: the *volte-face* in the Christian view of Judaism was heralded by nothing less than a conciliar declaration of the Roman Catholic Church, the 1965 document, *Nostra Aetate* ('In Our Time'). The authority of such a document is, for Catholics, unsurpassable. Moreover, its impact was felt well beyond that communion. *Nostra Aetate* is revered across many Christian traditions and often assumed as the starting point for all subsequent reflection on Jewish-Christian relations.

What does it say? *Nostra Aetate* is not actually about Judaism: it is a general statement of how the Roman Catholic Church sees the major world religions. A remarkably new note is sounded. The Church, hitherto regarded as the one ark of salvation in a troubled world outside which all would perish, now emphasised the good to be found in other religions, and how they reflect 'a ray of that Truth which enlightens all men'.[1] Other religions are no longer considered primarily as systems of idolatry drawing people away from God, but as expressions of yearning for Him. The Church trusts, of course, that that yearning will ultimately be fulfilled in encounter with Jesus Christ, the incarnation of the truth all people long for. Nevertheless, the Church is now not so much an ark as a magnet, attracting all that is good towards itself. Therefore, 'the Catholic Church rejects nothing which is true and holy in [other] religions'. Christians should not denounce other creeds but, 'through dialogue and collaboration with the followers of other religions, … and in witness to the Christian faith and life, [they should] recognize, preserve and promote the good things, spiritual and moral, as well as the socio-cultural values found among these men'.[2]

Within that overall framework, the Second Vatican Council then insists that Christians share a unique bond with Jews and Judaism, forged in God's original call to Abraham in which the Church believes its own existence to have been envisaged. Furthermore, the Church received the revelation of the Old Testament from the Jews. This is not merely a long-past gift, still recalled with gratitude. Rather, the Church goes on drawing sustenance from the roots of that good olive tree, onto which have been grafted the wild branches of the Gentiles.[3] This draws on Pauline metaphor (Romans 11:17-24) to show that there is something ineradicably Jewish at the heart of Christianity.

Nostra Aetate goes on to state definitively that the Jewish people have not been repudiated or cursed by God, who does not repent of the gifts He makes or of the calls He issues. Once again, the reference is to Paul in Romans 11:28-29. This is understood as teaching that God's fidelity means that, even if most Jews never accepted Jesus as the Christ, nevertheless,

---

1. *Nostra Aetate: Declaration on the Relation of the Church to Non-Christian Religions Proclaimed by His Holiness Pope Paul VI*, 28 October 1965, para. 2. The text is widely reproduced and available online at: http://www .vatican.va/archive/hist_councils/ii_vatican_council/documents/vat-ii _decl_19651028_nostra-aetate_en.html.
2. Ibid.
3. Ibid., para. 4.

God's promises to them hold good. At the very least, their eternal destiny is not dependent on whether or not they become Christians: 'In company with the Prophets and the same Apostle [Paul], the Church awaits that day, known to God alone, on which all peoples will address the Lord in a single voice and "serve him shoulder to shoulder".[4] Christians should approach the Jewish people not as lost souls, but confident they remain beloved of God and destined for eternal joy.

Crucially, the Council next repudiates any attempt to blame the Jews collectively for the death of Christ. Admittedly, certain Jews, especially among the leadership of Jesus' day, pressed for his execution. However, his death 'cannot be charged against all the Jews, without distinction, then alive, nor against the Jews of today'.[5] This renunciation of the 'deicide' charge is perhaps the single most famous move in *Nostra Aetate*, although it is not wholly original: official Roman Catholic doctrine since the sixteenth century had been that blame for the death of Jesus could not be attributed to the Jews alone.[6] Nevertheless, this had not had much effect in popular Western Christian tradition, and even less so in the East, and Vatican II drew some sharp criticism for restating the point so emphatically. The Jacobite Patriarch of Antioch and the Orient, Ignace Jakub III, fiercely condemned 'this Roman heresy, which contradicts the clear truth of the Bible and the teachings of the Christian Church throughout the centuries.'[7]

As the Jews are not deicides, *Nostra Aetate* concludes, they are no exception to the general principle that no human being should be persecuted. The Church 'decries hatred, persecutions, displays of anti-Semitism, directed against Jews at any time and by anyone'.[8] This is, in effect, to deplore much of the Church's own past behaviour – consider, for instance, the Fourth Lateran Council of 1215 which, *inter alia*, required Jews to dress distinctively, barred them from public office and banished them from the streets during Holy Week. What was that if not anti-Semitic?

All this represents a stunning reversal of nineteen hundred years of Christian teaching about Jews and Judaism. At the very least, the tone has changed utterly, and it would take a very determined advocate of what

---

4. Ibid.
5. Ibid.
6. Gavin D'Costa, *Vatican II: Catholic Doctrines on Jews and Muslims* (Oxford: Oxford University Press, 2014), p. 117.
7. Cited in D'Costa, *Vatican II*, p. 138.
8. *Nostra Aetate*, para. 4.

Pope Benedict XVI called 'a hermeneutic of continuity' in interpreting Vatican II to claim that the substance itself remained unaltered.[9] *Nostra Aetate* is highly unusual among the council documents in that it makes no reference to previous councils, or to the Early Church Fathers. The omission is highly symbolic, for *Nostra Aetate* really represents an implicit confession of how terribly wrong the teaching office of the Church had been for centuries. It is as if even the Second Vatican Council teetered on the brink of accepting that, while the Church may not have disproved the Gospel, the fantasy of an immaculate and infallible magisterium had been punctured for ever.

Two Covenants?

Nostra Aetate was short, simple and punchy. However, this left room for debate afterwards about what *exactly* was meant – on some very important questions. Take, for instance, supersessionism: the view which holds Christianity to have replaced Judaism in the purposes of God and sees the old covenant as defunct. Such teaching is now viewed by many as repellent. To be accused of supersessionism is to be tainted with appalling moral error, judged to sympathise with one of the principal intellectual streams that led to the death camps. Yet, *Nostra Aetate* is ambiguous. On the one hand, it echoes Paul in Romans 11:28-29: 'God holds the Jews most dear to God for the sake of their Fathers; He does not repent of the gifts He makes or of the calls He issues'. Yet, the Church is also described in an unqualified way as 'the new people of God', which can be read as succinctly supersessionist.[10] If Christians are now God's people, perhaps Jews no longer are?

The strong trend in Catholic reception of *Nostra Aetate* has, though, been to exclude supersessionism firmly. More and more emphasis has been placed upon the ongoing vitality of Judaism and on what Pope John Paul II (among others) often described as God's unrevoked covenant with the Jews. In 2001, Cardinal William Kasper reflected the growing Catholic consensus when he said that: 'Judaism, i.e. the faithful response of the Jewish people to God's irrevocable covenant, is salvific for them, because God is faithful to his promise.'[11] Indeed, Christians have increasingly been urged not just to respect Judaism, but to delight

---

9. D'Costa's *Vatican II* valiantly makes the attempt.
10. *Nostra Aetate*, para. 4.
11. The developing Catholic trajectory is traced in Philip A. Cunningham, '"God Holds the Jews Most Dear": Learning to Respect Jewish Self-Understanding', in Gilbert S. Rosenthal (ed.), *A Jubilee for All Time:*

in its continued vibrancy and to expect to encounter God in their relationships with Jews. The recent Church of England report, *God's Unfailing Word* (2019), even argues that contemporary Judaism should be approached as a God-given 'sacrament of otherness': 'encounter with the contemporary reality of the faithfulness of Jewish people – in readiness to learn by attentive listening and to be surprised by what is received – can be confidently relied upon to be a means of God's grace to us and an occasion for the renewal of our own faith'.[12]

A possible (though not inevitable) destination for this trajectory of affirmation is what might be called 'two-covenant' theology. Placing great emphasis upon Paul's declaration that 'the gifts and the calling of God are irrevocable', this position maintains that God's faithfulness is called into question, even denied, by any suggestion that His promises to Israel have ceased to hold.[13] If Christianity is indeed a 'new' covenant, this cannot mean that the first one is dead. Instead, the two now exist side by side, not competing with each other but simply *different*. Judaism is how God deals with Jews; Christianity what He provides for Gentiles. This idea has proved very influential among the Churches: surveying the North American scene in 2001, the Archbishop of Canterbury, George Carey, described it as 'the established new orthodoxy'.[14] It has also appealed to some Jews: Rabbi Jacob Emden of Amsterdam suggested something similar as far back as 1757 and, in the new climate produced by Christianity's post-Holocaust renunciation of supersessionism, many more Jewish thinkers, (such as those involved in the influential 2001 statement *Dabru Emet*) have begun to explore further along these lines.[15]

The Copernican Revolution in Jewish-Christian Relations (Cambridge: Lutterworth Press, 2017), pp. 44-58, p. 53.

12. Faith and Order Commission of the Church of England, *God's Unfailing Word*, p. 46.
13. Essays representing this perspective are collected in Mary C. Boys (ed.), *Seeing Judaism Anew: Christianity's Sacred Obligation* (New York: Rowman and Littlefield, 2005).
14. George Carey, 'Jewish-Christian Relations: From Holocaust to Hope', Donald Coggan Memorial Lecture, Washington National Cathedral, 24 April 2001, available at: https://www.anglicannews.org/news/2001/04/inaugural-donald-coggan-lecturejewish-christian-relations-from-holocaust-to-hope.aspx (accessed 31 March 2022).
15. '*Dabru Emet*: A Jewish Statement on Christians and Christianity' is widely available online and reproduced, along with an illuminating set of essays, in T. Frymer-Kensky, D. Novak, P. Ochs, D.F. Sandmel and M.A Signer (eds), *Christianity in Jewish Terms* (Boulder, CO: Westview Press, 2000), pp. xvii-xx.

Under such a view, it is an article of faith that Christians should not try to convert Jews: 'in a post-Shoah world, [this is] simply unconscionable'.[16] Such evangelism is even sometimes regarded as a spiritual cousin to the Holocaust, inviting the charge that, whilst 'the Nazis wanted Jewish bodies; the churches wanted Jewish souls'.[17] The Jewish theologian Abraham Heschel famously told Pope Paul VI that he would rather go to Auschwitz than convert. The occasion was an early draft of *Nostra Aetate*, which explicitly called for the evangelisation of the Jews. Following the encounter with Heschel, a chastened Pope struck the noxious passage.[18] Paul VI also altered the Good Friday liturgy, replacing a prayer for the conversion of the Jews with one that asked simply 'that they might continue to grow ... in faithfulness to God's covenant'.[19] As *God's Unfailing Word* notes, many Christians today are deeply reluctant to evangelise Jews, 'because we find ourselves at a point where such activity is inevitably shadowed by a legacy that is bound to trigger mistrust and estrangement'.[20]

For the fully fledged, two-covenant view, however, evangelising Jews is not only impossibly sensitive, but quite unnecessary: 'Jews do not need Christianity in order to know the one true God. They can know him already through their Judaism.'[21] Jews – at any rate those who adhere to the covenant (there is an interesting and usually unasked question about the many who do not) – are part of God's people already. Their covenant with God may indeed be old, but it is emphatically *not* defunct. David Tracy even suggests that Christians should 'drop talk of a "new" [i.e. traditionally, often a supersessionist] covenant, and hold, with Judaism to YHWH alone'.[22]

16. Elena Procario-Foley, 'Teaching, Learning and Relationships: *Nostra Aetate* and Education', in Rosenthal (ed.), *A Jubilee for All Time*, pp. 189-206, p. 196.
17. Edward Kessler, 'A Jewish Response to Gavin D'Costa', *Journal of Theological Studies* 73, no. 3 (2012), pp. 614-28, p. 616.
18. Gilbert S. Rosenthal, 'Introduction', in Rosenthal (ed.), *A Jubilee for All Time*, p. xvi.
19. Ibid., p. xvii.
20. Faith and Order Commission of the Church of England, *God's Unfailing Word*, p. 58.
21. Richard Harries, *After the Evil: Christianity and Judaism in the Shadow of the Holocaust* (Oxford: Oxford University Press, 2003), p. 126.
22. David Tracy, 'God as Trinitarian: A Christian Response to Peter Ochs', in Frymer-Kensky, Novak, Ochs, Sandmel and Signer (eds), *Christianity in Jewish Terms*, pp. 77-84, p. 77.

Can matters really be so straightforward? Christians, after all, did not invent the phrase 'new covenant', which came from Jesus himself (echoing Jeremiah). Can it be so easily jettisoned? Can its newness reside only in the fact that Gentiles are now brought into covenant relationship with the God of Israel? Is the first covenant left wholly unaffected? We have noted the importance of Romans 11:29 to the two-covenant view, but that verse is part of Paul's larger argument that Jews who refuse to acknowledge Jesus as Messiah have for now been 'broken off' from the one tree which symbolises God's people. Paul hopes they will one day be grafted back in again, 'if they do not persist in unbelief' (Romans 11:23). Meanwhile, however, their refusal severs them from the covenant people. This is why Paul suffers 'great sorrow and unceasing anguish in my heart. ... I could wish that I myself were accursed and cut off from Christ for the sake of my own people, my kindred according to the flesh' (Romans 9:2-3). If the two-covenant theory is correct, Paul should instead have been intensely relaxed about the condition of the Jews, secure in the knowledge that the gifts and calling of God are irrevocable.

Equally, if Paul did believe that the first covenant was still what God wanted for the Jewish people, it is difficult to understand passages like 2 Corinthians 3:10-16:

> what once had glory has lost its glory because of the greater glory. ... [T]o this very day, when they [the Jews] hear the reading of the old covenant, that same veil is still there, because only in Christ is it set aside. Indeed, to this very day, whenever Moses is read, a veil lies over their minds; but when one turns to the Lord, the veil is removed.

Moreover the 'Apostle to the Gentiles' did try to encourage the lifting of that veil by also seeking Jewish converts to Christ (1 Corinthians 9:20; Acts 13:13-43). In short, it is an injustice to Paul to give the impression that Romans 11:29 was the only thing he ever said about the Jews and Judaism.

The more difficult texts in Paul and elsewhere in the New Testament (the letter to the Hebrews is especially fierce) are not though always evaded by supporters of a two-covenant theory. Philip Cunningham's approach is typical:

> [the] writers could not have imagined that people would be reading their words two thousand years later. Nor would they have seen any need to ponder the ongoing role of Judaism

in a human history that they saw as reaching its climax. ...
[T]he shorter-range vision of the New Testament authors
is inadequate as the sole basis of Christian theological
approaches to Judaism.[23]

It is tempting to read this as simply a circuitous way of saying 'the
New Testament is wrong', which would clearly be a difficult (though
not necessarily impossible) position for Christian theology to adopt.
The Church of England statement, *God's Unfailing Word*, offers a more
nuanced approach. *Something* was indeed superseded by Christianity,
but not Judaism *per se*. Rather, the particular form of Second Temple
Judaism (*c*. 515 BCE-70 CE) was indeed replaced – on the one hand, by
Christianity and, on the other, by rabbinic Judaism. The letter to the
Hebrews, for instance, was explicitly aimed at the end of the Temple
cultus. It says nothing about any form of Judaism which then lay in an
unknown future, and Christians are therefore free to respond to such
Judaism free from New Testament negativity.

Whatever is made of such arguments, the key reason for rejecting
two-covenant theology is not that it contradicts some apparently
supersessionist texts in the New Testament. It is, indeed, intriguing
to ask what Paul would have made of rabbinic Judaism if he had the
advantage of peering three, four hundred years into the future and
seeing his 'kindred according to the flesh' still going strong. We simply
cannot know the answer to that question, although those who wish to
answer it in a way utterly affirming of Judaism would have to admit it
would represent a startling twist from the general thrust of the New
Testament witness. The more basic problem for fully developed two-
covenant theology falls rather in the related areas of, first, its inability
to distinguish between fulfilment and betrayal and, second, its weak
Christology.

On fulfilment and betrayal, a standard move in the two-covenant
case is to present a binary choice: *either* God's covenant with Abraham
and Moses remains in full effect (as Paul says in Romans 11:29) *or* God is
unfaithful. Mary Boys is typical: 'to claim that God's covenant with the
Jewish people endures forever is an act of faith in God's fidelity. What
kind of God would betray divine promises?'[24] Is this, though, how Paul
would have understood matters? Given that he wanted Jews to embrace

---

23. Philip A. Cunningham, 'Covenant and Conversion', in Boys (ed.), *Seeing Judaism Anew*, pp. 151-62, p. 157.
24. Mary C. Boys, 'The Enduring Covenant', in ibid., pp. 17-28, p. 24.

Jesus as the Messiah, did he think God had 'betrayed' the original covenants? Unsurprisingly, no: for him, Jesus instead represented the *fulfilment* of all God's promises (2 Corinthians 1:20). As Tom Wright puts it, scathingly:

> it is impossible to imagine [Paul], or any second Temple Jew in a comparable position, supposing that [the] Messiah could have his followers while 'Israel' could carry on as though nothing had happened. That, indeed, would be the route to the true 'supersessionism': the idea that Jesus had started a new movement discontinuous with Israel's history from Abraham to the present. To claim, instead, that this history is affirmed, validated, *and now fulfilled*, however surprisingly, by the arrival of Israel's Messiah – to call this 'supersessionism' is a cynical misuse of words.[25]

The Christological point is closely related. It is difficult to read the whole New Testament – not isolated passages which might be aimed merely at a particular, transitory, historical-cultural form of Judaism, but the *whole* New Testament – and to resist the impression that Jesus is presented as the universal Saviour. The consistent basic claim of the New Testament is that the destiny of the whole world and of every individual in it, without exception, is worked out in relation to Jesus. A position which sees Israel as carrying on 'as though nothing had happened' testifies to a much-diminished Christology. This is why, despite George Carey's 2001 observation that two-covenant theology had become the 'new orthodoxy', *God's Unfailing Word* in 2019 all but ruled it out as an acceptable position for Anglican or Christian theology more broadly.[26]

This critical weakness means two covenant theology is unlikely to be the best lens through which to understand the meaning of *Nostra Aetate*. Even Church Councils are bound by the fundamental trajectories of Scripture! So how then should we understand Vatican II's emphasis on the fact that the gifts and calling of God are irrevocable, and the confidence with which the Church awaits the ultimate salvation of the Jewish people?

---

25. N.T. Wright, *Paul and the Faithfulness of God: Parts III and IV* (London: SPCK, 2013), p. 985. Emphasis in the original.
26. Faith and Order Commission of the Church of England, *God's Unfailing Word*, pp. 34-35.

Nostra Aetate starts from the promises of the old covenant, which because God is faithful will not be annulled even if human beings are faithless. However, the focus then shifts. We are told that the Church 'awaits that day, known to God alone, on which *all peoples* will address the Lord in a single voice and "serve him shoulder to shoulder"'.[27] '*All peoples*' – it is not that Christians are saved through faith in Christ, and Jews by the promises given to Abraham and Moses. Rather, here is a universally available salvation in which all peoples are swept up – and the point which the Council is making, against centuries of popular and magisterial teaching, is that Jews are not by definition excluded from this common destiny of joy. God loves the Jews, God has called the Jews, God will never abandon the Jews – but this does not mean that they are saved by some means other than Christ. If Vatican II said anything else, it would be starkly at variance with the whole Christian tradition, which has emphasised the central role of Jesus in salvation – both in how it was secured and what it means to enjoy it. As Paul puts it, before Him '*every* knee shall bow, every tongue confess, that Jesus Christ is Lord' (Philippians 2:10-11). No exception is made for the Jews – in Scripture or in later church tradition, including *Nostra Aetate.*

This is why Pope Benedict XVI was not being inconsistent with Vatican II when in 2008, in contrast to Paul VI, he authorised a prayer for the Good Friday liturgy which spoke in terms of the conversion of the Jews, 'that they might recognise Jesus Christ as Saviour of all men'. Cardinal Kasper was given the task of explaining why this was not a call for mass evangelistic effort to convert Jews; his answer was that the prayer left matters in God's hands: the Church need not 'orchestrate the realisation of the unfathomable mystery' but simply commends the Jews to God.[28] The Church has no desire to return to days of crusades, pogroms and forced baptisms: there must be nothing violent, intimidatory or manipulative in our approach to the Jews. One might even say the less effort the Church puts into converting Jews the better! Whatever St Paul would make of *that* sentiment, he would share the Pope's basic conviction that, when the mystery of salvation is realised, it will involve salvation through Jesus Christ alone for all people. There is no other name through which we may be saved – and 'we' includes the Jews. There is but *one* covenant of salvation.

How, though, can this teaching that in some sense – even if only beyond this life and, indeed, beyond all of history – Jews 'need' to embrace

27. *Nostra Aetate*, para. 4 – emphasis added.
28. Cunningham, '"God Holds the Jews Most Dear"', p. 55.

Jesus, be reconciled with the insistence that the gifts and calling of God are irrevocable? Why is this not just bad old supersessionism? Once again, fulfilment is not supersessionism – at least if the latter means condemnation, rejection or replacement. The old covenant has no more been superseded than a seed is by its flower. It was always a temporary stage in God's saving purposes. It had always been destined, as occasional glimpses in the Hebrew scriptures themselves suggest (*inter alia*, Genesis 12:3, Isaiah 19:23-25 and 49:5-6, the stories of Ruth and Jonah) to end in the inclusion of the Gentiles – in the glory of God indwelling all peoples and the whole creation. This had always been meant to happen, Paul saw, through the strange events of the death and resurrection of God's Servant Son, Jesus. There is certainly radical newness here, which means that the old forms of covenant and law have fallen away (hence, Paul's passionate rejection of the need for circumcision or strict dietary law), but this newness cannot be construed as a simple *break* with the old – rather, it is its glory.

This way of thinking should not be foreign to Christians. Consider, for instance, the relationship between the resurrected body of Jesus and the body born of the Virgin Mary. In 1 Corinthians 15, Paul spells out the astonishing newness of the resurrection body – and yet, there remains real continuity with what has gone before. The body born of the Virgin is not discarded or left behind but caught up in stupendous transformation and made unimaginably more than itself. Analogously, we might consider that the Church is not a replacement for Israel, but what Israel looks like at this new stage of its unfolding destiny – Paul does, after all, bless the Church as 'the Israel of God' in Galatians 6:16.[29]

A similar line of thought might be suggested by John 12, which records the approach of some Gentiles to Jesus. For John, this moment is critical: Jesus' looming 'hour' has arrived. Jesus immediately relates the arrival of the Gentiles to his death: 'Very truly, I tell you, unless a grain of wheat falls into the earth and dies, it remains just a single grain: but if it dies, it bears much fruit' (12:24). The implication seems to be that Jesus' death will bear fruit in the inclusion of the Gentiles within God's people. We can go further: if Jesus is the true Israelite, who in some sense represents and embodies the whole people (a fairly common idea in the New Testament), can we see his fruit-bearing death as also,

---

29. A phrase which, of course, is open to much interpretation but, as N.T Wright shows convincingly, is used here by Paul to designate the mixed Jewish and Gentile Church. See Wright, *Paul and the Faithfulness of God*, pp. 1142-51.

in some sense, the death of Israel? Or, at least, as the death of what Israel has been to this point: a people who dwell alone, separated from the nations by circumcision, sabbath and food laws? This Israel was not a bad thing, any more than the body born of the Virgin was. Like that body, however, it dies to bear fruit: to become the burning heart of the renewal of all things.

Revelation 7 suggests similar reflections. The visionary sees 144,000 figures robed in white assembled in Heaven to praise God and carefully takes us through how this total represents 12,000 for each of the twelve ancient tribes of Israel. It seems at first sight an odd emphasis – what have the tribes of the beginning got to do with the revelation of the end? However, that vision is swiftly followed by another, of 'a great multitude that none could count, from every tribe, from all nations and peoples and languages, standing before the throne and the Lamb' (7:9). According to many commentators, the second vision is a reiteration of the first: there are not two vast assemblies, but one.[30] In brilliant, pictorial terms John is suggesting that the multi-ethnic, multi-cultural, truly catholic church is what happens when the promise first made to Asher, Dan, Gad and the rest is fulfilled. Look what Israel, through the mystery of Christ crucified and risen, has given birth to! Look at what Israel now is! Israel is no more 'superseded' here – rejected, condemned, replaced – than my own past is by my present and future.

Tom Wright has described Paul's understanding of the Church in terms very similar to those suggested here and summarises it as 'a kind of fulfilled Judaism'.[31] This instantly begs the question: what of those Jews who do not embrace their fulfilment? Paul himself hoped that, when Jews saw the transformation of the Gentiles who came to worship the God of Israel, their hard hearts would melt and they too would come to Jesus: 'And so all Israel will be saved' (Romans 11:26) – but 'all Israel' means what it meant in Galatians 6:16: the new Jewish and Gentile people of God, the Church. Jews will not be saved just because they are Jews, resting on the promises made to Abraham and on the Mosaic Covenant. If that were so, Paul's grief in Romans 9:1-2 would make no sense. Furthermore, God could justly be accused of partiality, of favouring Jews over Gentiles – something which Paul rules out. No, according to Wright, Paul's take on Jews who will not become Christians is bleak: 'There is no hope for those who stay in that condition and do

---

30. Richard Bauckham, *The Theology of the Book of Revelation* (Cambridge: Cambridge University Press, 1993), p. 76.
31. Wright, *Paul and the Faithfulness of God*, p. 1261.

not move forward into the covenant renewal which has now taken place in the Messiah and is being implemented through the Spirit.'[32]

This seems a convincing reading of at least some of Paul's writing but is it a sustainable position for Christian theology? Where would it leave those Jews murdered by Christians and Nazis? If we read Paul with Wright, we cannot be confident of their place in eternal joy: 'There is no hope for those who stay in that condition.' Alarmingly, Wright does not pursue the question either in his magisterial work on Paul or his more popular *Surprised by Hope*.[33] Yet, the difficult must be faced head on: whatever Paul thought, this cannot be the final word on the matter. A God who finishes Hitler's work for him is not a God worth worshipping.

Thankfully, there are plenty of resources in Paul for saying something much more hopeful. Take, for instance, Romans 5:18: 'just as one man's trespass led to condemnation for all, so one man's act of righteousness leads to justification and life for all'. The argument is especially striking because Paul is trying to make the point that what happens in Jesus is far more powerful than what happened in Adam: 'For if the many died through the one man's trespass, much more surely have the grace of God and the free gift in the grace of the one man, Jesus Christ, abounded for the many' (Romans 5:15). '*Much more surely*': through Jesus an all-but-overwhelming power of salvation has been set loose in creation. The 'all-but' here is important, as we shall see in chapter seven when assessing the case for universalism (the confident assertion that all *must* be saved). Paul is not a universalist, at least not consistently: his warnings are too frequent and heartfelt for that. However, he holds that sense of risk within a larger confidence in the grace of God working for the salvation of the world. As I shall argue more fully in the final chapter, it is, indeed, possible not to be saved but it is not the murdered Jews who need to fear that fate. It is, rather, their killers who should tremble.

However, this confident hope for Jewish salvation is not based on their Jewishness, or on the promises to Abraham and Moses. No, true Christian hope for the Jew, and for everyone, is based on Jesus Christ, and his Cross and Resurrection. If anyone at all is saved, it is through His work. Christians can have an astonishingly large and wide hope for salvation, falling just short of dogmatic universalism – but it turns on an equally astonishingly particular point: Christ alone is the Saviour of the world. A theology which abandoned that would abandon its claim to be Christian.

---

32. Ibid., p. 1229.
33. N.T. Wright, *Surprised by Hope* (London: SPCK, 2007).

So, we need have no fear for the eternal destiny of Jewish people. Individual Jews, like anyone else, might indeed steer themselves into eternal misery. It will, however, have nothing to do with their Jewishness, but only with their own hate, greed, fear and violence – all the things that damn anyone if they are not repented of. In terms of eternal salvation, the Jew stands in exactly the same place as every other human person: caught up in the all-but-overwhelming 'Yes' which erupts from Christ's tomb to transfigure the universe in joy, but with the tragic possibility of saying 'No' – and having that 'No' honoured by God. Truly, God shows no partiality (Romans 2:11).

But if a person's Jewishness isn't *bad* news for their eternal destiny – is it in any sense *good* news? Is the Jew's faithful obedience to God as they understand Him simply irrelevant to their eternal destiny? Is being a good Jew in no way *good* for you, spiritually speaking? Moreover, how, if Judaism has failed to see its own fulfilment in Christ, if two thousand years of post-biblical Judaism are just a kind of misguided or blind staggering on, has it not only survived in the most hostile of circumstances but flourished? How has it generated wisdom and goodness and holiness in abundance, if the glory has indeed departed?

Such questions are not hard to answer. Of course, post-biblical Judaism is not bereft of grace. Of course, God's Spirit is at work in the lives of Jews and in the corporate life of Judaism. Of course, wisdom and goodness and sanctity are at least as possible in Judaism as in any other world religion, or in the lives of agnostics and atheists – indeed, possibly more so, since the faithful Jew is formed through God's own self-revelation in the texts of the Hebrew Scriptures, the canon which is also the matrix for all post-biblical Judaism. Being a good Jew is *very* good for you, spiritually speaking. A good Jew might have much to teach a Christian about all manner of things. That Jesus is the Saviour of the world does not exclude God's grace finding a way through many channels. Christ is not magnified by the denigration of non-Christians or their religions.

Our answer to the question of whether Christians should evangelise Jews must therefore be nuanced. We need to start from the frank admission that such evangelism has often been grossly crass, when not actually wicked and violent. Christians have so much to repent of in this respect that one might justly think a period of evangelistic silence is now required. More positively, we can acknowledge that the Christian-Jewish encounter is not one where only Jews have something to receive, and that the spirit of any approach now should be one of friendship, dialogue and collaboration. We can do all this without anxiety, free of the terrible fear that anyone's eternal destiny depends upon them having accepted Christ as their personal Lord and Saviour during this lifetime. As Cardinal Kasper so wisely glossed Pope Benedict XVI's Good Friday prayer for the conversion of the Jews:

> the Church does not take it upon herself to orchestrate the realisation of the unfathomable mystery. She cannot do so. Instead, she lays the *when* and the *how* entirely in God's hands. God alone can bring about the Kingdom of God in which the whole of Israel is saved and eschatological peace is bestowed upon the world.[34]

It is not up to the Church to force the recognition of Jesus and, when the Church behaves as if it is, disaster follows. To that extent, 'No' to the evangelisation of the Jews. Yet that 'No' is held within the bigger conviction that Jesus Christ is the 'Yes' to all of God's promises, for Israel and for the whole world. He was and is the one Jews wait for, and their destiny – no less than that of all other human beings – is wrapped up in and determined by Him. In the end, every knee shall bend and every tongue confess that Jesus Christ is Lord (Philippians 2:10-11). If that is the end, it cannot be wrong to proclaim it now and to invite its anticipation now. It cannot be wrong to – lovingly, sensitively, without anxiety – invite anyone to see who Jesus is and to own his Kingship. So, to that extent, 'Yes' to evangelising the Jews. They are destined to share with every tribe, tongue and nation in the eternal happiness which is God's kingdom, centred on Jesus of Nazareth. Our murderous history makes it hard for Jews to hear that Gospel. However, Gospel it really is and, lovingly, sensitively and without anxiety, we must proclaim it.

Coda: Christians and the State of Israel

Gavin D'Costa describes the question of Christian mission to the Jews as probably the most contentious in Jewish-Christian dialogue today, 'second only to the Land'.[35] The Holy Land and the state of Israel, and its relationship with its Arab neighbours and the Palestinian people, are indeed sharply controversial questions, and not only within Christian-

---

34. Cited in Cunningham, '"God Holds the Jews Most Dear"', p. 55.
35. Gavin D'Costa, 'What Does the Catholic Church Teach about Mission to the Jewish People?', *Journal of Theological Studies* 73, no. 3 (2012), pp. 590-614, p. 590.

Jewish dialogue. Christians themselves are keenly divided over how to respond to this set of issues. For some, staunch support for the state of Israel is central to biblical faith. Others focus more on the Palestinian experience of *nabka* ('catastrophe') in the events of 1948 and beyond. They pose critical questions about how Israel conducts itself and, on grounds of justice, sometimes even call for its disappearance.

All of this is closely related to issues already discussed. The promise of the land was central to the covenant God made with Abraham and Moses: He was summoning a people to live in such a way as to exhibit His glory and manifest His character. Being the people of God was not a matter of what individuals did with their solitude, as Archbishop Temple once defined religion: it was about every aspect of communal life – diet, labour, legislation, defence, agriculture, everything – referred to God and ordered under Him. Of necessity, this involved dwelling together, in a particular territory, joined in one polity. The same insight underpins religious Zionism today. As Jonathan Sacks has put it:

> Judaism is the constitution of a self-governing nation, the architectonics of a society dedicated to the service of God in freedom and dignity. Without a land and a state, Judaism is a shadow of itself. In exile, God might still live in the hearts of Jews, but not in the public square, in the justice of the courts, the morality of the economy, and the humanitarianism of everyday life. … Only in Israel can Jews live Judaism in anything other than an edited edition.[36]

Not all Zionism, of course, is religious: the Zionist movement of the late nineteenth and early twentieth centuries was more inspired by the European nationalisms it sought to emulate than the Bible. Indeed, religious Jews were often rather suspicious of Zionism, suspecting it as a hubristic attempt to pre-empt the proper action of the Messiah in restoring the Jewish state. However, this situation is now decisively changed. Although secular Zionism remains very strong, and some religious Jews still oppose the very existence of Israel, today the vast majority of religious Jews are committed Zionists. After the Nazi horror, most came to see the existence of the state of Israel as a vital bulwark against future genocides – and some also saw in her birth the strange

---

36. Jonathan Sacks, *Future Tense: A Vision for Jews and Judaism in the Global Culture* (London: Hodder & Stoughton, 2009), p. 136.

providence of God, bringing a Jewish national renaissance out of the ruins of European Jewry (more of this in the next chapter).

Religious Zionism is also now a powerful presence in Christianity, especially, but not exclusively, in the United States and circles inspired by the nineteenth-century Pentecostal preacher, J.N. Darby. His influential interpretation of Scripture predicted a mass return of the Jews to the Holy Land and the re-establishment of Israel as a state as a vital prelude to the Second Coming of Jesus.[37] The Old Testament promises of the land to the people of Israel are considered as still fully valid and Christians should use all their energies to see them realised. Alongside this theology came horror at the Holocaust and the conviction that only a strong, well-armed Israel could guarantee it would not be repeated. Add to that the instinctive kinship felt by many Americans for the Israeli foundation myth – bold pioneers making the wilderness bloom – admiration for Israel's economic and political liberalism in a region of autocrats, and fear of Islam – and you have the recipe for strong American Christian support for Israel, often known by friend and foe alike as Christian Zionism.

Such support is not universal, even in the United States, and in Europe the Churches are more likely to be deeply critical of Israel. They are generally much more alert to the questions of justice and peace raised by the creation of Israel – it was often *not* wilderness that was being settled, but Palestinian (and often Christian) towns and villages and farmland being stolen. European Christians tend to view Christian Zionism with angry derision, scorning its uncritically literalist understandings of biblical prophecy and lack of interest in what happens to the dispossessed Palestinians. If it were not so malign, Christian Zionism would be almost funny: easy to lampoon for the way in which it reads Scripture without regard to historical context, making prophecies made long ago the material for speculation about next week's news headlines. Television ministries such as 'The Hal Lindsey Report', from the author of *The Late Great Planet Earth* (1970), are typical of the genre – and provide easy fare for academic knock-about.[38]

---

37. For an overview of the theological assumptions underpinning Christian Zionism, see Gary M. Burge, 'Theological and Biblical Assumptions of Christian Zionism', in Naim Ateek, Cedar Duaybis and Maurine Tobin (eds), *Challenging Christian Zionism: Theology, Politics and the Israel-Palestine Conflict* (London: Melisende, 2005), pp. 45-58.

38. See https://www.hallindsey.com/.

Interestingly, however, more respectable developments in contemporary theology also lead (sometimes unwittingly) to Zionist conclusions.
Advocates of the two-covenant position discussed earlier in this
chapter, for instance, usually do not realise that this at least strongly
suggests the existence of a divinely mandated Jewish claim to the Holy
Land. The first covenant was never just about on what basis individuals
might 'get into Heaven'. That is a typically Christian misunderstanding.
The covenant was about politics and geography, and the creation of a
flourishing society under God's rule. If it is still in force, so is the Jewish
claim to the land – or at any rate, that is how most Jews will understand
matters (even if some would maintain that the claim should only be
realised when the Messiah comes).

Traditionally, Christians did not think this. They took the view that
the promises concerning the land had been radically redefined by the
coming of Jesus. The land had always been envisaged as the place where
God's will was done, as the place of the Kingdom of God. For Christians,
that had only ever come true in the person of Jesus. He was the only one
in whom the Law was lived out, in whom God's glory and character
was revealed, in whom the covenant was fulfilled. The whole promise
of his new covenant was that, now, the Kingdom of God was a reality
dawning within and among those who were 'in Christ' – and that could
be in Corinth or Rome just as well as Jerusalem. As Gary Burge puts it,
from the traditional Christian perspective, 'the land no longer has an
intrinsic part to play in God's program for the world. ... [T]he fusion of
national politics and religious mandate is gone.'[39]

There is the rub: it is precisely that traditional Christian perspective
which is rejected by advocates of two-covenant theology, because for
them 'fulfilment' is indistinguishable from 'supersessionism' with all its
terrors. Without the older Christian tradition, however, they have no
rationale for refusing the logic of the first covenant with its promise of
the land to the Jewish people. Which means that they end up, effectively,
in the same position as the Christian Zionists they would usually deride.

Rowan Williams offers a different rationale for Christian support for
the state of Israel. He is not impressed by Christian Zionist arguments
from biblical prophecy. Nor is he an advocate of two-covenant theology:
he writes that 'only in connection with Jesus can Israel be fully itself,
become a transforming and inviting sign of God's justice.'[40] Like Paul, he

---

39. Burge, 'Theological and Biblical Assumptions', p. 54.
40. Rowan Williams, 'Holy Land and Holy People', in Ateek, Duaybis and
    Tobin (eds), *Challenging Christian Zionism*, pp. 293-303, p. 300.

believes that Israel's destiny is wrapped up with Christ and the Church, and that a two-covenant approach does not do justice to the 'single divine purpose for covenant that has a universal horizon'.[41] In the end, there is one common destiny of joy, centred on Jesus Christ. So far, so traditional.

In the meantime, however, Judaism continues to exist, and Christians must be able to see some positive meaning in this: 'The Christian, instead of being resentful or puzzled at this persistence, needs to understand that the testimony offered in the face of Christianity's own claim can become the most significant and necessary definition of the meaning of the whole idea of covenant.'[42] That is, Christians should understand the Jewish 'No' to Jesus as embodying something of the utmost positive importance: the insistence that God is faithful to His promises, which once made are never cast aside – any more than the people to whom they were made.

Moreover, because the ongoing existence of Jews and Judaism is theologically important for Williams, so, too, 'the existence of a homeland for the Jewish people remains a theologically positive matter'.[43] His support for Israel is not just as a bulwark against genocide; it is a matter of theology. Even in the Christian era, the *point* of Israel is to exist as a corporate, political entity – to show that humans can live the totality of their lives ordered under God: 'Israel is called to be the *paradigm nation*: the example held up to all nations of how a people live in obedience to God and justice with one another.'[44]

Of course, contemporary Israel may betray that vision. It is marred by social and economic injustice, it has been *nabka* for the Palestinians, and its relationships with its Arab neighbours are morally complex. For all this, it should be held to account by the biblical vision. Its Christian friends, whilst acutely conscious of their own failure to live under God's law, must offer that accountability. However, the critic 'has to earn the right to be heard; a criticism that does not recognise the full and complex reality of the other and is not prepared to stand in solidarity with the

---

41. Rowan Williams, 'The Place of Covenant in Judaism, Christianity and Jewish-Christian relations', Centre for the Study of Jewish Christian Relations, Cambridge, 6 December 2004, available online at: https://www.anglicannews.org/news/2004/12/lecture-at-jewish-christian-relations-centre.aspx (accessed 20 May 2022).
42. Ibid.
43. Williams, 'Holy Land and Holy People', p. 298.
44. Ibid., p. 294. Emphasis in original.

other will never earn that right'.[45] In other words, do not criticise Israel until you have demonstrated that you are unreservedly committed to her survival and flourishing, and realistic about the threats that she faces.

Robert Tobin offers a sharp critique of all this. He argues that at the heart of all religious Zionism, however nuanced, the idea remains of a chosen people dwelling in a land where others are in some sense alien and subordinate. Yet, such 'tribal exclusiveness' has been replaced in the new covenant by a theology of radical inclusiveness.[46] God's dealings with the world have a history and, even if a Jewish state was once intrinsic to His purposes, it is so no more. Tobin suspects what is really driving Williams to find a theological justification for Jewish statehood is Western Christian guilt over the Holocaust. However, 'this cataclysm cannot be used indefinitely to rationalise the political and military hegemony of a Jewish State in the Middle East in the 21st century'.[47]

Holocaust guilt also leads Williams, Tobin suspects, to fail to take the sufferings of the Palestinians seriously. They appear, he suggests, in Williams' argument primarily as those who inflict violence upon Jews, drawing Israel into the morass of defensive anxiety and retaliation which Williams laments – but there is no real attention paid to the violence first visited upon them by the very creation of Israel:

> if one is willing to entertain, even for a moment, the Pal-
> estinians' view of themselves as a people who have been
> systematically deprived of their land and liberty over the past
> five and a half decades by an aggressive military state, there is
> something perverse in the Archbishop's conclusion that 'the
> question for both Israeli and Palestinian must be how each
> encourages lawfulness and stability in the other'.[48]

This is like requiring the victim of a beating to think first of securing the welfare of his assailant, before actually getting the beating stopped. It is the existence of the state of Israel, Tobin argues, which created the

---

45. Ibid., p. 301.
46. Robert B. Tobin, 'On Knowing One's Place: A Liberationist Critique of Rowan Williams' "Holy Land and Holy People"', in Ateek, Duaybis and Tobin (eds), Challenging Christian Zionism, pp. 308-18, p. 317.
47. Ibid., p. 314.
48. Ibid., p. 313.

fundamental problem. To be unreservedly committed to it is to block the only possibility of true peace and justice for both Jews and Arabs.

Furthermore, adds another critic, the state of Israel was never even intended to be the paradigm nation envisioned by Williams. Helen Lewis argues that, for Herzl, Ben-Gurion and the majority of Israel's founding fathers, 'Israel was explicitly intended as a Western nation state like Britain or France, and its identity was to be ethnic, not religious or ethical.'[49] Rosemary and Herman Ruether go further, suggesting that in this respect Zionism even bears some resemblance to the dark energies which fuelled Nazism: 'Jewish nationalism ... was shaped in response to an ethnically or racially exclusivist European nationalism, and reproduced a similar racial-ethnic exclusivism of its own. Its plan for a Jewish state was for Jews only.'[50] If the state of Israel were really to operate as a paradigm of peace and justice, it would soon vanish. For this would entail, *inter alia*: the right of return for Palestinians or their full compensation; withdrawal from all occupied territory and an end to settlements; the return of all confiscated land; the equitable distribution of all natural resources; and the abolition of all discriminatory practices. The result, Lewis suggests, 'would almost certainly be the loss of a specifically Jewish state. The biblical ideals of which [Rowan Williams] writes cannot be fulfilled without the loss of what he sees as the very condition needed to sustain it.'[51]

Small wonder then that many Jews had deep misgivings about the Zionist project from the beginning. Albert Einstein put the point eloquently:

> The very nature of Judaism resists the idea of a Jewish State. I am afraid of the inner damage Judaism will sustain. ... [W]e are no longer the Jews of the Maccabean period. A return to a nation in the political sense of the word would be equivalent

49. Helen Lewis, 'A Response to Rowan Williams' Message to the Sabeel Conference', in Ateek, Duaybis and Tobin (eds), *Challenging Christian Zionism*, pp. 319-38, p. 322.

50. Rosemary and Herman Ruether, 'The Vatican, Zionism and the Israeli-Palestinian Conflict', in Donald E. Wagner and Walter T. Davis (eds), *Zionism and the Quest for Justice in the Holy Land* (Cambridge: Lutterworth Press, 2014), pp. 118-38, p. 121.

51. Lewis, 'A Response to Rowan Williams', p. 324.

> to turning away from the spiritualisation of our community, which we owe to the genius of our prophets.[52]

Such perspectives suggest another problem with Williams' position. Like Sacks, he believes that the existence of Israel is essential to the full flourishing of Judaism, because Judaism is essentially political. Statehood 'is the condition for Jewish people of faith and conscience to be able to exercise their historic calling'.[53] As Lewis points out, however, this is 'a hugely contentious statement, not least because it appears so dismissive of the contribution made to human civilisation by Jewish communities in the diaspora'.[54] *Does* Judaism really need a state? Many devout Jews have greatly doubted it.

The difficulties in sustaining a Christian theological case for supporting the state of Israel are, it seems, cumulatively overwhelming. Christian Zionism in its Hal Lindsey form is easy to lampoon, but Williams' more nuanced version is also flawed. Those who favour a two-covenant model of Christian-Jewish relations often fail to realise its Zionist implications, but, as we have argued throughout this chapter, their basic assumption is mistaken. Altogether, there is simply no compelling *theological* reason why Christians should support Israel – and all sorts of reasons why we should press on her the urgent questions of peace and justice posed by the occupation and the treatment of the Palestinian people.

However, there remain very important non-theological factors to consider. Christians – and women, gays, atheists and agnostics, be they Jewish or Arab – enjoy much more freedom in Israel than in almost any other Middle Eastern state. It is, by some distance, the most democratic state in the region. Against those who equate it with apartheid South Africa (or even more outrageously, Nazi Germany), we might remember that it was *Arab* judges sitting in Israel's Supreme Court who sent first a former President (Katsav, in 2011 for rape) and then a former Prime Minister (Olmert, in 2015 for fraud) to prison. We might also note that those who are critical of the very idea of a Jewish state seem to have little trouble with the notion of Islamic Republics or, indeed, of countries with established churches in Europe.

Finally, it is unsurprising that a people who within living memory have barely survived genocide, who were abandoned by their neighbours and

---

52. Ibid., p. 322.
53. Williams, 'Holy Land and Holy People', p. 299.
54. Lewis, 'A Response to Rowan Williams', p. 320.

refused refuge when they fled from their killers, should feel the need for a well-armed state of their own. It is, of course, unjust that Palestinians should pay the price for European crimes. However, it is not at all obvious that addressing that injustice should mean the dismantling of Israel. For most Jews today, the state of Israel represents a place to flee to and resist from. It is their guard against a second Holocaust. Christians, who bear so much responsibility for the first, should be the last people to suggest it is unnecessary.

Chapter 6

Where Was God?

I have more faith in Hitler than in anyone else. He alone has kept his promises, all his promises, to the Jewish people.

An Auschwitz inmate[1]

Why didn't God stop the Holocaust? Christians and Jews traditionally believe in a God who is Lord of history, working to bring about His purposes in the world. He is the Almighty. Most ordinary believers pray to Him for all sorts of things: cures from illness, new jobs, even – though at some point the sense of incredulity needs to kick in – parking spaces on busy city streets. How can such faith endure the reality of the Holocaust – and God's apparent absence? Why did He not tear the heavens and come down, and stop the wicked in their tracks? Since He did not, what sense can we now make of describing Him as the Lord of history, and of praying to Him for aid?

Such questions are not, of course, raised only by the Holocaust. There have been other genocides. If the Holocaust is unique, its distinction is to be found more in the degree of scale, and the mass organisation and technological sophistication required for its execution, than in the simple fact of mass innocent suffering. Equally, the fact that both Christianity and enlightened modernity are deeply implicated in the evil is startling. However, the problem of innocent suffering, radical wickedness and the absence of God is not in itself, as the Jewish scholar Eliezer Berkovits

---

1. Elie Wiesel, *Night* (London: Penguin, 1972), p. 81.

noted, a new one: 'as far as our faith in an absolutely just and merciful God is concerned, the suffering of a single innocent child poses no less a problem to faith than the undeserved sufferings of millions'.[2]

One possible approach to the question is suggested by that qualification: 'undeserved' sufferings. A long-standing traditional answer to the question of suffering is that in fact it must be in some sense *deserved*. In the case of Jewish suffering up to and including the Holocaust, we have seen this suggested by many Christian and anti-Semitic thinkers, beginning from Matthew's curse: 'His blood be upon us, and upon our children.' According to this school of thought, Jews were simply getting what they deserved for killing Jesus. Even if the actual Jews suffering at any one time were not directly involved in that killing, by the mere fact of their Jewishness they shared a collective guilt and punishment.

The Christian world has been largely shamed out of that way of thinking by the Holocaust and any attempt to vindicate God like this would now be met with anger and derision. It is worth noting, however, that a deeply traditional *Jewish* approach to the question of unjust suffering is also to explain it as deserved punishment. Rabbi Elchonon Wasserman of Baranovitch (1875-1941) can be taken as representative of much Orthodox Jewish thought on this point. The Nazi onslaught against the Jews, Wasserman taught, was due to three Jewish evils: secular nationalism in the form of Zionism; Reform Judaism's assimilationist tendencies; and contempt for the Torah in modern scientific study of Judaism: 'For Wasserman, the Nazi assault was ultimately God's appropriate response against those who had proved unfaithful to his Torah.'[3] Just as in ancient days, God chastised his people with the rod of the Assyrian king, so Hitler became the unwitting instrument of divine judgement. God did not intervene, because – despite himself – Hitler did His will.

Such interpretations find few advocates today. Wasserman taught before the full scale of the Nazi annihilation of the Jews was realised. Before very long, the sheer numbers of dead made his teaching seem, to most, incredible: what sin could possibly merit such disproportionate divine discipline? However, a significant variation on the same idea suggests that Jewish suffering in the Holocaust was not on account of

---

2. Berkovits, *Faith after the Holocaust*, p. 132.
3. Richard L. Rubenstein, *After Auschwitz: History, Theology, and Contemporary Judaism*, 2nd edn (Baltimore and London: Johns Hopkins University Press, 1992), p. 159.

Jewish sins, but was rather intended – or at least, *used* – by God as a way of freeing the world from evil: in other words, the Holocaust is a seen as a redemptive sacrifice for sin. Ignaz Maybaum writes that the victims are 'holy martyrs: they died as sacrificial lambs because of the sins inherent in Western civilisation. Their deaths purified Western civilisation so that it can again become a place where man can live, do justly, love mercy, and walk humbly with God.'[4] Indeed, to a certain extent the genocide did have just such a purifying effect: Western civilisation recoiled in horror from what it had done, and set in place all sorts of cultural and legal prohibitions against its recurrence. Nevertheless, even if this moral transformation had been complete, there would still be a question mark over the justice of God: why did this gain require the slaughter of so many? Was God right to barter their lives in such a way? Moreover, the most cursory glance at contemporary Western civilisation begs the question of whether the sacrifice was at all as efficacious as Maybaum suggests.

Less ambivalent perhaps, from a Jewish perspective at any rate, is perhaps the most obvious historical fruit of the Holocaust: the creation of the state of Israel. Why did God not intervene in the Holocaust? Because, some would say, through it He was bringing about the most glorious of all His works – the restoration of the Jews to sovereignty in their homeland, the messianic dream of generations. Hayyim Kanfo writes:

> the Holocaust constitutes the darkness and terrible absence that will cause the events of salvation to spring forth. The previous condition of the Jewish people – the debasement of the Diaspora and the severance from *Eretz Israel* – was excised, so that a new, fresh shoot for which we hope may come forth: the shoot that will constitute the foundation for the restoration of the Davidic line and the return of the Divine Presence to Zion.[5]

The great difficulty with all such arguments (quite apart from the rights and wrongs of Zionism) is the question of the justice of God. It is one thing to acknowledge that certain good things may have come

---

4. Ignaz Maybaum, *The Face of God after Auschwitz* (Amsterdam: Polak & Van Gennep, 1965), p. 83.
5. Hayyim Kanfo, 'Manifestation of Divine Providence in the Gloom of the Holocaust', in Rabbi Yehezkel Fogel (ed.), *I Will Be Sanctified: Religious Responses to the Holocaust* (Northvale, NJ: Jason Aronson, 1998), p. 22.

about as a result of the Holocaust, or even to say that God may have been at work to draw these good things out of the evil. To claim, however, that God *willed* the Holocaust so that the good might come is to make Him the worst kind of utilitarian ethicist – treating the six million as pawns to be sacrificed for the greater good. It shares with Nazi thinking a refusal to respect the dignity of each human person as created in the *imago dei* and therefore of inestimable value. The point is still sharper when it is recalled that the vast majority of Maybaum's 'holy martyrs' had no comprehension at all that they were dying for God's purposes: they were indeed, like sacrificial sheep, dumb animals. The martyr gives her life consciously and willingly as a testimony to God: the lives of the six million were *taken* – and on these kinds of account, if pressed, taken only secondarily by the Nazis. God, whatever His good intentions, was the real killer.

This is why Richard Rubenstein holds that the Holocaust calls for a radical revision of traditional Jewish (and Christian) belief about God. On their traditional assumptions, he argues, neither Jews nor Christians can 'avoid the conclusion that the National Socialist extermination of the Jews during World War II was a fulfilment of God's purposes. ... Given the Judeo-Christian conception that God is the ultimate actor in the historical drama, no other theological interpretation of the death of six million Jews is tenable.'[6] On all traditional accounts, Rubenstein thinks, there is some kind of divine plan: something into which the Holocaust fits and which justifies it (even if, for now, the plan remains veiled to us). Rubenstein finds this morally appalling and so offers a wholly new account: there is no Lord of history and no divine purpose. There is simply 'an absurd and ultimately tragic cosmos'.[7] Israel is not the Chosen People, as there is no divine actor to do the choosing: there is simply wild chaotic nature throwing up lives as the ocean throws up waves, lives which like waves come and go, merging into the ocean.[8] God did not intervene in the Holocaust because God (in anything like the sense implied in the protest against His passivity) does not exist. Instead, there is simply reality: filled not with loving purpose but mere 'sound and fury, signifying nothing'.

In responding to Rubenstein, we do well to remember two very basic points. Firstly, his atheism – for it is avowedly atheism, even whilst

---

6. Rubenstein, *After Auschwitz*, p. 17.

7. Ibid., p. 19.

8. Rubenstein explores the analogy of waves and the ocean in *After Auschwitz*, pp. 298-303.

claiming to offer a viable future for Jewish religious practice – actually vitiates the very root of his moral protest against Nazism. If, in fact, human beings are *not* made in the image and likeness of God, if they are not beloved creatures with a purpose but simply remarkable collections of atoms, thrown up by a purposeless, valueless, bleakly indifferent process of evolution – why should it matter if they die, torture or kill? They are just flotsam, of no more significance than the wave that dissolves back into the ocean. There is no particular reason to rage against the Nazis: what they do is no more or no less in tune with the purpose of things than the greatest of the saints, for there *is* no purpose of things. Why, anyway, should we be so attached to living or to the value of others living? Rubenstein offers the spirituality of Ecclesiastes unrelieved by the rest of the biblical canon: truly, all is vanity.

Secondly, although he pronounces with confidence that, if one believes in the traditional biblical conception of God, one must believe that in some sense God planned and used the death of the six million, this is quite wrong. We encounter here a crucial and ancient distinction: whilst on the traditional understanding God is indeed in some sense responsible for the Holocaust, in that He created a world where it is permitted to happen, He does not directly plan and bring it about. He *allows* the Holocaust, a claim which indeed itself raises profound moral questions, but which still remains a very different one from saying that He commands the killing.

Why, then, might God allow extreme evil, if He does not desire it? Berkovits offers a classic Jewish answer, which has much in common with traditional Christian approaches: God has created human beings with the dignity of freedom. The whole point of creation is that human beings should freely, responsibly be what God wants them to be, and through collaboration with Him bring the world to its divine intended destiny. It follows that God must respect His creatures' freedom, which of necessity will often seem like divine absence or indifference: 'Since history is man's responsibility, one would, in fact, expect [God] to hide, to be silent, while man is about his God-given task. Responsibility requires freedom, but God's convincing presence would undermine the freedom of human decision.'[9] If God were to intervene to stop the wicked in their tracks, and to end all innocent suffering, He would in fact abandon the whole rationale of creation. It is not any particular historical outcome (the purification of the West, the creation of the state of Israel) which justifies the divine restraint. It is rather the whole

9. Berkovits, *Faith after the Holocaust*, p. 63.

meaning of creation itself: 'The question therefore is not: why is there undeserved suffering? But, why is there man? He who asks the question about injustice in history really asks: why a world? Why creation?'[10]

To reiterate: God is indeed, in a sense, ultimately accountable for the Holocaust as for all innocent suffering. The free world He chose to create involves the possibility of terrible wickedness and pain. God does not engineer or plan this, but its possibility is implicit in the very nature of creation. God could indeed, theoretically, sweep in and end the horror – but, in doing so, He would end the project of creation itself. The act of creation therefore involves a certain renunciation of power on the part of God. As Berkovits writes:

> God is mighty for He shackles His omnipotence and becomes 'powerless' so that history may be possible. In spite of His infinite power, He does not frighten man but lets him find his own way, extending to him His long-suffering. God is mighty in the renunciation of His might in order to bear with man.[11]

The almightiness and goodness of God are not disproved by Auschwitz: rather we come to see these attributes as primarily describing God's faithfulness to His creation. Not even the worst of human wickedness will persuade God to give up on His original intention in creation and to return all things to nothingness. Were it so, Nazism would truly have been triumphant.

It is in the very nature of creation, then, that the sovereign power of God is largely hidden. However, divine self-restraint does not mean total absence. Berkovits' central point is that God remains faithful to His intent in creation: it therefore follows that He will not allow the creation to wholly destroy itself. There comes a point beyond which evil must be checked, lest the divine purpose be irrevocably defeated:

> that man may be, God must absent Himself; that man may not perish in the tragic absurdity of his own making, God must remain present. The God of history must be present and absent concurrently. ... Because of the necessity of His absence, there is the 'hiding of the face' and the suffering of

---

10. Ibid., p. 108.
11. Ibid., p. 112.

the innocent; because of the necessity of His presence, evil will not ultimately triumph; because of it there is hope for man.[12]

The creation project will never be allowed to fail completely, so evil can never be allowed to gain final triumph.

For Berkovits, the most tangible sign of the divine presence, even in the face of Auschwitz, is the survival of Israel and its renewed flourishing as a state exercising sovereignty over Jerusalem: 'no matter how empty of God vast tracts of the wastelands of history may appear to be, we know of His presence as we stand astounded, contemplating our own existence'.[13] The existence of Israel is not only a near miracle – Berkovits might omit the 'near' – but also represents God's offer of new life to the world. Just when, with the development of nuclear weaponry, the nations arrived at the point where the continued pursuit of the politics of domination would lead inevitably to global destruction, the state of Israel emerged to embody a different kind of politics – one infused by the spirit of the God who is long suffering and refuses to dominate. This nation, Berkovits contends, represents 'the renunciation of force as the arbiter of human destiny'.[14] Truly, Israel is become the light to the nations: 'mankind is entering upon its "Jewish era" or else upon an era of self-immolation'.[15]

Berkovits was writing long before Israel obtained nuclear weaponry, and just before the long occupation of territory seized during the 1967 Arab-Israeli war. It would take determined eyes of faith to see in the state's course since then a consistent embodying of the politics of the spirit, as opposed to those of force. In many ways Israel seems to have become as one of the nations. Zionism remains in large measure the secular nationalism it always was. To point out that Berkovits is starry-eyed here ('there has never been a less militaristic army than that of Israel. There has never been a victorious army as desirous of peace as that of Israel')[16] does not, however, invalidate his central point: that, though God is long suffering and though His hiddenness within history means that the innocent will suffer, nevertheless a limit is put to evil. Even within history – postponing for a moment the vital question of what might happen beyond history – Hitler's project fails. God's people flourish again and God's project continues.

12. Ibid., p. 110.
13. Ibid., p. 115.
14. Ibid., p. 144.
15. Ibid.
16. Ibid., p. 169.

From his Christian perspective Tom Wright thinks in a very similar way, observing in the Bible:

> a pattern of divine action, to judge and punish evil and set bounds to it, without destroying the agency of human beings themselves; and also, both to promise and bring about new moments of grace, events which constitute new creation, however much they are themselves necessarily shot through with ambiguity.[17]

One can, that is, with reverent caution trace the hand of God in history – see, for instance (though Wright never uses this example), the creation of the state of Israel as one of those moments which, while indeed shot through with ambiguity, are at least from one perspective a sign of the triumph of life over Nazism. Such moments of grace are not indisputably or even obviously divine events, they are brought about through human agency: the long-suffering God works with human freedom even as He seeks to contain and heal the evil human freedom does: '[God acts] from *within* the world he has created, affirming that world in its created otherness even as he is putting it to rights.'[18]

Part, then, of the Jewish and Christian answer to the question, 'Why did God not stop the Holocaust?', is to say that, ultimately, He did. The heavens were not torn open, and He did not swoop down, but in and through human agency – the Allied armies, in all their terrible ambiguity – divine judgement fell with shattering force upon Nazi Germany. It proclaimed itself a thousand-year Reich; within twelve it was in smoking ruins. It aimed for the destruction of the Jewish people; its actions led to the new Jewish state. It presented itself as the great bulwark against Soviet communism; it delivered all of Eastern Europe and half of Germany into Soviet hands. It stood for the restoration of German pride and military power; it discredited both for generations. Nor did judgement fall on Germany alone. The West was only too willing to tolerate Nazism as a counter to communism and – until the end – did almost nothing to rescue the Jews. Now it bears its judgement: the war ended the great power status of both Britain and France, and our whole culture is crippled by knowing that it both gave birth to the Holocaust and, when confronted, failed in the starkest and simplest of moral tests:

---

17. N.T. Wright, *Evil and the Justice of God* (London: SPCK, 2006), p. 43.
18. Ibid.

'this post-Holocaust era is charged with the nemesis of history. This is the ignoble twilight hour of a disintegrating civilisation.'[19]

God then is not absent in history. He is present, doing new deeds of salvation (albeit shot through with ambiguity) and in terrifying judgement. In it all, He works with the grain of human freedom. His action never involves the abrogation of the world's otherness from Him. Points on a railway line are not miraculously switched, guards are not overpowered by angels, the chemicals in the poison cylinders work as they always do. God does not 'interfere'. He is no *deus ex machina*, who swoops in from beyond the world to set things suddenly right. No, God is hidden within history, waiting for human beings to collaborate – consciously or not – with His purposes. He is always at work, but His work is not the magical solution we hoped and prayed for. It comes in strange and hidden guises and waits on human freedom for its effect.

It was thoughts like these that Dietrich Bonhoeffer was groping towards in the last months of his life. On 16 July 1944, he wrote to his friend Eberhard Bethge:

> we have to live in the world – *etsi Deus non daretur* ['as if God does not exist']. And this is precisely what we do recognise – before God! God Himself compels us to recognise it. ... Before God and with God we live without God. God consents to be pushed out of the world and onto the cross: God is weak and powerless in the world and in precisely this way, and only so, is at our side and helps us. Matt. 8:17 makes it quite clear that Christ helps us not by virtue of his omnipotence, but rather by virtue of his weakness and suffering. Here is the decisive difference between Christianity and all religions. Human religiosity directs people in need to the power of God in the world, God as *deus ex machina*. The Bible directs people to the powerlessness and the suffering of God: only the suffering God can help.[20]

Bonhoeffer was writing a letter to his best friend, not a carefully worked out theological treatise. To some extent, what he meant is not entirely clear, and the theme of 'the suffering God' has been sharply contested

---

19. Berkovits, *Faith after the Holocaust*, p. 137.
20. Bonhoeffer to Eberhard Bethge, 16 July 1944, in Bonhoeffer, *Letters and Papers from Prison*, pp. 473-80, pp. 478-79. Matthew 8:17 cites Isaiah 53:4: 'He took our infirmities and bore our diseases.'

in contemporary theology. Jürgen Moltmann famously developed it in his seminal *The Crucified God*, which proposed a rejection of classical theology's insistence on the divine impassibility.[21] God, thought Moltmann, could be changed by the world. That does not appear to be what Bonhoeffer intended. His vision is much closer to that of much Jewish thought – not least that of Berkovits, who also spoke of the suffering of God thus: 'God suffers not on account of what man does to Him. What could man do to God? He suffers because of what man does to himself and to his brother. He suffers the suffering of His servant, the agony of the guiltless. In all their affliction, He is afflicted.'[22] For the sake of the world He wants, the world which must be made through human freedom, God suffers what that freedom throws up: the destruction of His beloved children.

Indeed, Berkovits – who for understandable reasons was no great admirer of Christian theology – goes out of his way to praise Bonhoeffer and in that praise there is a clue to what Bonhoeffer's understanding of 'the suffering God' involves. Bonhoeffer, says Berkovits, understands more fully than other Christian theologians the authentic this-worldly emphasis of the Hebrew Scriptures.[23] He understands that the prophets' passion was for the real stuff of history: law, politics, justice, statehood. Most Christians have instead mistakenly focussed on an abstract salvation, an escape from the earth into a post-mortem heaven. 'God' has been made a special being found apart from the struggles of public, worldly existence: a matter for the private recesses of our hearts. Hitler can run the country, if he leaves the Church to save souls – we can see here themes already touched on in chapter two, when we dealt with Bonhoeffer's critique of the German Protestant response to Nazism.

'The suffering God' saves us from this religious abstraction. However, at this point, for all their kinship, Bonhoeffer and Berkovits part company. When Berkovits speaks of the suffering or hidden God, he means the self-restraint which God commits to in the act of creation. God cannot overpower His creation if His creation is truly to be. Bonhoeffer would not dispute this but, as a Christian thinker, his understanding of 'the suffering God' is inevitably focussed rather upon Jesus Christ on the Cross. The 'help' that Bonhoeffer sees the suffering Jesus as bringing rests on the fact that he was not primarily interested

21. Jürgen Moltmann, *The Crucified God: The Cross as the Foundation and Criticism of Christian Theology* (London: SCM, 1974).
22. Berkovits, *Faith after the Holocaust*, p. 130.
23. Ibid., p. 63.

in human beings' interiority or their souls. Jesus' overriding mission, according to Bonhoeffer, was to live in such a way that his neighbour could have life in all its fullness. He was utterly poured out for others, abandoning all status, all claim to righteousness (dying condemned by state and religion) and ultimately life itself. It is this 'for otherness' – concrete, costly self-offering for the neighbour – that his disciples are called to. This is true relationship to the true God, but it looks and is very different to received understandings of piety: 'our relationship to God is no "religious" relationship to some highest, most powerful and best being imaginable – that is no genuine transcendence. Instead, our relationship to God is a new life in "being there for others," through participation in the being of Jesus.'[24] That is: the real relationship to God is the one that lives like Jesus did – pouring oneself out sacrificially so that others might live. In Hitler's Germany that might look – must look, Bonhoeffer might urge – like costly resistance to the regime, binding up its victims and daring to 'put a spoke in the wheel', even to the extent of surrendering one's claim to moral righteousness (the good Lutheran conspiring to murder the head of state) and to life itself.

'Only the suffering God can help' because only Christ on the Cross, thinks Bonhoeffer, can deliver us, on the one hand, from looking for supernatural interventions which relieve us of *our* responsibility and, on the other, from all the constraints that prevent us from acting: from fear, from the urge for self-preservation, from false notions of respectability. He frees us, by His example and His Spirit breathed into us, to be fully human – human as God intended humans to be: self-offerings of love. It is through discipleship, through the actions of those made fully human, that the world will be saved – not through waiting for thunderbolts from heaven. Paul van Buren, much influenced by Bonhoeffer, notes that, 'had more Christians come to this realisation earlier, perhaps millions murdered by Hitler might have been saved'.[25] The founding of Israel teaches the same lesson:

> Israel was founded not by divine intervention from heaven
> or the sending of the Messiah, but by Jewish guns and Jewish
> effort against seemingly insuperable numerical and material
> odds. Had the early pioneers, the fugitives from the Holocaust
> or the supporters of the project from the Diaspora waited

---

24. Bonhoeffer to Bethge, 3 August 1944, in Bonhoeffer, *Letters and Papers from Prison*, pp. 498-504, p. 501.
25. Paul van Buren, *Discerning the Way: A Theology of the Jewish-Christian Reality* (New York: Seabury Press, 1980), p. 196.

upon a so-called act of God instead of daring to be the act of God, they would in all likelihood be waiting still, those who were still alive.[26]

Van Buren spoke of Jewish Zionists, but the point holds good: salvation happens when people are liberated from their smallness and fears so that they can dare to be the act of God. That liberation is how the suffering God on the Cross helps.

* * *

If all this is true, it comes with serious consequences for much traditional piety. Often, when the question as to why God did not intervene in the Holocaust is posed (or why any of the million other things we might plead with God for do not come to pass), we are told that, whilst God *could* have intervened, for one reason or another He chose not to do so. Those reasons may be forever beyond our ken: who are we to supervise the Almighty's running of the universe? Nevertheless, He *could* have done so and indeed – according to most popular and even many 'sophisticated' understandings of prayer and providence – regularly does. Stories of healings and other positive happenings are often claimed as answers to prayer, and not solely in the sense that human beings dared to be the act of God but as if there is indeed a *deus ex machina*, who from time to time intervenes from beyond history to set it on a new course. This God rains down fire to expose the prophets of Baal. He sends His angel to lead Peter from his death-cell, making the locked doors swing open before him. He alters the flight of a bullet so that it will not slay a Pope. He makes the weather suddenly brighten on the wedding morning. There is currently in Britain a plan to erect a 'Wall of Answered Prayer', where each of the million bricks 'will recount a personal, specific way in which God has answered a prayer for people both now and in the past, offering a vast amount of experiences all explaining how God has come through for individuals in the midst of life's storms'.[27] After all, Jesus himself taught that 'if two of you agree on earth about anything you ask, it will be done for you by my Father in Heaven' (Matthew 18:19).

Whatever that saying means, it quite obviously cannot be true in anything like its obvious sense. Perhaps there is a sophisticated and strange reading which can break truth out of it, or perhaps fantasy and

---

26. Ibid.

27. For more information about the 'Wall of Answered Prayer', see https://www.eternalwall.org.uk/about-us (accessed 31 March 2022).

wish fulfilment have found their way even into Scripture. However we approach the text, even the most ardent enthusiasts for the interventionist God must admit that very often, God does *not* give people what they ask for in prayer – no matter how united those doing the praying are, however sincere their intent and worthy their request. If Christians proclaim a God who intervenes to cure a cancer here, or provide a parking space there, they must explain why God did not similarly intervene to end the Holocaust. The standard apologetic answer tends to be that He could, but chose not to do so for reasons yet unfathomable, and that we must simply trust Him. In the end it will all be seen to be part of His great plan. God is in control and at work in everything. Rubenstein would recognise this model: by seeing God as the ultimate actor and planner in history, it makes Him directly responsible for the slaughter of the innocent.

There is an alternative way of approaching matters, shaped by the thought of Berkovits and Bonhoeffer. The creation of the world has involved God in a great loss of control. Yes, His purpose is constant – to bring the world to the glory He made it for, to see it filled with goodness and beauty and joy, to see created freedom exult in these things. However, there is no plan: no step-by-step design to reach that goal, as if God were a master chess strategist. The divine purpose is constant, but history is truly free – often wildly, chaotically free. Instead of directly supervising all events, God must work through the chaos, never overruling it, never depriving the world of its created freedom. He works largely – and perhaps exclusively, though here we reach the limit of what we could possibly know – through calling and inspiring human freedom to 'be His act', to subvert and counteract the gone-wrongness of the world, to return it to its proper course and destiny. The Christian and the Jew both say with confidence that, in the end, God's faithfulness will be vindicated and His decision to create will be proved good. In that careful sense, He is indeed Lord of history. But this is a far different thing from saying that each event within history is directly under His control, that He inspects every possible act and decides whether or not to intervene. No. Stuff – including the most horrendous torture and killing – really does just happen, and God could not make it *not* happen without renouncing the decision to create a free world in the first place.

To put the point at its sharpest: on the model of God presupposed by the Wall of Answered Prayer, when a young Jewish child is shoved into the gas chamber, it is because God – for reasons only known to Him – decreed it must be so. He *could* have chosen to make things otherwise and does so in many other circumstances. We must trust that His reasons were good reasons and that, when the whole plan of which the child's death was a necessary part is revealed, even the child will bless him for it. Our alternative view says no: when God created a free world, he surrendered the right to interfere. The decision to create a free world at all carries within it the possibility of children being shoved into gas chambers and, once made, there is nothing God can do – other than abandoning the whole creation project – to stop that from happening. The responsibility has been placed in human hands. By the same token, if God does not micro-manage the gas chambers, nor does He supervise each cancer treatment or job application. God does not decide, for reasons best known to Him, who will go into remission, or who will be appointed. There is no such minutely detailed plan: there is only God's constant purpose, entrusted to us to work out as best we can.

What then is the point of prayer, of asking God to do things in the world – to heal, to help? Two things must be said in advance of an answer. The first is to remember that this intercessory aspect of prayer is, after all, only one aspect of a much bigger reality. Prayer is primarily about deepening relationship with God, about aligning one's will and energies with His, about being freed to become the form of His action in the world. It is about confession, about refreshment, about drawing from the deep wells of divine wisdom and compassion. Even insofar as our prayer concerns the world, the primary thing is not so much to plead for divine intervention, but to become the people through whom God's will is done and the Kingdom comes.

The second is to remember that, even when thus put in context, the question retains its force. The Holocaust should have silenced much of our cheap talk about prayer. It is a disgrace to imagine God would arrange things for our convenience, or even meet our most urgent needs, whilst He tolerated Auschwitz. Many people's quite astute reaction to the Wall of Answered Prayer will be one of moral indignation. Equally, their reaction, for instance, to the list of the names of the sick called during the intercessions on Sunday morning is honest bafflement. Given the divine silence at Auschwitz, thoughtful Christians should be puzzled at what exactly we think we are asking and with what likelihood of 'success'.

Those two major caveats entered, what more can be said? The way forward lies in remembering the sense in which God is committed to, and is present and active within, creation. God wills to bring about a world of free, responsible, loving co-operation with Him and, despite all the ways in which His creatures refuse that purpose, He refuses to give up on it. He will not override our freedom to refuse Him (though, as in the case of the Third Reich, the abuse of that freedom usually carries within it the seeds of its own destruction). Instead, He waits for those who will work with Him. Prayer is the bringing together of human wills with the divine will and, when this happens, resources beyond the merely human – or certainly beyond what humans had previously known themselves capable of – come in to play. People are given the resource to do what had previously been beyond them – above all, in manifold ways, to love. They become people around whom new possibilities of grace happen.

God is hidden in His creation always and everywhere. He dwells deep within every fibre of created being, willing creation on to the destiny He intends for it. When there is a full, free, conscious response to that willing, the divine creativity flows most freely and effectively, and the healing of the damaged world is made possible – perhaps even in dramatic and apparently miraculous ways. This is why (assuming for the moment that the Gospels are reasonably historically reliable) there were so many miracles around Jesus: not because he was a magician or had a hotline to a *deus ex machina* interventionist God, but because his humanity posed no obstacle at all to the free flow of divine agency. Instead, his humanity became the perfect expression of that flow. Therefore, God's kingdom began to come around him, with the most astonishing moral, spiritual and physical transformations: 'The blind receive their sight, the lame walk, the lepers are cleansed, the deaf hear, the dead are raised, and the poor have good news brought to them' (Matthew 11:5).

Then he was executed. The one in whom the divine spring flowed perfectly, in whom the fullness of the Godhead was pleased to dwell, was cast among the dead, the hopeless and the condemned. In the ancient picture language, he descended into Hell: the utter extremity of human futility, the failure of God's creation. At this point only more picture language will suffice: what Jesus going to that place means is that even there, the spring of life which He was begins to flow. Even there, divine activity has its effect, and the dead themselves are brought into contact with the Prince of Life. The Crucifixion means that there is no human situation, however bleakly damned, which does not know the presence of Christ; the Resurrection shows that that presence brings hope and a future to all that was most wrecked and forsaken. There is, ultimately, only one human story, one story of creation, and at its heart is Jesus, who went into Hell so He could bring everyone back.

What then are Christians doing when they pray for those in terrible suffering? They are bringing together in their hearts and minds those desperate people and Jesus. They are trusting that those people, despite all evidence to the contrary, belong in Jesus' story. That however bleak their predicament, it is in contact with the perfect flow of divine creativity. The divine presence simply *cannot* be killed: that is what the Romans and the high priests learned on Easter Sunday. In prayer, Christians bring together the human situation in all its bleakness with the infinite resourcefulness of resurrection grace. They try to imagine, as best they can, what grace can do with such bleakness, what transformation might look like. They pour out their longing for this to happen. They do all in their power to make it happen, and to make themselves transparent to the divine energy pressing through them. In many instances, all they can feasibly do is express longing. We remember then the conviction that the story is *one* story, and that our actions where we do have agency may have indirect effects we cannot imagine elsewhere. We are used, after all, to hearing that a butterfly flapping its wings in one continent may contribute to a storm on the other side of the world. Prayer may be the same.

And, on rare occasions – perhaps staggeringly rare – the cancer is healed. The murderer repents. Things that seemed impossible happen. We have no comprehension why they do in one case, and not in another. We have no more of an overview than does the butterfly flapping its wings. Yet, somehow, resistance to the divine activity has been dislodged and resurrection grace enabled to flow freely. It is not that God has decided, like a master chess strategist, to interfere here and not there for the sake of some greater end. It is rather that the same divine energy which yearns to burst through in every situation has, for reasons we know not, been *able* to do so in one situation and not another.

Perhaps the difference is something to do with the intensity of evil: it may be easier for the divine activity to break through when all around are open to it and willing with it. Perhaps all those prayers for an end to Hitler's evil were always going to run aground on the hard hearts of a European civilisation prepared, by and large, to tolerate or welcome him. In all honesty, we cannot know. This agnosticism, however, is different in kind from that proposed in much conventional talk about prayer. It is not that we do not understand the stratagems of the divine chess player (who sacrifices so many pawns): rather, we imagine a love battering away from the inside of every situation, desperately longing to save and to heal, and we confess we do not know why – for now – its victory usually remains elusive.

That 'for now' is of the utmost importance and suggests where Bonhoeffer's approach is most open to criticism. He was so concerned to resist the magical solution of the *deus ex machina* and to refocus attention on the need for discipleship, for people here and now to be the act of

God they seek, that he neglected another part of the truth: the fact that the resurrected Jesus stands as what Jürgen Moltmann describes as an 'embodied promise' for the whole of creation.[28] That is to say, once again, that the story of the world is *one* story – and that the risen Jesus is not only at the heart of every human situation, but reveals and embodies the destiny of every human situation. Even if the divine agency does not yet run free in every human situation, *it will*. There will be comprehensive healing, comprehensive forgiveness. When we celebrate an instance of healing now, we do so because we recognise it as an anticipation of the great and universal healing to come. When we lament every stubbornly unhealed situation now, we do so in hope, groaning as if in labour pains until 'the creation itself will be set free from its bondage to decay and will obtain the freedom of the glory of the children of God' (Romans 8:21).

This hope does not excuse us from action now or make discipleship simply a matter of waiting: but it does emphasise what Bonhoeffer understates – that no matter how radical our discipleship, or total our collaboration with the will of God, it could not deliver all that we hope for. The Kingdom of God will not arrive because human beings try very hard. The hope symbolised by that expression, 'Kingdom of God', is simply too immense for us to do anything but testify to it, anticipate it, wait for it. To *produce* it is beyond our capacity. It is resurrection: *we* cannot raise the dead and heal them, *we* cannot make all the darkness of history end in brightness. That is God's act alone and, as Berkovits acknowledges, such hope is as much Jewish as Christian: 'there must be a dimension beyond history in which all suffering finds its redemption through God. This is essential to the faith of a Jew.'[29] Within the confines of history alone, suffering can never be fully relieved; God's purposes can never be fully vindicated. If the dead stay dead, then even the defeated Hitler remains at one level triumphant, and we may rightly question whether God was right to create. His purpose in creation, to make a world of joy and freedom, would indeed be doomed to fail.

It is not that the resurrection, or whatever language we choose to denote this hope beyond history (the Kingdom, eternal life), justifies the darkness of history or 'makes it alright'. Our horror at Auschwitz should not diminish one bit, nor our commitment to ensure that nothing like it ever happens again. Nothing defuses the outrage. The point, rather, is that, if there were no resurrection, as St Paul put it, 'your faith is futile and you are still in your sins' (1 Corinthians 15:17) – or, which means

---

28. Jürgen Moltmann, *The Way of Jesus Christ: Christology in Messianic Dimensions* (London: SCM, 1990), p. 258.
29. Berkovits, *Faith after the Holocaust*, p. 139.

the same, Auschwitz would be left to tell the final truth about the world. Just as the final truth about its victims would be that they are mere victims, dead and finished, so too would God's whole creation project be dead and finished. If Auschwitz, like all the dark places of history, is not somehow touched and transformed by resurrection grace, then the world is wrecked eternally and the nihilists are right.

Not, of course, that we have the first clue what such touching and transformation will look like. We cannot know what resurrection will look like and attempts to describe it usually end in banality. We do not, yet, have the mental apparatus fit for it. As St Paul says, 'Now we see through a glass darkly, but then face to face: now I know in part; but then I shall know even as I am fully known' (1 Corinthians 13:12). When he first met the risen Jesus on the road to Damascus, it was as a blinding flash of light; whatever Jesus now is simply overwhelmed all of Paul's senses and conceptuality. To think of resurrection now is like staring into the sun; and yet (again, following Paul), we know that it is all Jesus, that the same life of love and joy and vibrancy that flowed in the man from Nazareth, whom we could touch and see and know, whom we can describe, is what we will know magnified beyond imagination and running free throughout the world when resurrection comes.

All of which is why it is time-honoured Christian practice to pray for the dead. The custom became controversial at the time of the Reformation, when it was connected with dubious financial transactions and overly detailed speculations about the structure of the afterlife – and, above all, when it seemed that such prayers were taken as a 'work' which could effect salvation for the dead, apparently threatening the sole sufficiency of Christ's death and resurrection. That controversy need not detain us here. All we do is note that at the heart of the ancient practice was a wholly true insight: that, because of the death and resurrection of Jesus, no human being's story can be regarded as finally closed by death. Jesus is Lord even of the tombs. He is capable of touching and transforming even that which by all human standards is lost forever. The murderer, for all his pride, does not get to boast over his victims. Resurrection grace has the final word.

Does it really? Over *everyone*? We have said that resurrection life is capable of touching and transforming all things, even that it *will* touch and transform all things. Was this not a step too far? We may rejoice to see the victims of Auschwitz healed and restored, brought into the glorious sunrise beyond description which is resurrection. But what of those other ruined creatures – the killers? What is the Gospel for them?

Chapter 7

Is Hitler in Heaven?

According to midrashic teaching, at the time of the drowning of the hosts of Pharaoh in the Red Sea the angels in heaven, as is their wont, were preparing to chant the daily hymn in praise of the Almighty. But God silenced them with the words, 'The works of my hands are drowning in the sea and you sing my praises!' It is not an easy matter for God to execute judgement over the guilty. Even 'His failures' are the works of his hands.

Eliezer Berkovits[1]

In May 1945, on receiving news of Hitler's death, the Cardinal Archbishop of Breslau, Adolf Bertram, ordered a Requiem Mass to be said for the Führer's soul in all churches across his archdiocese. Unsurprisingly, for critics of the Church's role in the Holocaust, such as Daniel Goldhagen, this speaks powerfully of Christian accommodation with and complicity in Hitler's crimes.[2] We have already examined that broader charge. The Requiem Mass is mentioned in its own right now, because a Requiem Mass is, above all, a plea by the Church on behalf of a particular sinner that the salvation won by Christ upon the Cross might apply to that individual. The Cardinal need not have been intending to endorse the Führer as a fine, upstanding Christian (although, in fact, he seems to have regarded the provision of a Mass as a fitting tribute to an at least nominally Catholic head of state, and it is very hard not to side with his harsh critics on this point).[3] In principle, however, all he was asking was

---

1. Berkovits, *Faith after the Holocaust*, p. 135.
2. Goldhagen, *A Moral Reckoning*, p. 266.
3. Scholder, *A Requiem for Hitler*, p. 166.

that the Church should pray that this particular sinner, Adolf Hitler, might receive the benefits of Christ's atoning death – so that, despite all his crimes, Hitler might enter Heaven. To many, of course, this will be as scandalous as appearing to approve of Hitler. Is it even conceivable that Hitler could be in Heaven? Are we really to *hope* to see him there? Are his victims required to hope that? That is the question this chapter seeks to address.

We have framed the question in terms of Hitler but, of course, far more is at stake here than one individual – or even the other names that have joined his in infamy: Eichmann, Mengele, Himmler and the rest. Tens of thousands of killers bear the same guilt. The question extends well beyond the Holocaust; we might well ask the same question about Stalin and the NKVD, or Ian Brady and Myra Hindley, or so many others. There are many who might seem well beyond the scope of any possible reconciliation. The issue is not Hitler *per se* but the whole Christian theology of salvation. Is salvation potentially or actually *universal*, so that simply everyone will be gathered into the Kingdom at the end? Or is there a greater or lesser degree of exclusion – in simpler language, do some people go to Hell?

Why Even Ask the Question?

In recent years, of course, there has been something of a Christian pincer movement against such talk of Heaven and Hell. From one side, Tom Wright has led the charge against a version of Christianity which emphasises other-worldly, ethereal post-mortem destinations. Wright insists that the Bible knows little of this: the biblical hope is for the Kingdom of God established on this good earth, renewed and perfected.[4] There is a fascinating debate to be had here but, for our current purposes, it is immaterial: however the glorious future promised is conceived, the question is whether some might be shut out of it.

The other side of the pincer movement perhaps needs more addressing. Many contemporary Christians have begun to shy away from talk of Heaven and Hell for a different set of reasons. The shift is, in part, indicated by a famous Christian Aid slogan, 'We believe in life *before* death', the aim being to subvert the idea that Christianity is obsessed with the 'afterlife' to the neglect of the here and now. The question of what happens beyond death has accordingly been somewhat bracketed. The emphasis of preachers and laity alike has fallen more and more on what difference faith makes *now*. Recent research in one Church of

---

4. See especially Wright, *Surprised by Hope.*

England diocese highlighted this very clearly. Most clergy surveyed were supremely concerned with 'the beneficent potential of faith' – 'whether a faith is conducive to the individual and common good of people in this life, in this world. … Its concerns are with "earthly salvation".'[5] One minister summed it up as follows:

> Well, what is salvation? If we're referring to what happens after this life, I think we've missed the point. It's about … there are kingdom values, for want of a better expression, that are formed across the faiths, such as the Golden Rule. My perspective on salvation is that salvation is something that starts here and now. Salvation beyond this life is fairly, I think, to me, immaterial.[6]

It is tempting to see this shift from an older emphasis on post-mortem destiny as just one more element of the long process of secularisation, the gradual erosion of the Christian world view and traditional doctrine in general society and even among those who still belong to the Church. Even if that is true, however, such 'secularism' might also enable us to see again important Christian truths which the Christian religion itself had obscured. This is partly what Dietrich Bonhoeffer was saying in his *Letters and Papers from Prison* when he speculated about the 'religion-less Christianity' he thought was the Church's future. Religions are what you have in order to answer certain questions: Where did we come from? How can we deal with guilt? What happens when we die? Bonhoeffer suggested that what was different about twentieth-century people is that such questions no longer really gripped them. They just were not that interested; it did not matter much to them what happened when they died. That whole religious frame of reference was losing its significance. This was good news, thinks Bonhoeffer, because actually Christianity (like its Jewish parent) was not really about those questions in the first place. Bonhoeffer observes at one point that the Old Testament has remarkably little to say about what happens after death – and much, much more to say about how you live and organise your society here and now. To use our anachronistic categories, it is much more interested in

---

5. Sabine Bohnacker-Bruce, *Church of England Ministers' Beliefs about Other Religions: A Constructivist Grounded Theory Study*, unpublished doctoral thesis for the University of Winchester, 2016, p. 192.
6. Ibid., p. 193.

politics than religion. Moreover, says Bonhoeffer, a good dose of that Old Testament worldliness is just what contemporary Christianity needs.

There are, however, more problematic reasons – at any rate, problematic for orthodox Christians – why talk about Heaven and Hell as eternal destinies has waned in the contemporary Church. The general scientism of our culture is one. If a thing cannot be touched, felt, measured and tested, its reality is open to serious doubt. There is a kind of resolute determination amongst the scientifically minded not to think about the unverifiable and unknowable at all, and to some extent this has filtered even into the Churches. Of course, there is simply the contemporary knowledge of how vast reality is in terms of time and space. We know that our planet is just one among billions and billions of others spread throughout the universe. Even on this one, whole civilisations and epochs have lived and died and vanished without trace. Can it really be true that not even a sparrow falls to the ground without our Father knowing, and that we are worth more than many sparrows (Matthew 10:29-31)? That was easier to believe when things were smaller and we appeared more central. For many people, post-mortem, personal existence seems just implausible.

If science pushes in that direction, so does a certain kind of ethical seriousness and spirituality. On the one hand, older Christian language about the Last Judgement – especially insofar as it emphasised the eternal torment of the damned – served simply to turn off a great many people from thinking about eternal destiny at all. They knew they did not believe *that*, yet the tradition did not seem to offer them much else. So they learned to stop worrying about it, and that went hand in hand with a kind of stern moralism: you should do right, and avoid wrong, not because you are going to be rewarded or punished, but simply because they are right and wrong. You do one, and not the other, for its own sake. To focus on judgement comes to be seen as a kind of immaturity, a preoccupation with one own's ego and its reward.

This combines with what we might call a kind of popular Buddhism, though it does not often come badged as such, which says that, if you are going to think of what comes after death at all, think of it in terms of losing your ego. Think of it in terms of merging back into the cosmos from which you came, of all that is narrow and constrained and particular about you just gently ceasing. This has nothing to do with traditional Christianity, which definitely affirms that, whatever our destiny is, it is in some sense *our* destiny, a *personal* reality which you and I shall experience. However, though not Christian, it has a certain power and beauty which is deeply appealing to many. The lines traditionally attributed to Mary Elizabeth Frye put it well:

> *Do not stand at my grave and weep.*
> *I am not there. I do not sleep.*
> *I am a thousand winds that blow.*
> *I am the diamond glints on snow.*
> *I am the sunlight on ripened grain.*
> *I am the gentle autumn rain. ...*
> *Do not stand at my grave and cry.*
> *I am not there. I did not die.*

So: a kind of recovery of the biblical emphasis on *this* world and *this* life. A scientism which does not like what it cannot see and verify and measure, and which tells us that we are astonishingly insignificant in the universe. A reaction against the old language of judgement, punishment and reward, and the sense that ego – personhood – is just a passing thing anyway, destined to merge back into the universe. All these have combined gradually to erode confident Christian belief in personal life after death. How many of us *really* think that we shall one day stand before our Maker to offer account for our lives and hear the divine verdict?

However, close attention to horrors like the Holocaust drives home the recognition that this loss of confidence in personal destiny after death has very serious consequences. Quite apart from any concern for fidelity to Scripture or tradition, Christians should be pushing back against those forces which tend to neglect or exclude this aspect of the Gospel. We need to recall why belief in life after death first emerged in the later writings of the Hebrew Scriptures. Bonhoeffer is correct that their emphasis was strongly this-worldly; but this is precisely why Jews eventually came to expect the Resurrection. The basic Jewish belief is that the Creator God was good, that His world was good and that the demands of righteousness must therefore be vindicated: creation *fails* if it languishes under evil, if the faithful are killed and the wicked triumph. Israel was sharply aware that history itself does not deliver this vindication; more often than not, the righteous are crushed: 'The law becomes slack and justice never prevails' (Habakkuk 1:4).

Given this realism about history, either the fundamental conviction of God's and creation's goodness must give way – *or* the vindication must be reconceived as coming from beyond history, as the great Day of the Lord which breaks in upon and radically transforms the world order. Human agency cannot produce this Day; it can only wait and prepare for it. Given that meanwhile the righteous continue to be slaughtered and the tyrants die happy in their beds, it soon came to be understood that as part of that Day the dead must be raised. They must experience the vindication of God in their own persons: 'Many of those who sleep in the earth shall awake, some to everlasting life, and some to shame and everlasting contempt' (Daniel 12:2).

If there is no personal life beyond death, all this is lost. As the Polish-American poet Czesław Miłosz has observed, this would be the best Gospel of all for the tyrants and killers: 'A true opium of the people is a belief in nothingness after death – the huge solace of thinking that for our betrayals, greed, cowardice, murders we are not going to be judged.'[7] That is: if there is no personal destiny after death, then Hitler and the rest of them will never be held to account for what they did. Human justice, the Hebrew prophets would be unsurprised to learn, has proved woefully incapable of punishing the perpetrators of the Holocaust.[8] Yet, even had such justice not been thwarted by the suicides of the criminals, the *realpolitik* of the Cold War, or the presence of Nazis among the Nazi hunters, what human sentence could possibly suffice in this case anyway? What court order could force the perpetrators, inescapably force them, to confront the magnitude of their guilt and to bear it? We know that, after the event, many even of those killers brought before the courts minimised their involvement or excused themselves – and some, indeed, remained defiantly unrepentant. *Karma* did not operate. Nature and history did not rebound on them, and they often died content in their beds. If there is no judgement after death, and no personal existence in which to bear that judgement, then reality truly is characterised 'at bottom, [by] no design, no purpose, no evil and no good, nothing but blind pitiless indifference'.[9]

'Blind pitiless indifference' is an excellent description of how the Nazi system and its personnel processed six million victims and it is important to pursue that connection. The intellectual struggle to affirm that after death there is a personal judgement is related to the moral protest against the Nazis' depersonalisation of their victims. At the heart of Nazism was a denial of the dignity of the individual human person,

---

7. Czesław Miłosz, 'Discreet Charm of Nihilism', *New York Review of Books*, 19 November 1998.
8. For a depressingly exhaustive demonstration of this point, see Fulbrook, *Reckonings*.
9. Richard Dawkins, *River out of Eden: A Darwinian View of Life* (London: Wiedenfeld & Nicolson, 1995), p. 133.

at least as far as the Jews and other 'sub-humans' were concerned. They were just elements in a mass, with no innate worth or claim on anyone else's love and protection. The cattle trucks which carried them to their death were deeply symbolic: their human cargo was indeed just so much meat destined for slaughter. As Zygmunt Bauman has observed, 'for genocide to be possible, personal differences must first be obliterated and faces must be melted into the uniform mass of the abstract category'.[10]

The Christian tradition, by contrast, insists that the person can never be dissolved into the mass. Each one of us is the beloved creation of God, bearing a unique relationship to and responsibility before Him. That is why murder is such an appalling crime: because the victim is not an anonymous thing, but a son or daughter of God loved into existence. Nonetheless, what holds true for the victim also holds true for the killer. Neither denial nor death can free them from ultimately having to reckon with their relationship to God, and with what their deeds mean in that light. Before God, individuals matter. Neither killer nor victim slides gently into extinction, to merge again with the cosmos. The individual relationship to God endures. Which means, of necessity, that the question of God's judgement remains. In picture language (and it is impossible to use any other), each will stand before the judgement seat and render account for his or her actions. So, there is no escape from the question: is there any hope for Hitler before that heavenly tribunal?

A Very Popular, Wrong Answer: Universalism

One very influential answer in the contemporary Church is that there is every hope for Hitler: indeed, more than hope, there is certainty. The doctrine of universal salvation, or universalism, teaches that every single human being without exception will in the end be saved. This is no recent innovation in Christian theology – there are texts in Scripture which, taken in isolation, press in this direction: 'As in Adam all die, so in Christ shall all be made alive!' (1 Corinthians 15:22). The great second-century theologian Origen of Alexandria went even further, asserting that even Satan himself would one day to be reconciled to God, in the great *apokatastasis* or restoration of all things. We should note that Origen was condemned as a heretic for this view (among others) but, nonetheless, while universalism has never been the official teaching of the Church, it has always been the favoured view of a minority. The greatest Protestant theologian of the twentieth century, Karl Barth, is understood by many

---

10. Bauman, *Modernity and the Holocaust*, p. 227.

to teach universalism. It could even be claimed as the most obvious reading of Vatican II's *Lumen Gentium*, when it dares to hope that 'the entire world may become the People of God, the Body of the Lord and the Temple of the Holy Spirit'.[11] One recent and powerful exponent is the Orthodox theologian David Bentley Hart, who opens his case by claiming that, 'if Christianity taken as a whole is indeed an entirely coherent and credible system of belief, then the universalist understanding of its message is the only one possible. ... I say that without the least hesitation or qualification.'[12]

The attractions of universalism are obvious. First, it has to be understood as a reaction against what was the older orthodoxy: that anyone who was not a Christian (or, indeed, from the Roman Catholic perspective, in communion with the Pope) was destined for eternal damnation. It was perhaps just possible that in some quite exceptional circumstances – such as the 'invincible ignorance' of those whom no missionaries had been able to reach – a lucky soul might sneak in under the wire. In most cases, however, the gates of Heaven would remain firmly shut. This teaching was often reinforced by a lurid, often pathologically sadistic, emphasis on the torments of the damned. They would suffer conscious agony for all eternity, without hope of deliverance. By such means, generations of preachers sought to draw people to the God who loved them. There are Christians who still hold, to some degree, to this theological picture and evangelistic strategy – but for large swathes of the Church it has come to lack all credibility.

There are many reasons for this. To most, it has seemed simply incompatible with the claim that God is Love. Alongside this, there has been an increased awareness of the spiritual and moral depth of religions other than Christianity, and a self-critical perspective on the Church's own history. The justice of purely *retributive* punishment where there is no possibility of reform or reconciliation also came to be rejected by many, whether in campaigns against the death penalty or in the realm of theology and God's judgement. There was also (paradoxically, in the light of the horrors dealt with in this book) an increasing sense that human beings were not, after all, that bad. The Enlightenment and the French Revolution, to paint in very broad brushstrokes, were fundamentally optimistic about human beings and their capacity for goodness. The cultural air was gradually being cleansed of the sin

---

11. *Lumen Gentium*, ch. 2, para. 17.
12. David Bentley Hart, *That All Shall Be Saved: Heaven, Hell and Universal Salvation* (New Haven, CT, and London: Yale University Press, 2019), p. 3.

and doom-laden-ness of the pre-modern era. People no longer readily reckoned themselves as miserable sinners deserving of Hell, as the old prayer books would have it. How could a just God possibly condemn most people to eternal torment? The Holocaust itself raised the question of the justice of the traditional picture in the sharpest possible form. Did murdered Jews go straight to Hell? For many Christians, the credibility of the traditional doctrine collapsed in the face of such pressures.

Of course, there are a variety of alternatives between the rigidly exclusivist position ('Only committed Christians will be saved') and universalism ('Absolutely everyone will be saved'). The concerns outlined above do not all, necessarily, lead to the universalist decision. Other factors do, however, tend very strongly in that direction. So, for instance, universalists are powerfully struck by the biblical insistence that: 'God desires everyone to be saved, and to come to knowledge of the truth' (1 Timothy 2:4). To be sure, God might desire something without ever actually obtaining it – but, if this was the case most of the time (as the traditional position, unless carefully qualified, entails), then serious questions would arise over the power of God. As Hart puts it, even if only a small number fail to attain everlasting joy, this would still represent 'a measure of failure or loss preserved within the totality of the tale of divine victory. If what is lost is lost finally and absolutely, then whatever remains, however glorious, is the residue of an unresolved and no less ultimate tragedy.'[13] God's intention in creating the universe – that His creatures should flourish in love and joy – would have been irrevocably frustrated. The power of sin would thus appear ultimately stronger than the power of God, depriving Him of what He wants. Even if there was only one soul that in the end held out and in which the divine purpose failed, a serious question mark would have been placed against the divine omnipotence. God is not Almighty if in the end He cannot save.

Approaching the same dilemma from another angle, Hart considers the implications of recognising, as Christian tradition does, that people are who they are through their relationships with one another. We do not exist as atomised units but are constituted by our relationships; a mother, for instance, is who she is, at least in part, through her relationship with her child. Hart presses us to see the logic: 'either all persons must be saved, or none can be'.[14] For, if that child was damned for eternity, in what sense could the mother enjoy heaven – given that heaven is the perfection of joy? If we reject as obscene the idea that she might rejoice in the just damnation

13. Ibid., p. 187.
14. Ibid., p.155.

of her child (the option favoured by much Christian tradition),[15] it could only be through some kind of forgetfulness that she ever had a child and, yet, such oblivion would erase a vital element of her personhood. One could justly question in what sense 'she' was actually in heaven, if such spiritual dismemberment is required. The logic runs far beyond the mother/child analogy. Ultimately, we are all bound up with each other and, so, in the end (argues Hart) none can truly be in Heaven if any are in Hell.

Ponder the scope of Christ's work upon the Cross. St Paul, in one of the earliest reflections on this, draws a parallel with the mythological sin of Adam in the Garden of Eden: that decision to eat the apple determined not just his fate, but that of the whole human race. Paul suggests that what Jesus did on the Cross has at least as great – even greater – determining power:

> For if the many died through the one man's trespass, much more surely have the grace of God and the free gift of the one man, Jesus Christ, abounded for the many. ... Just as one man's trespass led to condemnation for all, so one man's act of righteousness leads to justification and life for all. (Romans 5:15, 18)

Those who object to universalism might protest that, whilst the Cross does indeed extend the *possibility* of life to all, that possibility needs to be freely chosen and owned by each individual to become real and effective. Perhaps, but that is not how the parallel with Adam works. Traditionally, the doctrine of original sin has not relied on this kind of wholly voluntary 'opting in' but has seen sin as going to work in each of us before our consent. Why should the same not be true of grace? Would this not be the best way to understand Paul's conviction that, 'As in Adam all die, so in Christ shall all be made alive' (1 Corinthians 15:22) and that, in the end, '*every* knee shall bow, and *every* tongue confess, that Jesus Christ is Lord to the glory of God the Father' (Philippians 2:10-11, emphasis added)? Paul is not, to be sure, consistently or even largely universalist – but there are undoubtedly universalising impulses in his thinking.

The case for universalism might then seem overwhelmingly strong. However, there are at least equally forceful reasons for refusing, in the end, to accept it. It is not only that, often, universalists appear not to grasp that some really do delight in torture and murder: that people

---

15. Hart notes that Tertullian, Lombard, Aquinas and Luther, among others, take just this view, ibid., p. 78.

were not always forced to do these things but embraced them willingly and never came near repentance for them. As Miroslav Volf has observed, the reluctance to believe in the fiery vengeance of God comes most easily to those who have had very sheltered lives.[16] What does it say about God if murder has no consequence and killers waltz into Heaven regardless? When this very obvious point is made, appeal is often made to the idea that the path to salvation will, of course, involve repentance. Yet, mentioning repentance marks a retreat from universalism proper, however generous and merciful and patient a God is envisaged. The human being is always free, after all, *not* to repent.

We shall return to this crucial question of freedom shortly but, first, note the principal reason for Christians to reject universalism. There are simply too many notes of urgent warning, and indeed of threat, in the teaching of Jesus and in the wider New Testament: 'The gate is wide and the road is easy that leads to destruction, and there are many who take it. The gate is narrow, and the road is hard that leads to life, and there are few who find it' (Matthew 7:13-14). Although sayings that we read as obviously being about post-mortem destiny are not always necessarily such, Jesus definitely seems to think that at least some of his hearers are at risk of eternal misery. This alarming note makes no sense if ultimately there is no question that all shall be saved.

Hart does not ignore this element in Jesus' teaching and the wider New Testament. It must, however, he suggests, somehow be reconciled with those texts which speak of God's ultimate and universal victory. The way to do so is to remember that 'the two sides of the New Testament's eschatological language represent not two antithetical possibilities, tantalisingly or menacingly dangled before us, posed one against the other … but rather different moments within a seamless narrative, two distinct eschatological horizons, one enclosed within the other'.[17] In other words, New Testament threats of eschatological misery do indeed describe a reality: those who live their lives closed to grace are headed for disaster. Darkness and fire and terror might well be apt metaphors for that experience; however, it will be but a preliminary experience, a necessary stage on the way of salvation. The darkness and fire are purgative, rather than ultimately destructive. The wicked suffer so that they might be saved. The terrible note of judgement is held within a larger and ultimately more final purpose of salvation.

---

16. Miroslav Volf, *Exclusion and Embrace: A Theological Exploration of Identity, Otherness, and Reconciliation* (Nashville, TN: Abingdon Press, 1996), p. 304.

17. Hart, *All That Shall Be Saved*, p. 103.

There is undoubtedly some merit in Hart's case. He is right that, in a world where 'as in Adam all died, so in Christ shall all be made alive', eternal damnation and salvation cannot be two equally real, equally possible, equally likely outcomes to either an individual's or the world's story. The Gospel is that an almost-irresistible power of salvation has been set at work in creation. One might even say that you would have to try quite hard *not* to be saved, have to set your face resolutely and grimly and unremittingly against grace. Yet, it is precisely that possibility which Jesus consistently leaves open – whether suggestively in the figure of the older brother in the parable of the Prodigal Son (Luke 15:11-32), or emphatically in the parable of the Sheep and the Goats (Matthew 25:31-46). There is no trace here of unshakeable confidence that all will ultimately be well for all. For that reason alone, dogmatic universalism should be resisted.

Back now to the idea of freedom: the second most powerful reason for resisting universalism. As noted in the last chapter, it is central to the Christian vision that God respects the freedom of His creatures. The entire point of creation was to bring forth that which was other than God, which freely came to express, share in, and magnify the nature of God – to join in with His life of love and joy and peace. However, love is in its essence free: it cannot be compelled. To use the sexual analogy, God longs for the consummation of union with the world, or the individual soul. He does everything to make that consummation possible, but He also refuses to violate the integrity of the other by *imposing* it. To do otherwise would be not love, but rape.

The logical consequence of this divine respect is that, if a human being so chooses, she must be allowed to shut herself out of God's purpose. Moreover, it must at least be possible that such choosing goes on forever: that no matter how long God coaxes and beseeches the response of the beloved, it is never given. Where the universalist sees this as an impossible affront to God's power, traditional doctrine sees it as self-imposed divine restraint – God will not overwhelm us, because He will be faithful to His nature as Love. To anticipate a further stage of our argument, this need not necessarily mean that He ever ceases to hold out the possibility of life. It does mean, however, that we cannot say with absolute certainty, as universalists do, that every single soul will finally be saved. In the end, says traditional doctrine, God has chosen for that not to be in His control.

Nonsense, says Hart: 'The infernalist argument from creaturely freedom is a silly distraction.'[18] The Christian tradition, he claims (and

---

18. Ibid., p. 52.

he is frank in recognising that it is, with a few significant exceptions, the vast weight of that tradition he is dissenting from), has let itself down here by adopting a sub-Christian understanding of freedom as something like arbitrary choice. On such a model, freedom is the power to choose between objects, without regard either to what I am or those objects are. I may 'freely' choose to cut off my arm or to end my own existence. By contrast, Hart urges, the Christian tradition has usually understood freedom as *the capacity to be what we are meant to be*. Freedom is not arbitrary but ordered towards a specific end: in the case of human beings, communion with their Maker. Our deepest and truest desire, according to the Christian tradition, is for unity with God. To enact this is freedom; to waver from it, however much a 'chosen' act, is to be un-free, to distort what we are meant to be. There can therefore be, Hart argues, no truly free rejection of God:

> The more one is in one's right mind – the more, that is, that one is conscious of God as the Goodness that fulfils all beings, and the more one recognises that one's own nature can have its own true completion and joy nowhere but in Him, and the more one is unfettered by distorting misperceptions, deranged passions, and the encumbrances of past mistakes – the more inevitable is one's surrender to God. Liberated from *all* ignorance, emancipated from *all* the adverse conditions of this life, the rational soul could freely will only its own union with God, and thereby its own supreme beatitude. We are, as it were, doomed to happiness.[19]

Only the truly free choice – one not made under any kind of constraint, in complete possession of the facts and with full, conscious, deliberation – could possibly merit utter, final condemnation. A soul not so free would have some excuse, not be so guilty, and divine justice would accordingly be tempered by mercy. Yet, a soul that was so free could not refuse God, because the soul is made for God and finds its joy in Him alone: 'The irresistibility of God for any soul that has truly been set free is no more a constraint placed on its liberty than is the irresistible attraction of a flowing spring of fresh water in a desert place to a man who is dying of thirst.'[20] The notion of choice is redundant here.

---

19. Ibid., pp. 40-41.
20. Ibid., p. 41.

Yet, has Hart truly weighed the gravity of sin? He presumes a situation where the soul sees God without distortion, where all the damage the sinner does to himself through sin has been undone, where there is no obstacle to freedom. Nevertheless, those obstacles were self-imposed: will God simply remove them, without any co-operation or even consent from the self? Hart may be correct that face to face with God, all distortion stripped away, the soul will leap to love Him as a thirsty man drinks from the spring. However, is he right to assume that God will strip away the distortions with which we have surrounded ourselves, even *against* our will? God might always be willing to bring us to Himself, but the soul might choose never to let Him: choose, as it were, to remain 'unfree'. As Volf puts it,

> we should not shy away from the possibility, the unpleasant and tragic *possibility* that there *might* be human beings, created in the image of God, who, through the practice of evil, have immunised themselves from all attempts at their redemption. Ensnared by the chaos of violence which generates its own legitimising 'reason' and 'goodness', they have become untouchable for the lure of God's truth and goodness.[21]

Once again, we circle back to the biblical warnings. If this cannot be so, if we are indeed 'doomed to happiness', why the urgency in the words of Jesus and the prophets?

A final reason for objecting to universalism was classically put by the novelist Fyodor Dostoevsky in *The Brothers Karamazov*. Ivan, a brilliant rationalist student, gives his reasons for rejecting Christian faith. Salvation, he thinks (correctly) means reconciliation: harmony re-established between victims and killers. There are crimes, however, which must radically and permanently cancel that possibility. Ivan asks us to imagine a situation wherein a nobleman orders a peasant child to be torn apart by hunting dogs, his mother looking on. The Gospel, says Ivan, promises a time:

> when earth and heaven unite in a single paean of praise, when all that lives and has lived will cry out, 'You are just O Lord, for your ways are revealed to us!' When the mother embraces the murderer whose dogs tore her son apart, and all three shall cry out weeping, 'You are just O Lord,' and

21. Volf, *Exclusion and Embrace*, p. 297. Emphasis in the original.

that of course will be the summit of all knowledge, and all will be explained. But here's the snag, that's just what I can't accept ... above all, I don't want the mother to embrace the torturer whose dogs tore her son apart! She has no right to forgive him! ... the price of harmony has been set too high, we cannot afford the entrance fee. And that's why I hasten to return my entry ticket.[22]

Ivan objects not just to universalism, of course, but also to the mere *possibility* of reconciliation after terrible evil. We shall return to his protest later to see whether any answer can be given – but, if there can be, it will be a tentative venture, made in fear and trembling. In the picture language of the tradition, we are talking about asking the Jews to embrace their murderers, to sit and eat with them at the same heavenly banquet as friends, rejoicing together. Quite possibly, this simply cannot and should not be done, and universalism's dogmatic insistence that it must be so is one of its most unattractive features. Notably, Hart only addresses Ivan's question briefly – and then to suggest that the truly unacceptable price is that required by the traditional understanding of salvation and damnation. In making Hitler (Hart's chosen example) suffer eternally – whether out of respect for freedom or to manifest divine justice – the tradition effectively makes him serve 'as my redeemer in some shadow eternity of eternal torment, offering up his screams of agony as the price of my hope for salvation'.[23] Eternal torment is not, of course, the only alternative to the universalist case. We might argue either that there is always the possibility for Hitler to begin the journey of repentance and reconciliation, or that damnation really means annihilation, and there is no longer any Hitler to be tormented. The key point, however, is that Hart simply does not show evidence of taking seriously the moral offence of presuming any reconciliation between murderer and victim. His dogmatic universalism simply rides roughshod over any cry for justice. Perhaps all Christians should be ashamed of the moral superficiality of our hope for salvation; certainly, the dogmatic universalist should be.

---

22. Fyodor Dostoevsky, *The Karamazov Brothers*, trans. with an intro-duction and notes by Ignat Avsey (Oxford: Oxford University Press, 1994), pp. 307-8.
23. Hart, *That All Shall Be Saved*, p. 84.

If Universalism Is Not the Answer, What Is?

Is there then any hope for Hitler?

The first element in our answer must be to affirm the tremendous scope and saving potential of the Cross and the Resurrection. It is fundamental to the Christian faith that we are saved not by our own moral performance, but by the grace of God made flesh in Jesus and enacted in his death and resurrection. If we are not saved by moral merit, however, then neither can moral failure (however terrible) automatically and irrevocably exclude us from salvation. Our sins are not the determining factor in salvation because, as St Paul put it, 'God proves his love for us in that while we were still sinners, Christ died for us' (Romans 5:8). One need not in any way minimise the depravity of Hitler to say that *even his* crimes cannot put him beyond the reach of God and that reach is intended for Hitler's good. It is basic to Christian belief that God 'desires everyone to be saved, and to come to knowledge of the truth' (1 Timothy 2:4).

The second element must be to affirm the freedom of Hitler *not to be saved* if Hitler so chooses. *Pace* Hart, Hitler might choose not to become truly free, might choose to remain immured in his self-deception, pride and hatred. To state the same truth in a different way, if Hitler is to be saved there must be *some* element of repentance and faith on his part. He must at the very least allow himself to begin to be drawn along the journey home. This is not to imagine that, if, just before his death, Hitler prayed 'the sinner's prayer', all would suddenly be well for him – and that, if he did not, it would not.[24] If we said that such a prayer before death was necessary, we would, on the one hand, be radically limiting the power of God to save – for many sinners have died unrepentant. On the other, we would lay ourselves open to the charge of moral superficiality. While many Christians rejoice in believing that 'The vilest offender who truly believes, / That moment from Jesus a pardon receives',[25] others understandably see this as suggesting a kind of 'get out of jail (or Hell) free card' which evacuates moral decisions of

---

24. 'The sinner's prayer' is a popular phrase in traditional evangelical Protestantism, indicating a short prayer uttered at the moment of conversion. There is no fixed formula, but the essence of the prayer is the acknowledgement of guilt and the plea for forgiveness on the basis of Christ's saving death alone.

25. A line from Fanny Crosby's popular hymn, 'To God Be the Glory', stanza 2 (1875).

all consequence: how can you let a killer just turn around at the end of his life, say he's sorry, and waltz into Heaven?

The protest is understandable but stems from a failure to grasp the sheer difficulty of being forgiven. Forgiveness may indeed be *free*, in that our moral performance can never earn it, and it is always simply offered to us regardless of merit. However, it is decidedly not *easy*. Recall 1 Timothy 2:4: '[God] desires everyone to be saved, and to come to the knowledge of the truth.' What would it be for Hitler to come to the knowledge of the truth? It would involve coming to see his life from a wholly new perspective, through the eyes of God. It would involve understanding – not only on an intellectual level but, existentially, in the very core of his conscience and being – that every murdered Jew was the beloved child of God. It would involve bearing something of the divine pain at their destruction. It would involve bearing something of the victims' terror and sadness. It would be, for Hitler, the kind of overwhelming destruction of which biblical prophecies of judgement often speak. Nothing would be left of him but ruins and desolation. For Hitler, to repent means to unthink all his self-justifications, all his evasions and lies, and to let the bare truth of who he was and what he had done be exposed by piercing divine light.

The Gospel for Hitler, though, is that this light is ultimately kind. On the far side of destruction, there is healing. God sees and loves the person trapped inside the catastrophe of his own making and, in Jesus, promises to accompany him through the needed death to that old identity and out into new life. However, the courage required to trust that this is the case, and so to begin to face reality, is immense. It would be much easier, in Hitler's case, for the self-protective instinct to kick in, making even beginning the process impossible. It might well be that Hitler would rather remain sealed forever inside the lie of his own self-justification, than take the risk of knowing the truth. Using picture language, we might imagine Hell as a deep dungeon. The walls have been broken down and the doors flung open by Jesus. He stands in the doorway, calling the prisoners out – but some are so understandably afraid of freedom that they would rather remain crouched in the darkest corner, hunched into themselves. They are determined to be alone rather than risk being brought back into relationship with God and with their victims – because, whilst indeed free, their restoration would 'cost not less than everything'.

It should now be clear quite how far removed this understanding of salvation is from killers 'just turning around at the end of their lives, saying they're sorry, and waltzing into heaven'. We are talking about a long and arduous journey back from a far country, requiring immense courage and made possible only by the grace of God, reaching out in the crucified Jesus. It should be equally clear that it is quite impossible, in most cases, for this journey to be completed – or in many cases even begun – before the end of our natural lives. The cost of repentance is such that many will prefer to remain stuck in themselves, perhaps forever. That forever stuck-ness would be the proper context for language about Hell: these would-be people condemned to exist forever in the misery of their own falsity, self-deprived of all love and growth.

Yet, this is only 'forever' if the damned continued to have it so. It is quite possible that they will. In such a case, Hart's observations about the imperfect, damaged nature of resurrection hope hold good. If Hitler remains in Hell, then in him at least the divine purpose has failed. His mother's joy is gone forever, and to some degree all our joy is diminished, for our lives (however remotely) are all bound up with each other. Hitler is part of humanity and, if the bell tolls for him, it tolls for us all. Hart is correct that the affirmation of the possibility of Hell comes at a price for the Christian doctrine of Heaven: it cannot be a place of unalloyed rejoicing but is eternally shadowed by grief – if the damned never turn. The key question for Christians is whether we must imagine the love of God as having, as it were, a 'use-by' date: so that, if you have not responded by a particular moment in time, then the love is withdrawn and you have lost your chance.

Much Protestant tradition has identified such a moment and placed it at the time of death (and has also insisted on a conscious, if perhaps private, acceptance of Jesus as the content of the necessary response). Catholic theology, by contrast, has various ideas of Purgatory: a post-mortem state in which the layers of sin in which people have immured themselves are scorched away by the transforming love of God. In Catholic theology, it makes sense to speak of people in some way still responding to and growing in the love of God even beyond death. Something like this is necessary, it seems, if we are to avoid either saying that only a relatively small number of people are saved (those who achieved the requisite level of response to grace before dying), or grossly underestimating the personal transformation involved in being saved.

So perhaps we should imagine the situation of Hitler thus. Let us assume that there was no sinner's prayer at the last moment: that he died, like so many of the wicked before him, in defiant rage, full of hatred and self-pity. He remained firmly locked inside his lie. He remains, however, the beloved child of God: that was never based on his moral performance, but on the fact of his creation – and so cannot be undone by his sins. He remains surrounded by the love of God, which is beseeching him, knocking constantly upon the hardened shell of the lie, longing for him to unclench himself just the slightest bit – to dare to turn, in the slightest degree, towards the light. At the beginning, that is all that is required – just the faintest glimmer of desire for truth, for relationship, for love restored. Even that tiniest first step will take great pain and courage (although *not* to take it involves still greater misery). Yet, if he begins to turn, 'while he was still far off, his father saw him, and was filled with compassion; he ran and put his arms around him and kissed him' (Luke 15:20). He will be met by God, who will bear him and carry him through the great baptismal sea of transformation to the promised land of forgiveness.

It is that transforming journey that perhaps holds the key to the greatest objection to speaking of Hitler being in Heaven: Ivan Karamazov's protest that, if Heaven means reconciliation, then the price has been set too high. Ivan is correct: Heaven is indeed reconciliation. There can be no separate compartments in eternal destiny, where victim and killer enjoy private communion with God in isolation from each other. The New Testament vision is one where all of us belong with and for one another, and we become sources of joy and life to each other. However, perhaps Ivan has underestimated quite what it would mean for the murderer to come back from Hell. For Hitler to un-learn all that he had told himself about his righteousness, his victimhood, about the wickedness of his enemies and, above all, of the Jews – for Hitler to 'know the truth' – would mean in one sense that there was very little of Hitler left. As the Psalmist says, he had 'clothed himself with cursing like a garment: it seeped into his body like water, and into his bones like oil' (Psalm 109:18). Forgiveness means the deconstruction of this violence-soaked self, so that all the carefully erected and maintained pretences come crashing down. The Gospel is that, beyond all the destruction, someone is left: Adolf, the beloved child of God, who was lost and is found again.

So – to use our picture language – when the murdered Jew is invited to sit down at the heavenly banquet with Hitler, at one level it is no longer Hitler who sits there. Hitler's old self has died and is no more. It has been swept away with the lies. The one sitting at the banquet bears some relation to that past, but is not defined by that past, is not that past. Paul was not Saul. When the Apostle taught about the resurrection life, he saw continuity between our risen and our current bodies – but continuity set within and caught up by a still more staggering transformation, like the relationship between seed and flower (1 Corinthians 15:35-49). Reflecting upon the beginning of that transformation in the present life, Paul writes: 'It is not I who live, but Christ who lives in me' (Galatians 2:20) – getting at the fact that salvation involves the complete transformation of identity, where the old (in Paul's case, let us not forget, a murderer of Christians) is wholly and beautifully reconfigured – from one point of view, put to death; from another, given resurrection life. So, the Hitler who sits at the heavenly banquet both is and is not Hitler. Staggeringly, and beyond all human capacity and comprehension, he has become one who can give and receive joy in the one destiny which he and his victims share.

Beyond all human capacity and comprehension? It might be objected that that is just where this chapter has flown, that even trying to imagine Hitler and his victims sitting joyfully together at table in the Kingdom is an insult to the dead and to justice, and that the kind of transformation that would be required in Hitler envisaged is both incredible and inconceivable. It is impossible not to feel the deepest sympathy for this complaint. It is the single most compelling reason for rejecting the Christian Gospel.

However, Christians need to remember how much is at stake were we *not* to say something like what has been argued here. If it is *impossible* for Hitler to be in Heaven, if there can simply be *no* reconciliation between murderer and victim, then God's desire that all shall be saved must be thwarted (and thwarted often). We should be putting a severe limit on the power of God by saying that there were certain degrees of sin that are simply irredeemable. We should, ultimately, be denying the very principle of miracle: that God can raise the dead and call into being things that do not exist. Without question, Hitler has put himself beyond all human power to save. However, do we really think it is beyond *God*'s power? Or that God does not *want* to save him? That, when we say God wills all people to be saved, there are in fact exceptions to that rule, people whom God does *not* actually love? This is not falling back into the universalist error of proclaiming that all *must* be saved. It is simply to insist that even Hitler cannot fall outside the possible scope of grace.

In this light, let us turn again to Cardinal Bertram's instruction that the churches of his archdiocese celebrate Requiem Masses for Hitler's soul. Critics may well be right – they *are* right – that this order gave the impression that the Church somehow approved of Hitler or was in sympathy with him. From a presentational point of view, it was a disaster. However, from the strictly theological angle it was an entirely appropriate response. A Requiem Mass is not a declaration that a person is saved, let alone an indication that the Church views that person with moral approval. A Requiem Mass is a plea for God's mercy, enacted in the death of Jesus, to be at work in a particular soul – a soul confessed to be in desperate need. To offer Mass for Hitler is simply to affirm that he is loved by God, that Christ died for him also and that therefore, no matter how horrendous his crimes, the question of his ultimate salvation cannot be regarded as definitively and negatively settled. To say that Hitler will be forever in Hell is to set a limit on the saving power of Christ's death and resurrection. Christians cannot do that. If we are really followers of Christ, then we must learn to love as He loves – which means love even for the most bleakly loveless, in the great hope that grace will make them lovely once again.

Select Bibliography

Ateek, Naim, Cedar Duaybis and Maurine Tobin (eds), *Challenging Christian Zionism: Theology, Politics and the Israel-Palestine Conflict* (London: Melisende, 2005)

Augustine of Hippo, *Treatise against the Jews* (*Tractatus adversus Iudaeos*), in *Fathers of the Church*, Volume 27 (Washington, DC: Catholic University Press of America, 1955), pp. 387-414

Banki, Judith H., and John T. Pawlikowski OSM (eds), *Ethics in the Shadow of the Holocaust: Christian and Jewish Perspectives* (Chicago: Sheed and Ward, 2001)

Barnett, Victoria, *For the Soul of the People: Protestant Protest against Hitler* (Oxford: Oxford University Press, 1992)

Bauman, Zygmunt, *Modernity and the Holocaust* (Cambridge: Polity, 1989)

Beller, Steven, *Antisemitism: A Very Short Introduction*, 2nd edn (Oxford: Oxford University Press, 2015)

Bergen, Doris L., *Twisted Cross: The German Christian Movement in the Third Reich* (Chapel Hill: University of North Carolina Press, 1996)

Berkovits, Eliezer Rabbi, *Faith after the Holocaust* (Jerusalem: Maggid Books, 1973)

Bethge, Eberhard, *Dietrich Bonhoeffer: Theologian, Christian, Contemporary* (London: Collins, 1970)

Bonhoeffer, Dietrich, 'The Church and the Jewish Question', in Dietrich Bonhoeffer, *Berlin: 1932-1933: Dietrich Bonhoeffer Works, Volume 12*, ed. by Larry L. Rasmussen, trans. by Isabel Best, David Higgins and Douglas W. Stott (Minneapolis: Fortress Press, 2009), pp. 361-71

———, 'Ethics as Formation', in Dietrich Bonhoeffer, *Ethics: Dietrich Bonhoeffer Works, Volume 6*, ed. by Clifford J. Green, trans. by Reinhard Krauss, Charles C. West and Douglas W. Stott (Minneapolis: Fortress Press, 2005)

———, *Letters and Papers from Prison: Dietrich Bonhoeffer Works, Volume 8*, ed. by John W. de Gruchy, trans. by Isabel Best, Lisa E. Dahill, Reinhard Krauss and Nancy Lukens (Minneapolis: Fortress Press, 2010)

———, *Sanctorum Communio: A Theological Study of the Sociology of the Church: Dietrich Bonhoeffer Works, Volume 1*, ed. by Clifford J. Green, trans. by Richard Krauss and Nancy Lukens (Minneapolis: Fortress Press, 1998)

Boys, Mary C., (ed.), *Seeing Judaism Anew: Christianity's Sacred Obligation* (New York: Rowman and Littlefield, 2005)

Braham, Randolph A., (ed.), *The Vatican and the Holocaust: The Catholic Church and the Jews during the Nazi Era* (New York: Rosenthal Institute for Holocaust Studies, distributed by Columbia University Press, 2000)

Browning, Christopher R., *Ordinary Men: Reserve Police Battalion 101 and the Final Solution in Poland* (London: Penguin, 2001)

Burleigh, Michael, *Sacred Causes: Religion and Politics from the European Dictators to Al Qaeda* (London: Harper Collins, 2006)

———, *The Third Reich: A New History* (London: Macmillan, 2000)

Cesarani, David, *Final Solution: The Fate of the Jews 1933-49* (London: Macmillan, 2016)

Cohen, Jeremy, *Christ Killers: The Jews and the Passion from the Bible to the Big Screen* (Oxford: Oxford University Press, 2007)

———,*The Friars and the Jews: The Evolution of Medieval Anti-Judaism* (Ithaca, NY: Cornell University Press, 1984)

Cohn-Sherbok, Dan, *The Crucified Jew: Twenty Centuries of Christian Anti-Semitism* (London: Harper Collins, 1992)

———, *Holocaust Theology: A Reader* (Exeter: University of Exeter Press, 2002)

Conway, John S., *The Nazi Persecution of the Churches, 1933-1945* (Vancouver: Regents College Publishing, 1968)

Coppa, Frank J., *The Life and Pontificate of Pope Pius XII: Between History and Controversy* (Washington, DC: Catholic University of America Press, 2013)

Cornwell, John, *Hitler's Pope: The Secret History of Pius XII* (London: Penguin, 1999)

D'Costa, Gavin, *Vatican II: Catholic Doctrines on Jews and Muslims* (Oxford: Oxford University Press, 2014)

Dulles SJ, Avery, and Rabbi Leon Klenicki, *The Holocaust, Never to Be Forgotten: Reflections on the Holy See's Document* We Remember: *Commentaries by Avery Dulles SJ and Rabbi Leon Klenicki, with an Address by Edward Idris Cardinal Cassidy* (New York: Paulist Press, 2001)

Ericksen, Robert P., and Susannah Heschel, *Betrayal: German Churches and the Holocaust* (Minneapolis: Fortress Press, 1999)

Fackenheim, Emil L., *To Mend the World: Foundations of Post-Holocaust Jewish Thought* (Bloomington: Indiana University Press, 1982)

Fredriksen, Paula, *Augustine and the Jews: A Christian Defense of Jews and Judaism* (New Haven, CT, and London: Yale University Press, 2008)

Fulbrook, Mary, *Reckonings: Legacies of Nazi Persecution and the Quest for Justice* (Oxford: Oxford University Press, 2018)

Gerlach, Wolfgang, *And the Witnesses Were Silent: The Confessing Church and the Persecution of the Jews* (Lincoln: University of Nebraska Press, 2000)

Gilbert, Martin, *The Holocaust: The Jewish Tragedy* (London: Collins, 1986)

——, *The Righteous: The Unsung Heroes of the Holocaust* (London: Black Swan, 2003)

Goldhagen, Daniel J., *Hitler's Willing Executioners: Ordinary Germans and the Holocaust* (London: Abacus, 1996).

——, *A Moral Reckoning: The Role of the Catholic Church in the Holocaust and Its Unfulfilled Duty of Repair* (New York: Vintage, 2003)

Gutteridge, Richard, *Open Thy Mouth for the Dumb: The German Evangelical Church and the Jews 1879-1950* (Oxford: Basil Blackwell, 1976)

Harries, Richard, *After the Evil: Christianity and Judaism in the Shadow of the Holocaust* (Oxford: Oxford University Press, 2003)

Hart, David Bentley, *That All Shall Be Saved: Heaven, Hell and Universal Salvation* (New Haven, CT, and London: Yale University Press, 2019)

Hockenhos, Matthew D., *A Church Divided: German Protestants Confront the Nazi Past* (Bloomington: Indiana University Press, 2004)

——, *Then They Came for Me: Martin Niemöller, The Pastor Who Defied the Nazis* (New York: Basic Books, 2018)

Kaufmann, Thomas, *Luther's Jews: A Journey into anti-Semitism* (Oxford: Oxford University Press, 2017)

Kershaw, Ian, *Hitler* (London: Penguin, 1998)

Luther, Martin, *On the Jews and Their Lies* (1543) (Luther's *Collected Works*, Weimar Edition, Volume 53, pp. 417-552), available in English translation at: https://www.ccjr.us/dialogika-resources/primary-texts-from-the-history -of-the-relationship/luther-1543

Michael, Robert, *Holy Hatred: Christianity, Antisemitism, and the Holocaust* (London: Palgrave Macmillan, 2006)

Rittner, Carol, and John K. Roth (eds), *Pope Pius XII and the Holocaust* (London: Continuum, 2002)

Rosenthal, Gilbert S., *A Jubilee for All Time: The Copernican Revolution in Jewish-Christian Relations* (Cambridge: Lutterworth Press, 2017)

Rubenstein, Richard L., *After Auschwitz: History, Theology, and Contemporary Judaism*, 2nd edn (Baltimore and London: Johns Hopkins University Press, 1992)

Ruether, Rosemary Radford, *Faith and Fratricide: The Theological Roots of Anti-Semitism* (Eugene, OR: Wipf & Stock, 1996)

Sacks, Jonathan, *Future Tense: A Vision for Jews and Judaism in the Global Culture* (London: Hodder & Stoughton, 2009)

Schama, Simon, *The Story of the Jews: Finding the Words 1000 BCE-1492 CE* (London: Vintage, 2014)

——, *The Story of the Jews: Belonging 1492-1900* (London: Vintage, 2017)

Simon, Ulrich, *A Theology of Auschwitz: The Christian Faith and the Problem of Evil* (London: John Knox Press, 1979)

Steigman-Gall, Richard, *The Holy Reich: Nazi Conceptions of Christianity 1919-1945* (Cambridge: Cambridge University Press, 2003)

Ventresca, Robert A., *Soldier of Christ: The Life of Pope Pius XII* (Cambridge, MA, and London: Belknap Press of Harvard University, 2013)

Volf, Miroslav, *Exclusion and Embrace: A Theological Exploration of Identity, Otherness, and Reconciliation* (Nashville, TN: Abingdon Press, 1996)

Wagner, Donald E., and Walter T. Davis (eds), *Zionism and the Quest for Justice in the Holy Land* (Cambridge: Lutterworth Press, 2014)

Wiesel, Eli, *Night* (London: Penguin, 2006)

Wiesenthal, Simon, *Justice, Not Vengeance* (London: Weidenfeld & Nicolson, 1989)

———, *The Sunflower: On the Possibilities and Limits of Forgiveness* (New York: Schocken Books, 1997)

Wright, N.T., *Paul and the Faithfulness of God*, 2 vols (London: SPCK, 2013)

Papal Encyclicals and Other Church Documents

Communium Interpretes Dolorum, Encyclical of Pius XII, 15 April 1945, http://w2.vatican.va/content/pius-xii/en/encyclicals/documents/hf_p-xii_enc_15041945_communium-interpretes-dolorum.html (accessed 16 August 2018)

Faith and Order Commission of the Church of England, *God's Unfailing Word: Theological and Practical Perspectives on Christian-Jewish Relations* (London: Church House Publishing, 2019)

Holy See's Commission for Religious Relations with the Jews, 'We Remember: A Reflection on the Shoah' (1998), reproduced in Secretariat for Ecumenical Interreligious Affairs, *Catholics Remember the Holocaust*

Lumen Gentium, promulgated by Pope Paul VI, 21 November 1964, 'The Mystery of the Church', available at: https://www.vatican.va/archive/hist_councils/ii_vatican_council/documents/vat-ii_const_19641121_lumen-gentium_en.html (accessed 5 May 2022)

Mit brennender Sorge, Encyclical of Pius XI, 14 March 1937, http://w2.vatican.va/content/pius-xi/en/encyclicals/documents/hf_p-xi_enc_14031937_mit-brennender-sorge.html (accessed 14 August 2018)

Mystici Corporis Christi, Encyclical of Pius XII, 29 June 1943, http://w2.vatican.va/content/pius-xii/en/encyclicals/documents/hf_p-xii_enc_29061943_mystici-corporis-christi.html (accessed 16 August 2018)

Nostra Aetate: Declaration on the Relation of the Church to Non-Christian Religions Proclaimed by His Holiness Pope Paul VI, 28 October 1965, https://www.vatican.va/archive/hist_councils/ii_vatican_council/documents/vat-ii_decl_19651028_nostra-aetate_en.html (accessed 22 March 2022)

Secretariat for Ecumenical and Interreligious Affairs, *Catholics Remember the Holocaust* (Washington, DC: United States Catholic Conference, May 1998)

Summi Pontificatus, Encyclical of Pius XII, 20 October 1939, http://w2.vatican.va/content/pius-xii/en/encyclicals/documents/hf_p-xii_enc_20101939_summi-pontificatus.html (accessed 15August 2018)

Index of Subjects

Index of Authors Cited

Index of Scriptural References

You may also be interested in:

Reading Auschwitz with Barth

The Holocaust as Problem and Promise for Barthian Theology

by Mark R. Lindsay

It has been widely accepted that few individuals had as great an influence on the church and its theology during the twentieth century as Karl Barth (1886-1968). His legacy continues to be explored and explained, with theologians around the world and from across the ecumenical spectrum vigorously debating the doctrinal ramifications of Barth's insights. What has been less readily accepted is that the Holocaust of the Jews had an equally profound effect, and that it, too, entails far-reaching consequences for the church's understanding of itself and its God. In this groundbreaking book, Barth and the Holocaust are brought into deliberate dialogue with one another to show why the church should heed both their voices, and how that might be done.

'One of the most significant contributions of this book is its willingness to face what Lindsay calls the tremendum of the Holocaust and to continue to rethink Christian theology, liturgy, and practise in light of the horror of those events.' – **Ashley Cocksworth**, in *Modern Believing*, Vol. 57.2

Associate Professor **Mark R. Lindsay** is Director of Research at MCD University of Divinity. He is the author of two earlier books on Karl Barth – *Covenanted Solidarity: The Theological Basis of Karl Barth's Opposition to Nazi Antisemitism and the Holocaust* (2001), and *Barth, Israel and Jesus* (2007) – as well as numerous chapters and articles on Barth, Bonhoeffer, and post-Holocaust theology.

Published 2014

Paperback ISBN: 978 0 227 17471 5
PDF ISBN: 978 0 227 90281 3

You may also be interested in:

Reading Bonhoeffer

A Guide to His Spiritual Classics and Selected Writings on Peace

by Geffrey B. Kelly

The German theologian Dorothee Soelle once wrote that "Dietrich Bonhoeffer is the one German theologian who will lead us into the third millennium". Now as we near the end of the first decade of this third millennium, Bonhoeffer continues to inspire new generations of those who have recognised in him a spiritual guide in their actions on behalf of peace and social justice.

The author, Geffrey Kelly, Bonhoeffer scholar and past president of the International Bonhoeffer Society, provides a critical analysis and reading guide to two of Bonhoeffer's classic spiritual texts.

Reading Bonhoeffer offers a running commentary of each segment of these popular texts along with discussion questions suitable for the university and seminary classroom as well as for parish adult education programs using these two books.

In the final section of the book, Dr Kelly has excerpted and analysed three significant texts by Bonhoeffer on the need for world peace against the rising militarism and continued glorification of war in Germany and other European nations.

'both Bonhoeffer's and Kelly's passion for Christian discipleship comes through' – **H. Gaylon Barker**, International Bonhoeffer Society

Dr Geffrey B. Kelly is Professor of Systematic Theology at La Salle University, Philadelphia, PA. A prolific writer and spiritual guide, he has published eleven books in the fields of theology, ethics and Christian spirituality. He has lectured both nationally and internationally on the theology and spirituality of Dietrich Bonhoeffer.

Published 2008

Paperback ISBN: 978 0 227 17272 8
PDF ISBN: 978 0 227 90341 4

BV - #0024 - 171122 - C0 - 234/156/11 - PB - 9780227178454 - Matt Lamination